RIDE A STAGE OF THE TOUR DE FRANCE

The legendary climbs and how to ride them

Kristian Bauer

Wiesbauer

RIDE A STAGE OF THE TOUR DE FRANCE

The legendary climbs and how to ride them

Kristian Bauer

A & C Black • London

Note
Whilst every effort has been made to ensure that the content of this book is as technically accurate and as sound as possible, neither the author nor the publishers can accept responsibility for any injury or loss sustained as a result of the use of this material.

Published in 2011 by A & C Black Publishers Ltd, an imprint of Bloomsbury Publishing Plc
36 Soho Square, London W1D 3QY
www.acblack.com
First published in Germany in 2006 by Bruckmann Verlag GmbH, Munich under the title *Tour de France: die härtesten Anstiege*

ISBN 9781408133330

A CIP catalogue record for this book is available from the British Library.

Acknowledgements
Cover photographs: © Getty Images (front), Freier, Ute and Peter (back)
Inside photographs © All photographs are by the author Kristian Bauer with the exception of:
Hennes Roth, Pulheim: pp. vi, viii, ix, xiii, xviii, xx/1, 75, 121 (bottom), 123, 124 (top and bottom), 158 (bottom), 161, 185, 186 (bottom), back cover
Dr Elmar Bauer: pp. 104, 108, 114, 118, 186 (top), 192, 193
Tom Beck: p. 181
Picture library Corbis: pp. 70/71, 167
Jean-Michel Charassier: p. 33
Raymond Dobbins: pp. xii, xv, 68, 69 (all)
Freier, Ute and Peter: pp. 168/169
Hüseyin Apu and Eric Loew: pp. 13, 120, 121 (top), 130 (top), 139, 157 (top)
Fassa Bortollo: p. 167
Alois Furtner: pp. ii, 111, 138
Markus Golletz: pp. 100/101
Ulrike Huber: pp. 102, 107, 110, 116, 190
LUK: pp. 53 (top), 57
Phonak Cycling Team: pp. 126, 135, 147, 157 (bottom)
Johannes Sossalla: pp. v, 6, 18, 24, 27, 34, 36, 50, 52, 53 (bottom), 64,
Quintefilm: p. 98
Skoda Germany: p. 136
T-Mobile Team: pp. 60, 188
Peter Witek: pp. 51, 78 (top)
Witters Sports-Presse-Foto GmbH: pp. xi, xiv, xvii, 113

This book is produced using paper that is made from wood grown in managed, sustainable forests. It is natural, renewable and recyclable. The logging and manufacturing processes conform to the environmental regulations of the country of origin.
Typeset in 9.5pt on 11.75pt Myriad Pro by Saxon Graphics Ltd, Derby

Printed and bound in Singapore by Star Standard

CONTENTS

Tour de France: Lance Armstrong, Jan Ullrich and Michael Rasmussen on Col de Peyresourde.

The mountain stages are the high points of the Tour de France.

Southern Alps

PREFACE

Yes, I still love the Tour de France. Whether it's the bare peak plateau of Mont Ventoux, the consecutively numbered bends on the way to Alpe d`Huez, or the grandiose panorama from Galibier, the climbs of the Tour de France offer every amateur cyclist unforgettable experiences. All your cycling life, you`ll never forget the sweat that poured out of you during the ascent of Mont Ventoux, those burning thighs on Tourmalet, or the frozen fingers on Col de la Croix de Fer. All are contributing factors to my increased patience with the 'Tour de Farce', and why I stick with it, despite the eternal chaos surrounding the Tour. The last few years were a hard test for all cycling fans. They had to watch helplessly while a sporting discipline tore itself apart in front of their eyes. Barely had the Tour de France started, when the first doping rumours appeared, followed in quick succession by positive test results and signs of cheating. The dopers that were caught hid behind bizarre excuses and a few months later no one could say if the winner of the Tour would still be regarded as such. With the aid of testosterone plasters and blood doping, cyclists were racing up the mountains, while simultaneously viewer ratings were plummeting. But as is well known, hope springs eternal. And therefore I live in hope that the sport will recover, and wistfully remember the past. I've spent so many hours in front of the TV, in feverish support of those brave escapists fighting for the yellow jersey. Admittedly, I too ignored the signs of the doping problem, preferring to devote myself instead entirely to the duel between Armstrong and Ullrich. Also, Galibier, Tourmalet and Mont Ventoux are names that give me an indescribable rush and remind me of many decisive racing episodes.

Tom Simpson's memorial on Mont Ventoux.

The Alpine stages lend piquancy to the Tour.

Legendary passes – the emotion and the passion

To experience the legendary mountains and alpine passes myself on my racing bike was a long cherished dream of mine. Every ride also means submerging yourself in the history of the Tour, which can give you totally new insights into the race. And if you have experienced the pitiless final ramp of Galibier, or the searing heat of Ventoux, you see the Tour through different eyes.

It's incredibly good fun, and the feelings of happiness on Tourmalet are in a different league from those on other nameless passes. However, it's not just the legends alone that are attractive about the mountain reaches introduced in this book. The routes described here offer the chance to experience wonderful scenery, including shimmering turquoise reservoirs, gleaming white giant mountains or grey rocky abysses. Even the soberest of kilometre devourers waxes lyrical on the steep flank between Soulor or Aubisque, or in the hairpin bends 'garden' of Pailhères.

The good hard times

Strictly speaking, all passes of the Tour de France are easier today than ever before, as although the peaks are, of course, still the same height, the circumstances are dramatically different. The course was inching slowly forward, venturing first into the Vosges, then the Alps and finally even into the Pyrenees. Reports of the first Pyrenean stage in 1910 illustrate how arduous the riders found the conditions then. The stage extended from Perpignan to Luchon, a total distance of 289km, and mainly completed over forestry and gravel paths. Although this was only the ninth stage, the number of participants had been decimated to 62 from the original 110 through accidents, sickness and exhaustion. The race started at 3.30am in Perpignan and the first to cross the line after 14 hours and 23 minutes was Octave Lapize. He maintained an impressive average speed of 27km/h – and that without gears and over abysmal road conditions! But the drivers often presented a pitiful spectacle when they crossed the line. They were so badly marked by their ordeal that the spectators were shocked.

Total exhaustion

As is always the case with these very long stages, the cyclists arrived in a state that shocked the unweary observer. Their hard faces were brown, or blearily grey, they were dripping with sweat, their legs were covered with a layer of dust and mud, emblazoned with blades of grass. The sweat, and sometimes the blood, gave rise, especially in female spectators, to expressions of surprise and pity. As ever, there were some riders who gave the impression of total exhaustion and acted like automata. Others appeared still fresh and full of energy.

– Local paper *La Dépèche*
July 1910

At the finishing line, riders would greedily descend on an impromptu buffet, and would empty a bottle of lemonade or beer. In those days the Tour comprised a total of 5000km; individual day stages were approximately 400km long and road conditions were catastrophic. In old photographs and films, the passes look more like present-day mountain bike trails. At best they were fine gravel pistes frequently covered with large stones, soil or mud.

Hazards of the road

"Dortignac arrives late. He was the victim of an accident. In the vicinity of Lacourt, a cart stood in his way, whereupon he slammed violently into a rock face. This caused his front wheel to buckle. He explained that he would have to concede the race and take the train."

– Local press report from one of the stages in 1920

"In those days, we cyclists all shared the same conditions – only much harder than today," asserted the winner of the 1950 Tour, Ferdi Kübler. Even as late as the 1960s, cyclists had to gingerly search for a path between huge rocks, or stick to the route in the mud. "It's simpler for cyclists these days. The supply of materials and provisions is perfect. Even the roads are better. In the '60s we were still cycling on gravel paths and cobbled streets some of the time. We were only allowed to pick up provisions at the check points. There was cake, sandwiches, bananas and apples," reminisced Hennes Junkermann, who came fourth in the Tour of 1960.

The Tour and doping

Nostalgic recollections of the past are especially necessary now, because the present is an unmitigated disaster.

Since the revelations surrounding the Fuentes affair, the Tour has slithered from one scandal to the next.

Everyone has since become aware that doping was, and probably still is, occurring on a grand scale. The extent has amazed all concerned. The idea that this would go away overnight has sadly proved naïve. After all, there seems to have existed a parallel world for years, where many trainers and sportsmen have been publicly supporting the fight against doping, while eagerly resorting to pills and injections in private.

In defence of the cyclists, they were often in an environment which not only supported but demanded illegal methods. The shenanigans in and around the Freiburg University clinic, and the statements by Jörg Jaksche and other insiders speak volumes here.

However, that nothing has changed in the past two years, and that the same doping headlines still dominate proceedings, is sad. Many fans have deserted the sport, and if nothing is done, the Tour will deteriorate into a soap opera.

Cycling as a sport has its back to the wall, but many of the sport's official bodies, managers and competitors have failed to grasp this. Fans want to be able to cheer again, without discovering the next day that they have been betrayed yet again. The Tour offers unparalleled drama. It is high time the sport regained the upper hand, rather than the medics and judges!

The Italian cycling legend Fausto Coppi in the 1949 Tour.

EQUIPMENT

Off to the bike shop?

In the final time trial in 1989, Greg LeMond was the first Tour champion to use triathlon handlebars and won the Tour with an 8 second lead. Today, his bike would only attract the attention of enthusiasts in the market for a second-hand bike. If you compare the equipment of those days with a modern carbon racer, you see a quantum leap. But do you really need the most expensive equipment? Almost everywhere, I came across older racing cyclists who were climbing up the passes on their 10-gear steel racers. They have my greatest admiration, and those examples of true sportsmanship illustrate that you don't have to raid your bank account to be happy on the mountain.

Glossy pictures in cycling magazines encourage every cycling enthusiast to spend hundreds, or even thousands, of pounds in a bike shop. Today, lightweight carbon wheels are almost everywhere and more and more manufacturers are betting on carbon frames, which also reduces the price. But amateur cyclists usually only require an aluminium frame. Complete bikes are customary these days and weigh no more than 10kg even in the lowest price bracket. Although you won't win mountain time trials, you'll still be well kitted out. Personally, I managed on a 9.5kg aluminium racer and was very pleased with it.

For those of you who like to treat yourselves to the best and have the necessary cash, a lightweight aluminium or carbon racer will do the trick. You'll then be able to achieve a weight between 7 and 8kg, which of course makes the cycling easier.

Tough but doable: Tour ascents on a steel racer.

Accessories

A puncture repair kit, a spare inner tube, tyre levers, a mini pump and a set of Allen keys should definitely be included. A multi-purpose toolkit with screwdrivers is ideal for adjusting the transmission and making other minor adjustments. A set of lights is advisable for some rides, or at least a small LED rear light.

Cycle computers

In the past, I have used a cycle computer with an altitude meter on my tours. Always make sure to set the altitude again every morning, as with all barometric altitude meters. On my last tour, I used a Garmin GPS cycle computer. The device combines an altitude meter with satellite positioning. This eliminates the need for manual adjustments and even during the ride there is a data exchange between satellite and barometer.

Helmet

A helmet is naturally a must on the tours described here, even on warm days when you might not feel like donning a plastic lid, in the case of Jens Heppner, "You are on the verge of passing out. When someone tells me that air circulation is equally good with or without a helmet, I know they've never cycled through the Alps with such a steam kettle on their head".

That's why many cyclists strap their helmet to the handlebars during an ascent, a practice that has proved effective and saved a lot of sweat during decisive ascents. Downhill you spurn the helmet at your own risk.

Clothing

Clothing depends very much on the time of year. It can get very cold before and after the summer season. A helmet, overshoes and gloves are advisable, and even a warm jacket may be necessary. In very cold weather arm and leg warmers are recommended. In most cases, however, a cycling jacket or windcheater is sufficient. A base layer under the jersey is recommended even in summer. Ideally you should have different vests for cold and hot days.

Shopping in France

Those who discover they've forgotten something after all will find assorted cycle shops in France. A good tip for bargain hunters is the Decathlon sports supermarkets. They often have branded products at a reasonably good price. As always, you may have to sacrifice quality when going for own-brand products.

Safety

Before the start of any ride you should thoroughly examine your bike – you don't want to take a plunge into the depths at 50 or 80kph. If you take your bike apart for transit, it's advisable to check before the start that the quick-release levers and the break nuts are tightened. Tyre damage during the descent presents the greatest risk of a fall. Most flat tyres are preventable in modern tyres with puncture protection. However, possible causes for a flat for those without protection could be foreign objects getting between the tyre and inner tube (stones, sand etc.), a badly fitting or damaged rim tape and, of course, external damage to the tyre. In the event of a puncture, you should always look for the cause. It's also advisable to change tyres regularly. Those who are using pure carbon fibre wheels have to put up with reduced braking performance. Investigations by the specialist press have shown that these wheels present an additional high risk, as they can heat up on long descents.

A helmet is a must: Those who do without one expose themselves to unnecessary danger.

Among the nastiest surprises on downhill sections are loose chippings on bends. Especially around the brow area of passes, larger stones are often in the way, and occasionally animals leave undesirable traces on the tarmac. Therefore, always be sure to maintain 100 per cent concentration on the downhill sections. A thin film of ice on the road can be especially treacherous in cold temperatures.

Should anything actually go wrong, a mobile phone is invaluable. France uses the European emergency number 112.

GEARING

Where did it come from?

In the old photographs of the early days of the Tour de France, you can see the cyclists dismounting before ascents. In those days they had to move the chain over by hand and they only had two gears. Although they had already been invented, the Tour's directors prevented professional cyclists from using derailleur gears. The ban was finally lifted in 1937 but not every team used them in the first year.

Joop Zoetemelk caused a stir in 1979 as the first rider to use a freewheel with seven gears. The press was astonished and asked what advantages there were: "...to have an additional gear in the mountain stages. That's simply reassuring. And one can also optimise the range of gears. For example, we now have 13, 14 and 15 teeth for the valleys, and 19, 20, 21 and 22 for the ascents, which is significantly better for the muscles," explained Zoetemelk to the astonished press. That he was currently wearing the yellow jersey naturally lent his tactics even greater credibility.

These days, technology is still progressing. "I had them fit a 25 sprocket on the rear, because although the passes in the Pyrenees aren't as high as the Alpine ones, they're a lot steeper. Usually I use a 23. It's quite possible, that some of my colleagues were even using 27 tooth sprockets. But no one uses a triple chainset in the Tour," relates former professional cyclist Fabian Wegmann in the 2005 Tour diary.

What is it?

The subject of the correct gear ratio is much debated, especially where ascents are concerned. It's best to begin by reminding yourself of the basic principles.

The gear ratio, pedal travel and pedal power of a racing bike depend on the following factors:

- Number of teeth of the chain ring
- Number of teeth on the sprocket
- Length of the crank
- Diameter of the wheel

Francois Faber on Galibier in 1912: Without gears, pushing the bike up the mountain was normal in those days.

Using these individual values, we can calculate the gear ratio in centimetres:

Gear ratio (in cm) = number of teeth of chain ring divided by the number of teeth of the sprocket times the circumference (in cm) of the rear wheel. This calculates the distance a cyclist will travel with each revolution of the pedals.

But in cycling jargon gear ratio usually just refers to the number of teeth. In the case of a gear ratio of 52/42, we mean the number of teeth on the chain ring, for example, a typical triple chain ring would be a 52/42/32.

Most often 9-speed or 10-speed sprockets are used at the back, for example in gradations of 11 to 21 or 13 to 25. There is much scope for you to choose what suits you, and you should consider whether you want to use the same cassette in the mountains and/or on the flat.

Triple or double?

The big debate among cyclists is the choice of chain ring. A small religious war has developed around this; supporters on both sides are defending their advantages.

Before deciding to buy, you should be able to answer the following questions:

- How often will the bike be used on steep mountains?
- How good is my fitness?
- Do I prefer power cycling or a higher pedalling frequency?
- How important is it to me to keep on pedalling downhill?
- Do I want to take part in races?

Simply put, those who don't do much cycling in the mountains, and who therefore have a training deficit, have more reserves when using a triple solution. The triple chain ring offers the possibility of covering a broader range of gear ratios. You'll even be able to cycle in the mountains with a higher pedalling frequency and you won't have to desperately stand on the pedals, or rip off the handlebars. I'll never give up my triple ring again, especially on longer mountain rides, where I crank along quite happily, while others have to give their all to push bigger gears.

Those in the know can also achieve a suitable gear ratio with a double chain ring. This is especially true if you already have a racer and want to make it fit for mountain riding. In this situation, compact chain rings are an ideal choice (e.g. 50/34) combined with a carefully chosen cassette. Compact chain rings have a smaller diameter than standard chain rings; one can therefore still achieve higher pedalling frequencies even on climbs. Those in training and with a lot of power will cope well with a dual solution and need not be concerned.

All of these detailed discussions in cycling circles can be summarised by the following: there is no standard solution, only individual solutions, tailored to the needs of the individual cyclist.

Not for the faint hearted: Double chain ring.

TECHNIQUE AND TACTICS

Preparation

It goes without saying that you should not attempt the passes described here without preparation. While a targeted training plan is a wonderful thing, it's not necessary. What is important are sufficient cycling kilometres, whether on a racer or town bike, and a slow improvement in form through the cycling season.

Those who go out as hard and fast as they can up the mountain in spring haven't chosen a promising method. A training camp in spring is ideal for a relaxed build-up of basic endurance. If you start with a good foundation you will see improvements in your form. Variety is the key: alternate between short and sharp, then faster sprint intervals and then another steady but long rolling trip. With improved form, your pulse rate will raise, which increases your stamina.

If you're not out to win races, there's no need to overstress your body – make the fun of training and taking part a high priority. Those of you without mountain experience should start with a small pass in the Vosges, or train in the German low mountain ranges. You'll soon see that the secret to successfully cycling up mountains is primarily to maintain the correct speed.

Standing in the pedals

Those of you who are not actively competing in a race will spend most of your uphill cycling time in the saddle. With the gear ratios available today, this is usually not a problem. With a low gear you can manage all the ascents described here, without having to give the saddle a rest. If you have experience of cycling on steeper terrain, you will be used to standing up every now and then to loosen the muscles.

However, when you do stand up, remember to keep in mind that image of Lance Armstrong, out of the saddle, flying upwards, bowed low over the handlebars. His accident wasn't down to him running out of puff, quite the opposite – it was because he was producing a devilish pedalling frequency. On closer inspection you can see that Armstrong bends forwards to an extreme degree. This shifts his centre of gravity, meaning the majority of his weight pushes on the handlebars. This will create a lot of pressure on the arms which are usually not that involved in racing. The disadvantage to his extremely cramped posture over the handlebars is that he continually cycles a slight zig-zag course, because he can't easily steer straight ahead with tensed arms.

The Texan didn't just endure this exhausting posture for long periods, it also helped him to win tough mountain stages. So his technique can't be that bad.

This was also the opinion of the German cycle sports lecturer Georg Ladig, who examined Armstrong's method in detail. He came to the conclusion that his posture confers certain advantages. Measurements taken with the SRM power meter showed that Armstrong's technique and his classic way of standing in the pedals instantly apply power to the rear wheel. The big difference: "The legs are freer, can pedal more quickly and the athlete can can cycle for longer while standing in the pedals. Even the pedalling frequency becomes more flexible". According to Ladig, even his pedalling economy is improved, because the transfer of power to the pedals improves with his slightly raised centre of gravity.

Perhaps this provides an explanation for the legendary speed which Lance managed to achieve on the mountain. In any case, this technique is a clever way for the amateur cyclist to relieve the leg muscles for a few metres.

For many, the greatest cycle sport talent of the century: Eddy Merckx on Izoard in 1972.

Eating and drinking

"Because of the heat today, I must've used at least 12 bottles of drink. And I chucked another 12 bottles over my head and down the back of my jersey. Especially treacherous in temperatures above 30°C is the fact that you hardly feel hungry at all. You automatically remember to drink, but it's easy to neglect food," explains Fabian Wegmann, a professional cyclist from Gerolstein, Germany.

There he touched on two problems in one, both of which are also relevant for summer amateur cyclists in the mountains. You should always pay attention to your water consumption, while also remembering to eat. Unfortunately there are no water carriers, and you have to remember to bring enough, or hope for springs along the way. Two water bottles per racer is the absolute minimum.

It should be a given that you don't go on tour either starving or stuffed to the gills. Shopping opportunities are often limited – even though there is a restaurant at the pass, it may be closed. Energy bars are therefore also essential, and they don't have to be the expensive ones, as you can find cheaper alternatives in your local health food shop. Muesli, fruit and whey bars fulfil the same purpose and are easier on the wallet. Those of you who are quickly ascending Alpe d'Huez need not worry. But when you are simultaneously battling with cold and hunger on the Galibier or Izoard, you'll be grateful for every bite.

ON THE ROAD

Best time to travel

Although you can climb the first passes in the Jura and Vosges starting from mid April, an Alpine trip is only sensible from June onwards. The months following are ideal, but busier. French school holidays are in July and August and traffic increases during that period. It starts to get colder again from October onwards, with the first snow often falling at the end of the month.

Therefore every time of year has its advantages and disadvantages. Naturally it's quietest in June and September, outside the peak holiday period. A further advantage is that you avoid the greatest heat during this time. Those who are travelling outside the summer months should do some thorough research in advance on the weather and conditions on mountain passes. Snow is possible on Galibier and Iseran, for example, even in July. I experienced an outbreak of winter weather in the Vosges during the Easter holidays. In other years you could cycle up the lower mountains there without any problems.

Accommodation

Those of you who are travelling with a tent can find a campsite near all the tours described. Many campsites are closed very early (May) or late (October) in the year. Those in search of a room in a hotel or B&B should contact the local tourist information service. In the summer months (July and August) it's advisable to book in advance (for example over the Internet). Especially cheap, but often quite cosy, are *gîtes d'étapes* (similar to a youth hostel), mostly used as starting points by walkers.

A harsh climate reigns in the high mountains.

Tour descriptions

The degree of difficulty has been defined according to the categories allocated by the Tour de France. Hors Catégorie corresponds to the highest degree of difficulty, while a mountain in the third category (Troisième Catégorie) is noticeably easier.

The height profiles in this guide were based on the data recorded by a cycle tachometer with barometric altimeter. This equipment didn't always record precisely, so small deviations are usual.

Timings are very generous. Those who cycle steadily uphill will arrive significantly sooner at the pass. The descent is not taken into consideration, since it is often practical to build the ascent into a round trip.

There are no best opening times for passes. It just depends on the weather whether a pass is open or closed. Therefore the information here serves only as a rough guideline. Outside the peak season, you should always check the latest status on the Internet. Even if a pass is open all year, this does not mean it is suitable for bike riding all year round. Often a pass is only open all year because it gives access to a ski resort. In spite of this, snow and ice are usually present on the road.

More and more passes are equipped with a *vélodateur*, a mechanical time stamping system. You can get the time card at the Office de Tourisme.

Quick guide to fun passes

- The three easiest passes: Col du Hundsruck, Notschrei, Pra-Loup
- The three most athletically challenging passes: Col de l'Iseran, Galibier via Télégraphe, Mont Ventoux
- The three most beautiful passes: Port de Pailhères, Col d'Aubisque, Col d'Izoard

Recommended reading

- Klaus Angermann, *Der Traum vom Gelben Trikot*, Delius Klasing 2004
- Bernard Hinault, Serge Laget and Luke Edwardes-Evans, *The Treasures of the Tour de France*, Carlton Books Ltd 2010
- William Fotheringham, Roule Britannia: A History of Britons in the Tour de France, Yellow Jersey 2010
- Jan Ullrich, *Ganz oder gar nicht*, Econ 2004
- Serge Laget, *Col mythiques du Tour de France*, L'Équipe 2005
- Peter Leissl and Rob Van der Plas, *Ascent: The Mountains of the Tour de France*, Van Der Plas Publications, US (May 2005)
- Peter Winnens, *Post aus alpe d'Huez*, Covadonga 2005

Website links

- Information about open passes: www.infotrafic.com
- French Tourist Office: www.franceguide.com
- Cycle racing and cycle touring: www.cyclosport.com
  www.cyclozone.com
  www.cycling-challenge.com

Climb top is used to indicate the highest point (in metres) that the road reaches on the mountain.

Total elevation is the measurement in vertical metres between the top of the climb (climb top) and the base of the climb.

Key to symbols

HC

Mountain pass:
Ascent of greatest difficulty, literally 'beyond or outside categorisation'

Mountain pass:
Ascent of first degree of difficulty

Mountain pass:
Ascent of second degree of difficulty

Mountain pass:
Ascent of third degree of difficulty

** This tour is more of historical and athletic interest. The landscape does not present much variety.

*** This tour is scenically beautiful but not spectacular.

**** This tour guarantees a ride through impressive scenery. The ascent occurs in impressive surroundings.

***** Scenically unique experience, only to be found on a few ascents. The impressive scenery helps you to forget all stresses and strains!

PYRENEES

1 One of the most beautiful Pyrenean passes COL D'AUBISQUE

CLIMB TOP: 1709m
TOTAL ELEVATION: 1470m
DISTANCE: 29km
MAX GRADIENT: 10%
AVERAGE GRADIENT: 5%
STARTING POINT:
Argelès-Gazost (3400 inhab.), Département Hautes-Pyrénées (65)
APPROACH:
From Lourdes on the N21 to Argelès-Gazost
PARKING:
Car park Argelès-Gazost "Centre Ville"
ROAD CONDITION:
Good apart from a few places
AREAS OF RISK:
Unlit tunnel and tight bends between Soulor and Aubisque
MOUNTAIN PASS OPENINGS:
June to October

Previous double spread: After the Alps, the Pyrenees are the second highest mountain range which cyclists on the Tour de France have to conquer.

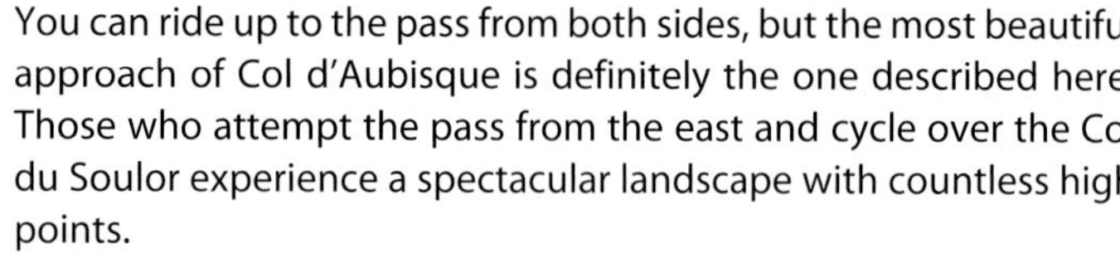

You can ride up to the pass from both sides, but the most beautiful approach of Col d'Aubisque is definitely the one described here. Those who attempt the pass from the east and cycle over the Col du Soulor experience a spectacular landscape with countless high points.

A Pyrenean classic

Traversed for the first time in the first Pyrenean stage in 1910, Col d'Aubisque still lays claim to being one of the great passes of the Tour. It remained part of the programme almost every year until 1972 and even recently competitors have tackled it. Very often the start or finish was in Pau, Luchon or Tarbes. There are three different routes over the pass and the Tour has explored them all. In addition to the tour over Soulor described here, the ascents from the west are also part of the usual standard routes. Starting from Laruns, you have to master 1190m of ascents and descents over 17km. With an average rate of climb of over 7 per cent, this is the most challenging variant. The variant from the north over Arbéost is rarely attempted, but is ideal as part of a round trip.

No navigation problems

The Col d'Aubisque cycle route is signposted from the roundabout at Argelès-Gazost onwards. You will begin the ascent up a good road right from the start, although you will need to beware of the traffic travelling in both directions. The gradient fluctuates between 5 and 10 per cent until you reach Arras, where it flattens out.

After Arras, the view opens out all of a sudden into a beautiful panorama. Ahead in the far distance is the outline of the imposing Pic du Midi d'Arrens (2267m) which you will pass on the right in Vallée d'Azun later. Next, there is a short flat section and the traffic decreases slightly. You will reach Aucun after 8.5km, where the climb begins again. In Aucun you'll go directly past a fountain (drinking water), a beautiful Romanesque stone-built church dating back to the 11th century, and a little local museum.

Between Soulor and Aubisque the road runs spectacularly close to the cliff face.

Pic du Midi d'Arrens in sight

After Aucun, it's immediately downhill again and you may have an anxious thought as to how those metres of ascent are to be climbed. The great Pic du Midi d'Arrens will now almost be within striking distance. Eventually you will reach Arrens, which is on the way to Santiago de Compostela.

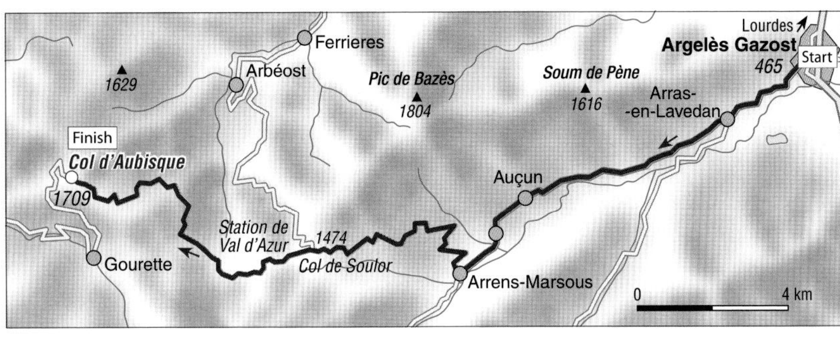

In town you will turn right and you'll finally find yourself climbing again. Both Col du Soulor and Aubisque are signposted here. Special signs for cyclists give details of the remaining kilometres to Soulor, current altitude and percentage gradients. In the meantime, the traffic abates and the surroundings are of a more rural nature: sheep stand alongside or on the road, shepherds offer their cheeses for sale and time and again beautiful traditional stone houses come into view. After 15km you will have reached the highest point of the route. It will then be a 100m rush downhill followed by a pedal up a short ramp with a 14 per cent gradient. But you'll barely notice the climb because it's only a few metres.

That was lucky!

At approximately this point of the ascent a tragic piece of cycle sport history was nearly written. In 2000, the perfectionist Lance Armstrong, of all people, made a catastrophic mistake. He tackled Aubisque and Soulor as part of his Tour preparation. The US Postal Team also wanted to practise the fast descent from Col du Solour. During the ascent, Armstrong had fastened his helmet to the handlebars, and plunged down the mountain without putting it back on again. After riding over a stone with the front wheel, the front tyre burst while he was doing 70kph. He lost control of the bike, continued into the ditch and hit his head against the stone wall on the edge of the pass. The unconscious Armstrong was taken to the hospital in Lourdes. A Canadian pair of doctors had witnessed the accident from a picnic spot and were convinced they would find a dead man. But the Texan was very lucky because his injuries were not life threatening. After his wounds had been stitched, he flew back to the US. He never again forgot to put on his helmet.

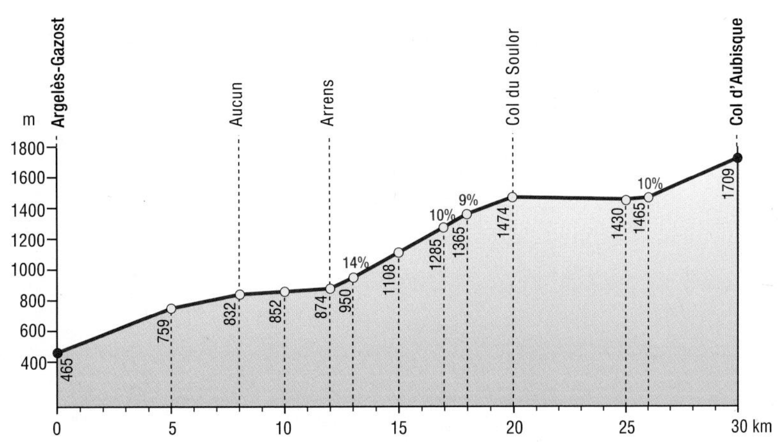

Keep going uphill

This acts as a warning, but it's hard to think of descending while the road is still meandering up a gentle wooded slope at around 7 per cent. There are no trees offering shade, and in high summer this ascent turns into a sweaty affair. It's fun to cycle past cow and mountain pastures, because the only thing to disturb the rural peace are the cow bells.

You will then head for Col du Soulor without any great difficulty. You'll come across the restaurant Les Marmottes, where you'll find a snack bar behind the pass.

Rendezvous for Tour fans

During the Tour de France the best places on Soulor are fiercely contested. Regardless on which side the cyclists are struggling up the mountain, the crowd are very close to the events of the race and can catch more than just a brief glimpse. The locals have been coming here for years to take up their usual places.

At the top of the pass a view of the most impressive part of the stage opens up where a very narrow road meanders along the left of a formidable, rock-studded precipice to Aubisque. Tour cyclists and their escorts spread out between Soulor and Aubisque like a colourful caterpillar. There are countless signs that remind you of the Tour de France. It's then downhill for 2km, where you'll lose the hard-earned height.

In some places the mountain plunges several hundred metres down on the right, and in the absence of barriers, you obviously need to tackle the decent with due respect. A perilous unlit tunnel awaits at the end of the descent. As far as I could make out without lighting, the tunnel consists of individual concrete sheets. Everything is extremely wet and covered with debris, but fortunately the tunnel is not very long.

A steep bit

Next you will pass a commemorative plaque; it was here that Wim Van Est plunged into the abyss (see 'Tour history', page 7). You need to take

The signposts on Col du Soulor are exemplary.

Well earned: The view from Col d'Aubisque over the rocky mountain landscape.

extra care here, because the bend on the descent is unexpectedly steep and there are no barriers along the edge.

At the end of the long, straight bit, you will go over a cattle grid. Immediately after it's uphill where you will once again fight to regain altitude. Where it was extremely rough and rocky until this point, you will see that the scenery will now change abruptly. You'll cycle along wooded slopes and gentle hillsides, which is quite surprising since you would expect more of the alpine scenery with every metre you gain. But that is precisely the attraction of this ascent: it is incredibly varied with regard to both athleticism and landscape.

At the pass

The route climbs briefly and then flattens out in a loop around the right of Mont Laid (1891m). Over the following kilometres short, very steep sections alternate with relatively flat passages. The gradient increases by up to 9 per cent on a significantly worse road. Ahead, the summit will already be visible, and you'll be able to make out the restaurant at the pass. Next you will go steadily up sweeping bends alongside a grassy slope at the rate of around 4 per cent. Time and again you will see old marker stones. At 6 per cent, you'll need to summon up all your effort for the final 500m, before you reach the pass, no doubt gasping for breath. At the top you'll be rewarded with a gigantic mountain panorama. A whole series of proud Pyrenean summits are within reach: Pic de Gabizos (2639m), Pic de la Latte de Bazen (2472m) and Pic de Ger (2613m) display their rocky flanks. You'll be in no doubt that you are in the Département Hautes-Pyrénées! Shopping enthusiasts can get their fix at the souvenir stalls and a restaurant offers refreshments.

Back into the valley

The descent is as unique as the panoramic view. You will notice how narrow the road is at the start, and how quickly the view of the valley can distract you. Octave Lapize, winner of the 1910 Tour, commented, "The Pyrenees are damned hilly and I prefer moving through the extreme bends of the Parc des Princes rather than descending Col d'Aubisque".

You will no doubt be motivated by the countless Tour inscriptions on the nearby climb to Soulor. Here too, you should have a break and cast a backward glance, because you will now be on probably one of the most beautiful passes of the Tour de France. It's almost a pity that you'll be riding downhill again!

Success all round

Those who fancy going back to Aubisque after this thrilling visit can make new plans immediately. An ascent from the western side is highly recommended for a second visit.

Those who start in Laruns expend the greatest effort at the start of the route. This is a wise decision, especially in high summer. Starting from the little village, the route follows the river valley at a mostly constant gradient. It's 17km to Aubisque. The well-known crossing to Soulor is along the D126 to Asson via Arbéost. There you will turn on to the D35 in a westerly direction towards Louvie which is already on the D934. This road will lead you back to Laruns. It's recommended that you take a map on the 85km round trip.

Above: You get back to the valley all too quickly.

Right: When the Tour comes this way, Aubisque is an ideal place for spectating.

The yellow jersey on the rescue rope

Fortunately there are some photos of this dramatic episode, as no one would otherwise believe it. On the 12th stage of the Tour de France, Wim Van Est became the first Dutchman ever to wear the yellow jersey. He had acquired the yellow jersey more or less by accident in a mass sprint and was rated as an insignificant talent. “He is equally bad uphill or downhill,” judged a contemporary Belgian journalist.

The stage from Dax to Tarbes was therefore a real challenge for him, and another day in the yellow jersey was rather unlikely. The riders climbed to the pass of Aubisque at very high speed and onward into the descent. Even at the first tight bend Van Est lost control of his bike and he fell down the grassy slope. In spite of this, he got back on his bike and raced onwards. In the meantime he had reached the crossing to Soulor. On the left there is a drop of several hundred metres without a barrier. The road was wet and covered in grit. In front of his horror-struck colleagues, he began to skid and once more fell into the depths. He miraculously came to rest on a narrow rocky ledge 70m down (as it states on his commemorative plaque). Although he had sustained only minor injuries, there was no rope available near by to rescue him. However, Kees Pellenaars, the athletics coach of the Dutch team, had a bright idea. He knotted all 40 spare inner tubes from his team together and let them down. Meanwhile, other helpers had climbed down to Wim Van Est. Together they finally managed to pull the injured man back up again. The Dutch team began the journey home to the Netherlands before the 15th stage.

Van Est instantly became famous to a wider audience. He became an ideal candidate for marketing campaigns: he advertised the Pontiac brand of watches with the convincing slogan, ‘My heart stopped, but my Pontiac kept on running.’

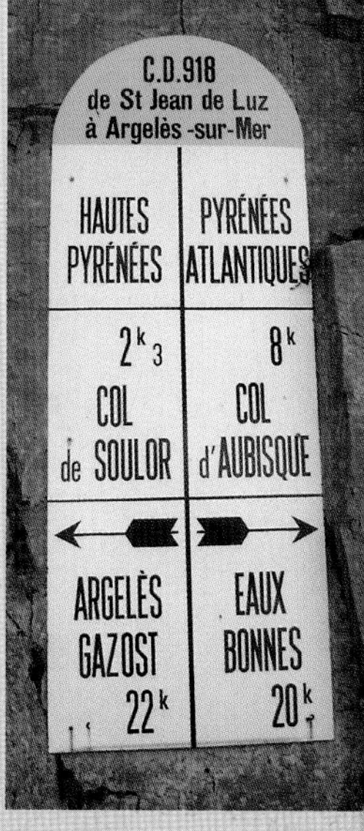

Above: The site of the accident is between the Hautes Pyrénées and the Pyrénées Atlantiques.

Left: Luck amidst bad luck: A commemorative plaque provides a reminder of the incredible incident.

Steep ramps and hairpin bends with grand panoramic views

LUZ-ARDIDEN

So far and yet so near, the panoramic view during the ascent enchants the senses.

CLIMB TOP: 1720m
TOTAL ELEVATION: 1380m
DISTANCE: 33km
MAX GRADIENT: 10%
AVERAGE GRADIENT: 4.2%
STARTING POINT:
Argelès-Gazost (3400 inhab.), Département Hautes-Pyrénées (65)
APPROACH:
From Lourdes on the N21 to Argelès-Gazost
PARKING:
Directly on the way into town by the supermarket
ROAD CONDITION: Very good
AREAS OF RISK:
Cycle path for the first few kilometres
MOUNTAIN PASS OPENINGS:
All year

Those who believe that the Tourmalet is the only cycling highlight in this neighbourhood are sadly mistaken. The ascent to the little ski station of Luz-Ardiden is a substantial athletic challenge. This is due to the fact that the stated average gradient refers only to the ride up to Luz-Saint-Sauveur. The average gradient of the ascent is in the region of 8 per cent.

Tame start

For the first 5km you'll be riding downhill or on the level, therefore the going is quite brisk. You will virtually fly towards the mountains. The traffic on the main road is heavy the cycle path along the disused stretch of railway between Lourdes and Pierrefitte-Nestalas therefore presents the perfect alternative. Seen from the supermarket in Argelès-Gazost, it is on the left, directly next to the main road. At the sign at the entrance to Pierrefitte-Nestalas, you will have to get back on to the road and follow the signs for Luz-Saint-Sauveur through the far more picturesque town, which is well worth a visit. The mining of silver ore brought prosperity to the town, which is still reflected in the facades dating back to the 16th and 18th centuries.

In the narrow valley

While the road to Hautacam goes straight on following a roundabout after about 8km, you will turn right in the direction of Luz-Saint-Sauveur. The great Tourmalet is also signposted in the same direction. You will then find yourself in a very narrow valley, the Gorge de Luz. On the left you will see a jagged rock face which is closely hugged by the winding road. To your right a broad river that is fed by a reservoir flows. That's why you will see frequent warning signs that inform you about potential flooding.

The little village of Grust on the way to Luz-Ardiden.

Jagged rock formations

The landscape is now a sheer joy, and the traffic not too bad. You will ride through several covered galleries which, although unlit, are light enough. After 14km you will be rewarded with a short downhill stretch and you'll then change over to the right side of the river (Gavarnie) at a bridge.

Still on the D921 you'll climb gently through a narrow valley. A few kilometres further on the view opens on to the pyramid-like, grass-covered mountain peaks behind Luz-Saint-Sauveur which encircle a ragged mountain giant in their midst. But no need to panic – you don't need to climb any of these peaks.

Decorative Luz-Saint-Sauveur

At the next roundabout the road from Tourmalet meets the road to our destination for this ride. Keep right and you'll reach Luz-Saint-Sauveur after a bridge. The thermal spa consists of small, exquisite houses, some of which will captivate you with their neo-classical marble facades. It offers a marked contrast to the ugly Alpine ski resorts. In the village you'll go noticeably downhill before you need to cross the river again and cycle uphill on the D12.

An information board immediately prepares you for the impending ascent. At 1km intervals, these boards offer the cyclist the usual Tour data. Details of the average gradients seem to be very precise here.

Strapping slopes

You'll then ride immediately along a wooded slope. The view ahead is obscured by thick deciduous woodland and the destination is therefore not visible. Meanwhile you'll gain height on long, straight ramps and tight bends at gradients of between 5 and 7 per cent.

There is hardly any traffic and you'll be able to enjoy the climb and beautiful view of the slate roofs of the village of Sazu below.

Shortly afterwards you will reach Grust, where a sign at the entrance warns of travelling too fast: *'Achtung Kinder – langsamer'* (Warning children – slow down) – a sign that Lance Armstrong must have ignored in 2003 ... On your right you will catch a glimpse of a gorgeous,

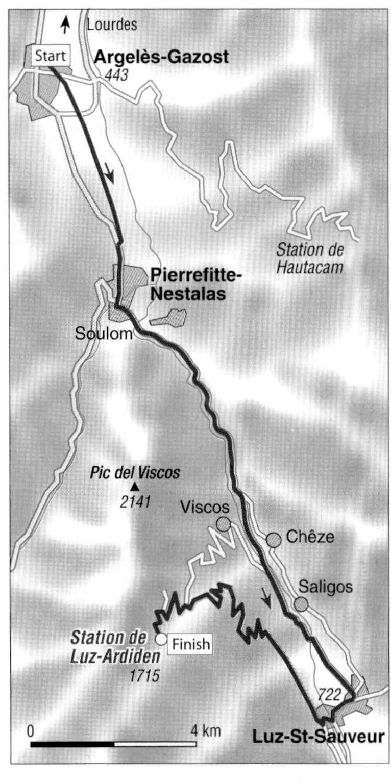

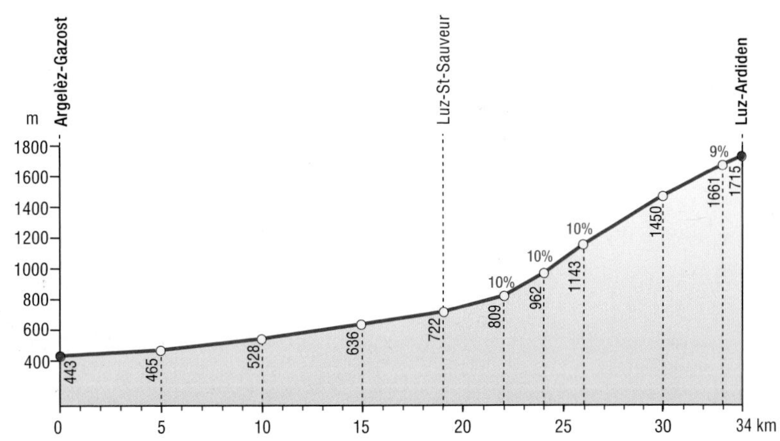

grass-covered mountain, Soum de Nère, which reaches the respectable height of 2394m.

You won't be aiming quite so high, but there is a bit more work to do to reach 1720m. So that it doesn't take too long, the gradient increases to 10 per cent. You'll no doubt feel your muscles creaking and the altimeter is buzzing.

Now you are approximately 8km from your goal and the gradient repeatedly reaches 10 per cent.

On a summer's day, the sun beats down on to the slope without protection and increases the agony of climbing. There is hardly any respite over the next 4km. Ride upwards through a wooded mountain slope where extended straights are followed by tight bends.

The final stretch

Shortly afterwards the gradient reduces and allows you to pedal comfortably along. Next follow two hairpin bends ridden with faded Tour graffiti. The rest of the way then unfolds in clear hairpin bends before you. Many sheep graze on broad grassy slopes, and sometimes stand in the middle of the road.

In long drawn-out bends you continue upwards at about 10 per cent. Your eyes may be drawn to some avalanche defences; the end of the stage lies to the left of them, next to the highest ski lift. You will go past a small place sign and reach a junction. Initially this presents a puzzle, but a signpost indicates left towards the ski school and Auleans. Crossing a cattle grid, you'll sprint towards the last of the steep hairpin bends.

Suddenly, and clearly sooner than anticipated, you will find yourself standing before a ski lift station and a gigantic car park. It's hard to believe, but you have really reached your destination – and in a rather more relaxed way than most professionals. "I don't believe that many people have

With gradients of up to 10 per cent, even the lowest gear finally gets used.

Before reaching Luz-Ardiden a quick glance back shows the course of the road.

reached that boundary where every step hurts and you believe that lactic acid is about to spurt from your ears," Jan Ullrich graphically described the agony on the mountain. Indeed, you won't have punished yourself in such an extreme fashion during the ascent.

The road is in very good condition which makes the downhill journey a real pleasure. Only when riding through villages are there some holes in the tarmac.

Welcome to the National Park

It's only when you study the map in detail that you realise you have just set foot in, or cycled into, the Parc National des Pyrénées. It feels a little strange that the ski lifts extend into this nature reserve, but then you are dealing only with the northern boundary of the park. In total, the French Pyrenean National Park extends for 100km along the Spanish border and covers an area of 457km^2.

A hallmark of the National Park is the many lakes, and the areas around the 'cirques' of Troumousse and Gavarnie attract walkers in their droves. Around 1.5 million nature lovers visit the park every year. This has transformed it into a significant economic contributor and no one wants to remember the protests against its creation. In the 1960s the understanding for the need to protect nature was less developed, and the park's founders had a lot of persuading to do until it was inaugurated in 1967. To reduce resistance, farmers were allowed to continue to cultivate the land in certain areas within the park.

Pure nature

The park has very diverse flora and fauna. The emblem of the National Park is the head of a chamois which is painted in

With a total elevation of up to 1000m, Luz-Ardiden proves to be great fun downhill.

red and white on the boundary stones of the park. More than 4000 chamois now live again in the National Park, while only a few decades ago the population was deemed to be under serious threat. Marmots, ptarmigans and royal eagles feel at home in the park, although the chances of seeing them are not very good.

The tree population consists largely of beech trees, firs and different varieties of pine.

Of special interest are rare orchid varieties, such as the Pyrenean Columbine which add touches of colour to the landscape.

No cycling in the park

You won't be affected by the 'no cycling in the park' rule unless you actually have a mountain bike with you, as well as your racer. But you don't really need a mountain bike to explore, since the park offers 350km of hiking trails, among them also the long distance footpath GR10.

Even where overnight accommodation is concerned, the park proves very flexible: it's forbidden to pitch a tent several nights running, but bivouacking for one night is allowed. There are also several rescue huts which make it possible to go walking over several days. Among the best-known starting points for excursions in the park are Gavarnie and Cauterets. Both places are in the vicinity of this cycle tour and therefore you'll be able to keep your eyes open for the road sign on your way back.

The road to Cauterets branches directly off the road to Argelès-Gazost in Pierrefitte-Nestalas. Cauterets is a little quieter than Gavarnie and you can get on the GR10 directly from here. Those who don't mind mass excursions can head from Luz-Saint-Sauveur in a southerly direction to Gavarnie. The place is very popular and extremely touristy. You will never be lonely here, even in the rain, so amateurs can end up feeling like a competitor in the Tour de France. From Gavarnie, it's perfectly signposted on to the Cirque de Gavarnie, a large valley which is one of the scenic highlights of the Pyrenees. This provides a unique experience and a perfect excuse for a day of rest!

2400m-high Soum de Nere on the other side of the valley sits amidst an imposing massif.

When Armstrong plunged to his Tour victory

The Tour de France of 2003 is surely up there among the most thrilling editions of recent years. Germany was fired up for Jan Ullrich who had risen from the ruins of his career and suddenly had a chance to win the Tour. After the thrilling duels on Pailherès, Aspet and Peyresourde, everything was up for grabs. Let's remind ourselves:

Ulle was still only 15 seconds behind Armstrong. High tension dominated the 15th stage leading from Col d'Aspin and Tourmalet to Luz-Ardiden. The difficult Pyrenean stage was ideally suited to be the deciding one of the Tour. Beginning with Tourmalet, Ullrich in his sky blue-coloured Bianchi-jersey, started several attacks, but Armstrong kept up. During the ascent of Luz-Ardiden, Ullrich dictated the tempo for much of the time and maintained the lead. Suddenly Armstrong attacked. He drove forward with strong kicks, behind him Iban Mayo and then Jan Ullrich.

Suddenly Armstrong's handlebars got entangled in the yellow bag of a spectator and he fell. Mayo also tumbled on to the tarmac. Only Ullrich managed to swerve and was suddenly in the lead. The man from Rostock didn't exploit this incident but kept turning around in the saddle, waiting for Armstrong. The latter pulled himself together and rejoined the field at a rapid pace. A few metres on, he almost fell again, as he slipped out of the pedals. Now the Texan was experiencing an adrenalin high. With a gigantic rage in his belly, he increased his pedalling frequency and chased up the mountain. Soon he had reached the group around Ullrich. Very briefly, he pedalled alongside him, then he virtually exploded, pulling past him no holds barred. Jan was totally unprepared for this attack and couldn't keep up. Armstrong rode the last 6km as if totally unfettered. He overtook the runaway Sylvain Chavanel, giving him a gentle tap on the back as he passed by.

At the finish, Ullrich's distance from Lance had increased to over a minute behind and he wouldn't be able to make it up until Paris – the chance of victory had therefore been lost. Rarely has a small fall had such huge consequences!

Lance surprised everyone in 2003.

Armstrong is rarely beaten on the mountain.

3 Another kind of pilgrimage
HAUTACAM

Hautacam – an athletic insider tip for the cycle racing fraternity.

CLIMB TOP: 1529m
TOTAL ELEVATION: 1050m
DISTANCE: 16km
MAX GRADIENT: 11%
AVERAGE GRADIENT: 6.6%
STARTING POINT:
Argelès-Gazost (3400 inhab.), Département Hautes-Pyrénées (65)
APPROACH:
From Lourdes on the N21 to exit Argelès-Gazost
PARKING:
Straight on at the roundabout near the Champion supermarket, right at the Total garage towards Hautacam; park in the street in front of the casino
ROAD CONDITION: Good
MOUNTAIN PASS OPENINGS:
All year

The climb up Hautacam is quiet and lonely once you leave the main road behind. That's because you will be travelling through the pastoral quiet of a thinly populated mountain landscape. It's only busy here in winter time, since Hautacam offers a dense network of cross-country ski runs and downhill pistes.

Pilgrimage on the mountain

The place is sometimes called Lourdes-Hautacam, although the well-known and bustling centre of pilgrimage is several kilometres away. Until the middle of the 19th century, Lourdes was an unknown provincial town. But then Bernadette Soubirous, a little farm girl, had a vision on 11 February, 1858. While out collecting wood, she saw a woman dressed in white: Mary, as she later found out. The hundreds who visited the place of the apparition at the beginning soon turned to thousands. Today, over 5 million visitors travel to Lourdes every year from all parts of the globe. They hope to be healed from serious illnesses, because the spring at Lourdes is credited with miraculous powers. A visit to the spring is the goal of every pilgrim, and taking part in the procession is equally a given. Naturally the whole of Lourdes is geared up for floods of visitors. The town offers countless souvenir shops, hotels and restaurants. The trade in cheap kitsch and dubious religious souvenirs is booming – bad taste has no limits here. The two cinemas in town have been screening religious motion pictures about the apparition of the Virgin Mary in Lourdes for years.

Global meeting place

The cycle trip up to Hautacam can naturally be combined with a trip to Lourdes. However, it might perhaps be better to make the

On the lonely mountain plateau, the vegetation takes on almost Nordic characteristics.

excursion by car, since the traffic is stressful and the signposts are not always easy to follow. After the Grotte de Masabielle the Basilica of the Immaculate Conception is among the best-known visitor destinations. The most important reason for visiting is the atmosphere created by pilgrims from all over the world. You rarely get to meet so many people from different nations in such a small space.

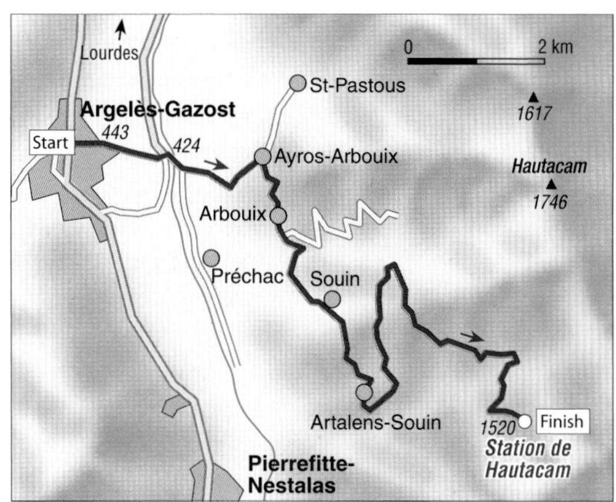

The end of Bartali's pilgrimage

The double winner of the Tour, Gino Bartali, was not put off by the masses of visitors and combined every Tour de France with a pilgrimage to Lourdes, even when the places of each stage were physically far apart. Perhaps no other sportsman has been received more often by the Pope than Gino 'The Pious'. Naturally he was therefore especially keen when in 1948 the Tour led from Biarritz to Lourdes. The devout Catholic did not allow anyone to wrest the victory from him and rode as shining victor over the finishing line in Lourdes. It's actually not easy to restrict the religious tourism in Lourdes to make room for the Tour. Therefore Lourdes has only twice been the stage town for the great loop.

The curse of the rain stone

You will see relatively little of the bustle of the busy centre of miracles in Lourdes-Hautacam. Instead, the Tour offers an empty country road alongside small villages. Hautacam is already signposted at the roundabout by the casino. Initially it's slightly downhill through the village. Here you will also go past the cycle path from Lourdes, which was created on a former rail track. Next you will head straight on over a river, where after 1.5km you will turn off on to the D100 (signposted). You will ride along on the level and reach Ayros-Arbouix, where it goes slightly convolutedly left, then immediately right again onwards to Hautacam. You will then be pedalling uphill, as the road winds tightly between the houses and the first steep ramp awaits you.

Past grazing sheep, you will wind your way upwards along a narrow road. On the right a beautiful view into

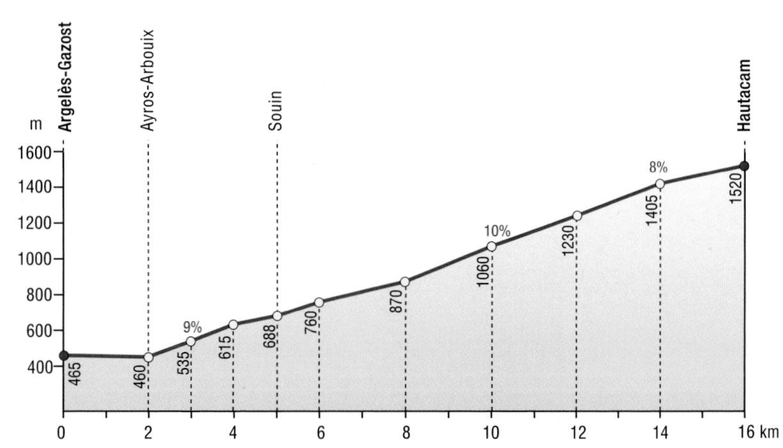

the valley will open before you – assuming the weather is up for it. In the far more common misty weather, visibility barely extends to the next corner. But perhaps that's no coincidence, since the church in Arbouix is host to a very special stone which was well known in the 17th century for its ability to conjure rain.

Steep climb to the finish

The road leads through Arbouix, a friendly little mountain village with a drinking water fountain. The quiet road meanders upwards along grassy slopes and deciduous trees. You will ride through several little places whose stone-built houses make them all look quite cosy. You will then begin your climb again past an inviting-looking restaurant. A steeper climb awaits you after a brief level stretch. At an inclination of around 10 per cent, progress will sap your strength, but you could allow yourself a little respite in Souin at around 6 per cent. On the left you will see the beautiful vista of rising wooded slopes. Depending on the time of day, you will be riding either in full sunshine or you might be able to take advantage of the shade afforded by the slope.

More little places with beautiful stone houses follow. After around 10km the incline increases markedly once more. Soon the vegetation dwindles and the first of the hairpins follow. A final trial of strength awaits you after around 16km with an incline of 11 per cent. Now the landscape is markedly different: many ferns and sparse shrubs shape the primeval picture.

Past grazing sheep, a windy approach leads towards your goal. On arrival in Hautacam there's not much on offer apart from sheep. But in fine weather the view is grand.

Doping has been an issue during the Tour for several decades.

Human – machine – doping?

The revelations of recent times make it easy to forget that medicinal aid has been part of the Tour de France from day one. The first scandal occurred in 1924, when Francis and Henri Pélissier left the race. Blazing with anger at the race's management, by whom they felt mistreated, they went in search of a few journalists. In a café they explained to the assembled reporters how the Tour supposedly really worked: without cocaine, chloroform and other pills it was impossible to cope with the physical punishment. Whether the two brothers exaggerated a little in the heat of the moment is a moot point – their words certainly contained a kernel of truth.

Only at the end of the 1950s did the subject once again become the focus of attention. In 1955 Ferdi Kübler made his legendary breakaway during the 11th stage, followed by a seizure in the evening, which suggested doping. But worse was to come in 1960, when the gold-medal winner Knud Jensen fell down dead at the end of the Olympic road race. And still, the battle against doping was only half-hearted. The first doping tests were carried out during the 1966 Tour de France, and six riders immediately tested positive. Obviously drug taking continued apace. In 1967 this led to a catastrophe for Tom Simpson. The British cyclist collapsed on the ascent of Mont Ventoux and died. Even this did not have much effect on doping practices: the 1970s and 80s in cycling were shaped by the ingestion of illegal substances.

The subject of doping reached its media high point with the 'Festina Affair' during the 1998 Tour. The scandal was unleashed by the Festina's team masseur, Willy Voet, in whose possession were found 400 ampules of EPO (a performance-enhancing drug). Following the arrest of the team's director Bruno Roussell and team's medic Eric Ryckaert, the Festina racing stable around mountain king Richard Virenque was barred from the Tour. Signs of the massive use of EPO had been apparent for some time, but only since the revelations about Team Telekom has it become clear: the Festina scandal is a misnomer, since it suggests that only individual black sheep reached for EPO.

In reality, large scale experiments with EPO were conducted from the early 90s. There are clear indications that it was in extensive use during the following years. Only in 2005 did the spotlight fall on Armstrong. The anonymity of frozen blood samples was lifted under peculiar circumstances. According to a respected laboratory, several of his samples had tested positive for EPO in 1999. "For the first time someone has told me that Armstrong had a prohibited substance called EPO in his body. We have all been deceived," explained Tour director Jean-Marie Leblanc back then. He ignored, however, that only some of the 12 positive samples from 1999 came from Armstrong. The year before it had been even worse: in 1998 out of a total of 70 anonymous samples, 40 were found to contain EPO. This discovery had no legal consequence, since 'B' samples were no longer possible. After an examination, the International Cycling Union (UCI) declared the seven-times Tour winner Lance Armstrong innocent. That nothing much had actually changed became clear as late as 2008, when Bernhard Kohl and Stefan Schumacher from the supposedly clean Team Gerolsteiner had their cover blown. Floyd Landis in 2010 admitted EPO doping for years and accused Lance Armstrong and other members of the US Postal Team, too. And many were not surprised when Alberto Contador, winner of the Tour 2009 and 2010 tested positive for clenbuterol in 2010.

Recommended reading

Jeremy Whittle, *Bad Blood: The Secret Life of the Tour de France*, Yellow Jersey (4 Jun 2009)
Laurent Fignon, *We Were Young and Carefree: The Autobiography of Laurent Fignon*, Yellow Jersey (10 Jun 2010)

4 King of all Tour passes
TOURMALET

Rolling along comfortably on the way to Luz-Saint-Sauveur.

HC *****

CLIMB TOP: 2115m
TOTAL ELEVATION: 1385m
DISTANCE: 18km
MAX GRADIENT: 11 per cent
AVERAGE GRADIENT: 7.7 per cent
STARTING POINT:
Luz-Saint-Sauveur (1120 inhab.), Département Hautes-Pyrénées (65)
APPROACH:
From Lourdes on the N21 then D921 to Luz-Saint-Sauveur
PARKING:
Car park in front of the tourist office in Luz-Saint-Sauveur
ROAD CONDITION:
On the whole good, slightly worse on the brow of the pass
MOUNTAIN PASS OPENINGS:
End of June to October

Without a doubt, the Tourmalet is the legendary Tour mountain par excellence, having been included 74 times in the Tour programme to date. Therefore you should approach this mountain with enormous respect, although it is definitely not unconquerable. Neither height difference nor gradient go beyond the usual scope of the other great Tour mountains. As long as the weather cooperates, it can be quite comfortable here even in summer.

Thick church walls

Nowhere were worshippers as safe as in the church in Luz-Saint-Sauveur. The fortified Église Saint-André is especially well protected. A thick wall, embrasures and a watch tower may remind you more of a castle. But the beautiful structure from the 12th century is by no means the only jewel in the old town. The affluence created by the visitors of the thermal spa is reflected in the ornamental facades of the houses. Culinary delights are catered for by speciality shops which sell locally produced sausages and cheese.

The dream of the Tourmalet

Rarely will you start the day with such euphoria. To conquer the great Tourmalet – which racing cyclist doesn't dream of that? Start by going left at the multi-storey, going uphill along a well-signposted route. Initially, you will ride between many houses and over the next few kilometres the road goes past many campsites. Unfortunately there is heavy traffic on the first part of the route. By the side of the road you will see the usual notices for cyclists about inclines and distances.

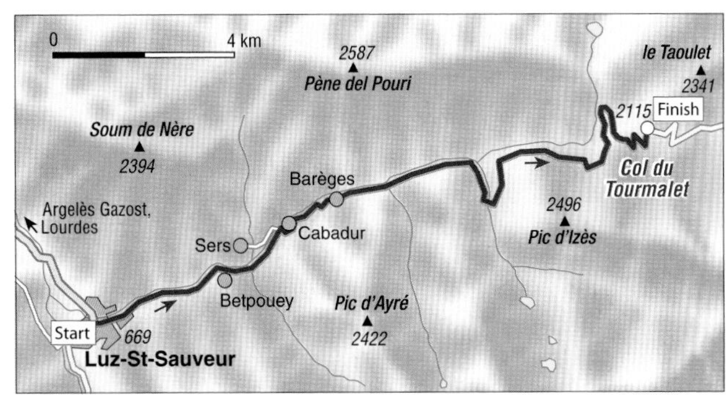

To the left you will see a beautiful slope, down which a stream tumbles after rain. You will find yourself in a little valley which widens gradually.

Next you will pass a sign advertising pony riding. Should your strength fail you, there is an actual alternative mode of transport 10km further on! After 4km the first hairpin bends will delight you and extend the view of the mountains on your left. You will still be cycling accompanied by the stream which is hiding behind the trees on the left. After the hairpin bends the panorama changes before you. On your left, the close, soft slope gives way to the rough, rocky flank of the 2328m-high Capet. The gradient reduces to a bearable 4 per cent and the Vallée de Barèges is noticeably more scenic than at the start.

Gold coins as a reward

After 6km you should finally catch sight of the stream which cleaves its way over rocks between the trees. You will reach Barèges, a place that already radiates a winter sports atmosphere which includes a nightclub. At the end of the village, the gradient increases to 9 per cent and the valley opens up. You will enjoy an extensive view over the steep slopes on your left. The rocky peaks give way to long grassy slopes. After 9km you will reach the first flat stretch where you can regain a bit of strength, before the next stretch at nearly 10 per cent. From here on in the landscape on this stretch is a special treat.

Jacques Goddet was director of the Tour de France from 1936 to 1986. Goddet permitted the use of gears and introduced the green and mountain jerseys.

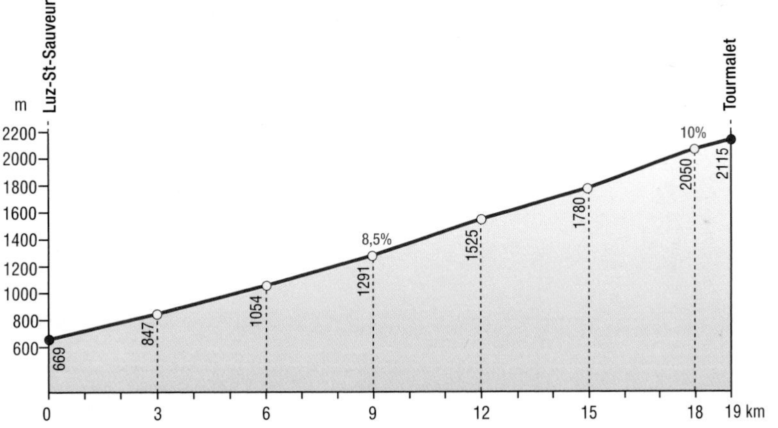

Next you'll see a right turn for the pony riding – the last chance to avoid the drudgery ahead! Shortly afterwards, your path is signposted as branching off on the right.

Along a wooded slope, you will go steadily upwards. You'll cycle with a view of a slope which already outlines the course of the route ahead. In a long sweeping turn to the left, the road ahead sweeps upwards around the 2500m-high Pic de la Caoubère. Before then, however, you'll go past a restaurant, before passing underneath a ski lift. On your left you'll now have a panorama of countless Pyrenean summits, all of which reach around 2500m. Ahead of you will be a bleak mountain range and you'll be surrounded by fantastically beautiful mountain slopes frequented by only a few hill walkers. An unpleasant wind often blows here and on the previous slope. The pass is visible in the far distance, and in case of any signs of weakness you should remind yourself of the heroic days of the Tour. In those days, any rider who climbed the Tourmalet without getting off their bike was rewarded with a gold coin.

At altitude

The road continues in very good condition but is often covered in debris. Crossing underneath a ski lift you will have a wonderful view ahead of a jagged rock massif. Further along you will see the observatory of the 2876m-high Pic du Midi de Bigorre. You'll be surrounded by moss-covered rocks and slopes full of rubble and debris. It is also possible to witness a herd of llamas actually crossing the road – from personal experience!

Now follow the last hairpin bends which offer the steepest part of the route as the finale. Located at the pass is the restaurant Col du Tourmalet, a souvenir shop and the monument to the Father of the Tour, Jacques Goddet, and perhaps also the well-known cycling sculpture. This, however, is dismantled in early autumn so that it doesn't get too damaged by the weather.

The view from the pass is stupendous, and pride in the 'victory

It's unpleasantly cold on the Tourmalet in autumn. By then, the cycling memorial has already been dismantled.

Summer after summer, the bleak meadows of the Pyrenees are home to herds of sheep and, especially on the Tourmalet, even llamas.

over the mountain' is entirely justified. After traversing the pass, you will ride downhill through several covered galleries which, although not dark, are nevertheless unpleasantly wet.

Crowds on the Col

Next to Alpe d'Huez and the Galibier, the Tourmalet is especially venerated by the cycling community.

Ever since its first inclusion in the Tour, true fans have been standing faithfully by the side of the road. They, too, will endure serious hardships to get up here. On foot or by bike, spectators have been attracted to the pass since 1910. Over the years the Tourmalet has attained almost mythical significance. It therefore requires a certain amount of enthusiasm to follow the Tour de France with your own eyes at this particular point.

Those who haven't reserved their place two days in advance, are often too late. The chances are slightly better in La Mongie, where there is also room for parked cars.

Eastern ascent via La Mongie

Spectating is one thing, to climb it on a bike is another, altogether more attractive experience. The Tourmalet is also climbable from the east via La Mongie. The landscape on this route through the Vallée du Campan is not quite so attractive. La Mongie is a large ski resort which has served several times as a stage destination. From an athletic perspective, the eastern approach of the Tourmalet also fulfills all expectations. The distance from Sainte-Marie-de-Campan to the pass is 17km. With an average gradient of 8 per cent you can easily relive the torments endured by cyclists in the early years of the Tour. Riding on fixed gears the Tour riders of old would have had no chance to recuperate, unless they dismounted.

The father of all Tour passes

The cycle sports journalist Peter Leissl has designated the Tourmalet 'the father of all passes' and with that has aptly described the significance of this mountain. The Tour de France without the Tourmalet is almost unthinkable. No other ascent has been mastered as often by the riders since 1910. But the Tourmalet is not only a superlative in terms of numbers. Rather it combines everything that represents the legend of the Tour de France: a handful of tall tales, tragic defeats and heroic victories. Eugène Christophe's broken fork in 1913 is legendary. He used the Tourmalet to go into the overall lead and was leading by 18 minutes, when his front fork suddenly broke. There were no support cars or spare bikes, and regulations decreed that every rider had to carry out their own repairs without outside help. He reached Sainte-Marie-de-Campan after 14km on foot. Since regulations prohibited outside help, he began to hand-craft a new fork in the local forge. After hours of labour, and on the verge of physical collapse, he finally crossed the finishing line. However, the race officials punished him with a time penalty of 1 minute: a little boy had fanned the flames with bellows, which was deemed to be unacceptable help. Christophe suffered two further (1919 and 1922) broken forks – not a good advertisement for his bike manufacturers.

The long way down to the valley: Eugène Christophe had a long march on foot ahead of him after his breakdown in 1913.

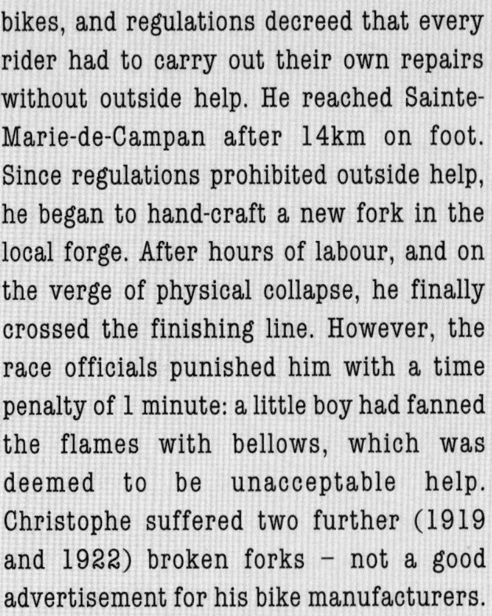

Even the 'discovery' of the Tourmalet by the Tour's management is a story of adventure in itself and owes much to Alphonse Steinès, a young colleague of the Tour director Henri Desgrange. In search of new attractions for the young Tour de France, Steinès submitted an audacious proposal to his superior: why shouldn't the Tour go through the Pyrenees? Desgrange thought this idea was totally absurd. In those days the Pyrenees were crisscrossed primarily by narrow paths for herding livestock, and bad gravel paths for woodsmen. Apart from that it was teeming with bears, wolves, and other wild animals, and avalanches were a threat. Therefore a visit seemed life-threatening. Nevertheless, in 1910 Desgrange despatched his co-worker on a mission. One month before the start of the Tour, Steinès was supposed to assess the situation in situ. Starting from Sainte-Marie-de-Campan, he battled up the road in a chauffeur-driven car. An overheating motor forced a break, then 4km below the pass, metres-high snow prevented further progress. It was now 7pm at night and pitch dark, but Steinès remained stubborn. He decided to cross the pass on foot and asked the driver to pick him up again on the other side. By then it was mainly a matter of keeping face after such a daredevil proposal. The primary reason, mainly the enrichment of the Tour, had long receded into the background.

The rest of the trip deteriorated into a fiasco: in metre-high snow the road was barely discernible, and Steinès wandered about aimlessly. As if by a miracle, he came across a shepherd who accompanied him to the pass. But the view on the other side was sobering. A metre-high blanket of snow covered the whole mountain for the next 10km. Gingerly he dug his way downwards through the deep snow. To speed things up, he slid downhill on his backside, but lost control and tumbled into a ravine.

Finally he landed abruptly in the snow and slid into an icy mountain stream. With his strength ebbing fast, he stumbled onwards and down; several hours had passed already. Meanwhile, a team of local mountain guides began to search for him. When there still was no trace of him at midnight, he was deemed lost. At 3am he staggered, exhausted, into the arms of the gendarmes from Barèges.

Next morning, Steinès telegraphed Paris as agreed. "Road over Tourmalet pass perfect; free of snow and undoubtedly drivable," read his note. Was it fear of professional consequences, or the certainty that the snow would melt during the remaining weeks? In any case, his deception assured the addition of Tourmalet to the Tour schedule.

However, at the premiere of the Aspin, Aubisque and Tourmalet, the Tour director Henri Desgrange suddenly got cold feet. He feared a catastrophe and had the feeling that he had gone too far. Dreading a total fiasco, he travelled back to Paris and anxiously awaited the outcome of the adventure. "This is murder. Those bastards want our scalp," complained Lucien Petit Breton at the start. Thus the officials on Aubisque waited fearfully for the riders. Hour after hour passed and no one could be seen.

But suddenly a filthy and utterly exhausted Octave Lapize appeared. "Assassins," shrieked Lapize at the representatives of the Tour and swore he would leave the Tour; a threat which he quickly forgot during the rapid descent – he was, after all, in the lead.

Neither the hair-raising road conditions, nor the inadequate equipment could stop the 'giants of the road'. Even the Pyrenees, hitherto regarded as 'unconquerable', had been tamed.

The opening up of the Pyrenees was significantly hampered by its dense valleys. The mighty 3000m-high peaks are adorned with snow right up into summer.

5 In the shadow of the great Tourmalet
COL D'ASPIN

The Col d'Aspin is only a small hill – nevertheless it can make you sweat a lot.

CLIMB TOP: 1489m
TOTAL ELEVATION: 800m
DISTANCE: 12km
MAX GRADIENT: 10%
AVERAGE GRADIENT: 6.7%
STARTING POINT:
Arreau (845 inhab.), Département Hautes-Pyrénées (65)
APPROACH:
From Saint-Lary-Soulan on D929 to Arreau
PARKING:
Car park near the Office de Tourisme, in front of a chapel
ROAD CONDITION: Very good
MOUNTAIN PASS OPENINGS:
February to November

You may wish to go for a stroll around Arreau immediately on arrival because the little place is so inviting. Right next to the car park is the Saint-Exupère chapel with its gorgeous Romanesque portal. So it's just as well that this tour's programme is not too taxing, so that you could do a little sightseeing before you start.

With its total elevation of 800m, Col d'Aspin is a relatively easy challenge. The pass flatters with a perfect road but the elevation poses an interesting challenge. With steeper sections of 10 per cent you certainly cannot take it for granted.

Little prelude

In the history of the Tour de France, the Aspin plays only a subordinate role. When compared to the 2115m-high Col du Tourmalet, the Aspin (1489m) is a much friendlier climb and that affects the appearance of the landscape. While a stony mountain world surrounds the Tourmalet, the Aspin is surrounded by gentle grassy slopes. Indeed, the Aspin does not measure up when compared to the other classic ascents on the Tour because of its low height. That it's nevertheless been included over 70 times in the Tour's itinerary is thanks to its proximity to the great Tourmalet.

Decisive for racing events is, naturally, the direction from which the Aspin is to be ascended. If the participants come from the west, the competition is usually already in full swing. Since the Tourmalet has already been crossed, the result of any attacks are clear. However, if the field approaches from the east, then the Tourmalet is yet to come. In this case, opponents still eye each other cautiously. Nobody wants to attack on the Aspin only to be mercilessly punished for it.

It's done: The obligatory summit picture is proof of 'summit euphoria'.

Leisurely running-in

The starting point of this tour is the little town of Arreau in the centre of the Aure Valley. You will leave the main road heading south and turn off left after a few metres. From here the exemplary signposting for cyclists begins again. Up to the summit, distances and inclines are provided at kilometre intervals.

Initially the road meanders up the mountain in tree shadow. Soon, however, you will leave the forest and enjoy a view of the mountain slope on the right. For the time being, you won't be able to make out the pass. You'll ride over a bridge and reach a steeper stretch after about 3km. The way goes along rough stone walls that fortify the slope. Since the road leads to the Tourmalet and to Bagnères, a slight increase in traffic is possible at the weekend.

Next you will pass soft grassy slopes with only a few trees beside the road. The gradient increases again and after 7km you'll face the steepest part at around 10 per cent. Soon after you will pass a barrier and will already be able to see the pass.

Up the mountain

You will be heading steadily for the pass which consists only of an insignificant cut. Cows and sheep graze alongside the road and on the left you will have a view deep into the Aure Valley. Along slopes thickly covered with ferns, it's more steeply uphill again. At one of the bends you will pass a snack bar, still heading in the same direction.

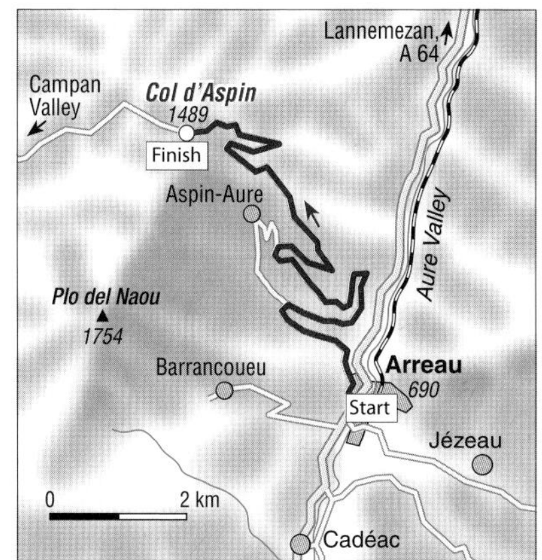

On reaching Col d'Aspin, you will enjoy a wide panoramic view, with the imposing Pyrenean giants showing themselves in outline in the distance. The reward is the beautiful panorama, because the pass itself lacks special attractions. But inscriptions on the road will remind you of days gone by: "I don't know how I managed it; the people virtually shouted me up the mountain," described Thomas Voeckler after his strength-sapping fight on the Aspin in 2004.

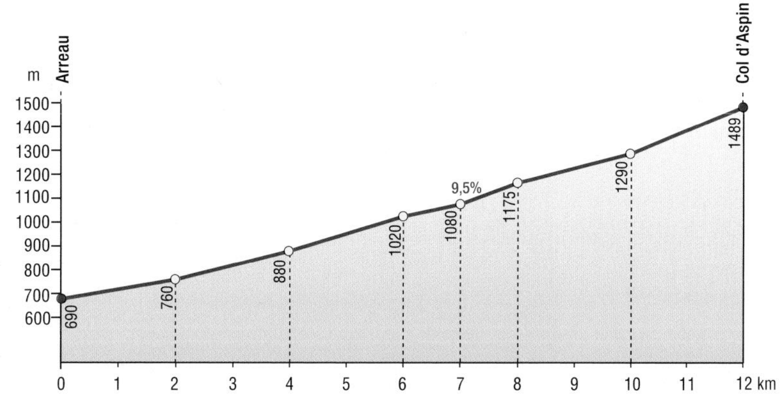

A stroll around Arreau

You won't need long for the ascent and then it's smoothly downhill. At the end of the descent, tighter bends will force you to break but you will arrive quickly back in Arreau. You should use the opportunity for a stroll through the town which used to be one of the most important stations for pilgrims on the way to Santiago di Compostela.

The central location at the confluence of the valleys of the Aure and the Louron did not only bring welcome visitors. Roman legions and Arab soldiers also pitched their camps here. Numerous well-preserved historic buildings grace the pretty old town. The half-timbered houses from the 16th century and especially the historic market building create a medieval atmosphere. The beautiful location right by a little river also delights the holiday maker's heart.

A walk through the place is therefore totally worth it. On market day the farmers from the region provide an additional attraction with their specialities.

In view of the shortness of the ascent, a longer round trip is indicated. On offer are, for example, crossing the pass and riding onwards to Bagnères-de-Bigorre. From there you can either proceed as far as Tarbes, or turn off earlier on to the D938 towards La Barthe-de-Neste. From there the D929 leads back to Arreau. Because of the countless alternatives on offer, you can vary the length of the tour with the aid of a map. Between 80 and 120km can transform the little ascent into a day-long undertaking. Those who tackle Col d'Aspin from the west have to cope with an average gradient of 5 per cent and a total elevation of barely 640m. From Sainte-Marie-de-Campan it's barely 12km to the top of the pass. This leads naturally to another consideration. Why not turn Aspin and Tourmalet into a twin pack? Those who have an accompanying vehicle at their disposal can hardly resist this combination.

Above: The Romanesque portal of the Saint-Exupère chapel is the jewel of Arreau.

Opposite: Enough space for everyone. When the Tour comes, Aspin transforms itself into a huge campsite.

Right: Beech, ash and pine trees dominate the lower reaches of the Pyrenean landscape.

The era of Miguel Indurain

One of the greatest cyclists of all time inaugurated his reign on Aspin. Miguel Indurain hails from a little village in the vicinity of Pamplona. The farmer's son was presented with a racing bike by his father at age 11 and knew how to make the most of the present. Even in his first race he landed on the winner's podium. Victories in regional competitions were finally followed by the big one in 1983. On his 19th birthday, he gave himself the nicest present when he won the Spanish amateur championships. This made his talent public knowledge and the Reynolds Team quickly brought him on board with a professional contract. During his first Tours, in 1985 and 1986 respectively, he only rode a few stages, but in 1987 he made it to Paris for the first time. A slimming programme had made him about 10kg lighter, thereby multiplying his chances. In the meantime he had become an important part of his team and was heading slowly towards his own breakthrough.

On 19 July, 1991, on the stage from Jaca to Val Louron, Miguel Indurain began his dominance of the Tour, which was to last several years. It was the second Pyrenean stage and Indurain was well and truly under pressure. It was Indurain's seventh Tour already and the whole of Spain was expecting him to deliver the Tour victory on that occasion. But the triple Tour winner Greg LeMond seemed to dominate the Tour again and the spectators became impatient. But Indurain kept his cool; he knew that his chance was yet to come. The 13th stage led over the Aubisque, Tourmalet, Col d'Aspin and eventually to Val Louron. This stage was made for an early decider; however, it wasn't Indurain but LeMond who initially attacked. During the ascent of Tourmalet, the American succeeded briefly in riding ahead, but 500m before the summit Indurain turned the tables. He overtook LeMond who was already riding at the limit. Indurain then went full throttle and, together with Claudio Chiappucci, he rode away from the field. LeMond was isolated without teammates and also had some bad luck: he was struck by a support vehicle which cost him valuable seconds. Nevertheless, he had almost caught up again on Col d'Aspin. But the Indurain/Chiappucci duo was unbeatable and the Spaniard granted the Italian Chiappucci the stage victory. He himself took over the yellow jersey; for him this realised a childhood dream. He had ridden to a 7-minute lead and won the Tour for the first time. "To win the Tour, one only has to attack once. But it has to be a knockout blow," is the Spaniard's credo.

Indurain's attack on Tourmalet began an exemplary era which was only to be surpassed by Lance Armstrong. Indurain celebrated five Tour victories in succession and drove his adversaries to despair. It was Indurain's talent for time trials in particular, that made him so unbeatable. In the fight against the clock, he ran like a well-oiled machine. His sensational performance in this discipline in 1992 is legendary: he won the first time trial over 65km with the lead time of 3 minutes over De Las Cuevas in second place. During the second single time trial of the Tour in 1992 he reached an average speed of over 52kph over the distance of 64km.

On the mountain, Indurain climbed powerfully and held his opponents at bay. This even though he had an apparently unsuitable physique for mountains: with his imposing height of 1.88m he weighed in at 80kg. The mountain stages were therefore really hard work. Claudio Chiappucci and Tony Rominger were among his toughest adversaries. The 125km-long solo attempt by Chiappucci in 1992 during the stage from Saint Gervais to Sestrière is unforgettable.

Even this desperate rebellion did not bring Indurain down. During his attempt to dethrone the Emperor, Rominger experienced repeated unhappy setbacks. Several flat tyres and bad weather during time trials put paid to the Swiss rider's attempts to unseat Indurain.

The press did not prove enthusiastic about the superiority of the 'cold' Spaniard. Indurain was described as emotionless, he seemed to ride from one victory to the next like a robot. It was probably mainly his dominance during the Tour that gave rise to the image of the cycling robot. "You're up for it, but that Indurain just moves up a gear and kills you," was the desperate verdict of Richard Virenque about his colleague. That Indurain was suffering as much as his colleagues was no secret. He was merely better at covering up and protecting himself from attack at the wrong moment. Only a good strategist can win the Tour, and thus Indurain did not allow public opinion to put pressure on him. Wisely, he kept track of the distance to his opponents and wasn't fazed by their partial successes. Generously he distributed stage victories among his fellow combatants. Coldheartedness is therefore not something one can accuse the Spaniard of. Because he was taciturn towards the press and didn't have a special sense of humour, his public image was less than brilliant.

One thing distinguished Indurain from the five-times Tour winners Anquetil, Merckx and Hinault: before his first triumph, he had slaved away for his countryman Pedro Delgado. Perhaps that's why he became reticent with the press and did not like to reveal his cards in public. He had perhaps learnt how transient fame is and how strong pressure from the media can be. And therefore he always behaved modestly and stayed away from cameras and microphones.

Only in 1996 could the giant Spaniard be pushed off the podium. The Dane Bjarne Riis won his first Tour – to a large extent thanks to a hitherto unknown helper: Jan Ullrich.

The French postal service honoured Indurain on the occasion of the 100th anniversary of the Tour with a postage stamp.

6 Steep paths to the ski station
PLA D'ADET

Totally 'in': The pilgrim's way to Santiago di Compostela is fashionable again and also goes past Saint-Lary-Soulan.

CLIMB TOP: 1680m
TOTAL ELEVATION: 860m
DISTANCE: 11.5km
MAX GRADIENT: 12%
AVERAGE GRADIENT: 7.5%
STARTING POINT:
Saint-Lary-Soulan (1040 inhab.), Département Hautes-Pyrénées (65)
APPROACH:
From Arreau on D929 to Saint-Lary-Soulan
PARKING:
Straight on into the town, car park directly in front of the Office de Tourisme
ROAD CONDITION: Perfect
MOUNTAIN PASS OPENINGS:
All year

The route into the ugly ski resort of Saint-Lary-Soulan is short and sharp. But never fear, although the place itself is off-putting, the journey there is gorgeous. With gradients of up to 12 per cent you definitely won't get bored!

High Pyrenean peaks

Saint-Lary-Soulan is a typical Pyrenean town with beautiful old houses and a church dating back to the 16th century. But in the last decades the place has undergone a drastic transformation. In 1963 the communities of Saint Lary and Soulan united to forge ambitious and promising plans for tourism together.

What was then a daring vision of ambitious villagers has since proved itself to be the wise master plan for the prosperity of a region. In the meantime, Saint-Lary-Soulan has developed into one of the most important ski centres of the French Pyrenees. The incredible 35 pistes extend over an area of over 500 hectares.

The number of visitors has increased steeply and they continue to come in their droves, even in summer. The nearby Réserve Naturelle Néouvielle and the Parc National des Pyrénées especially attract nature lovers in the warmer months. Part of the pilgrim's way to Santiago di Compostela comes this way and offers lots of hiking opportunities.

Pyrenean bears

A heated argument rages across the whole of the Pyrenees: how dangerous are the bears that have made themselves at home in the Pyrenees? In Saint-Lary-Soulan in the Maison de l'Ours you can find out more about the history of the bears in the Pyrenees. An exhibition

Guaranteed fun along the bends: The way to the ski station goes over hairpin bends.

with multimedia components will broaden your knowledge of the Pyrenean bears. There are also living examples, albeit carefully kept in cages. But even the most beautiful exhibition won't keep you from the main reason for the visit: the cycling. From the Office de Tourisme you will go diagonally right at the roundabout, along narrow little streets and between houses. Past the Parking du Stade, you'll follow the signs for 'Saint-Lary 1700 Le Pla d'Adet'. First you will roll past two roundabouts, straight through the town in the direction of Vignec. After a small, cosy campsite you will head straight for the mountain. At a wooded slope the immaculate road then goes stoutly uphill, winding alongside the mountain.

Shortly after the start, a glance upwards and to the left reveals where you will need to go. There are bunker-like tower blocks on the horizon which are the winter sport resort you're aiming for. After 2.5km you will corkscrew your way up the first hairpin at over 10 per cent. During my visit the road was virtually littered with Tour graffiti, the proximity to the Basque country is reflected on the tarmac. To the left beckons a gorgeous panorama with 3000m giants along the Spanish border. In good visibility you should be able to see Pic Schrader, Pic Perdiguère and Pic des Crabioules.

Idyll in Soulan

Next you'll continue to ride along a wooded slope. You'll then corkscrew upwards on steep hairpin bends and quickly gain height.

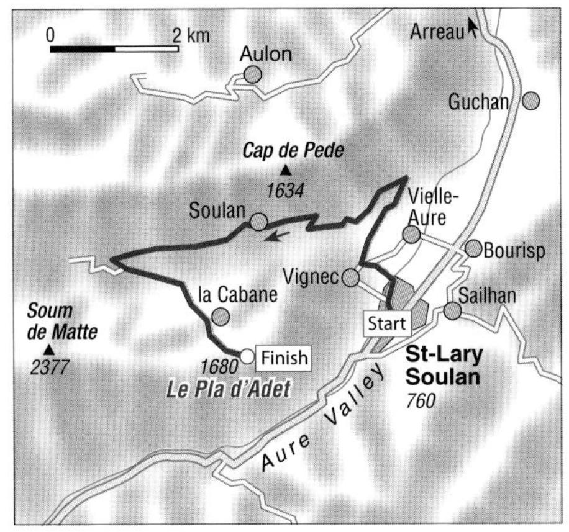

After 6km you'll reach Soulan, a small and cosy mountain village, which is such an unexpected contrast to the concrete castle on the other side! A little church, a well-maintained fountain, flowers – these places in the mountains can be so beautiful. The gradient reduces only for a short distance, only to jump back up to 7 and later 10 per cent.

On the left a beautiful wooded slope is now closer and you'll already be able to see the ascent to come. There are still more beautiful mountain landscapes to be admired; dense mountain forest dominates the picture.

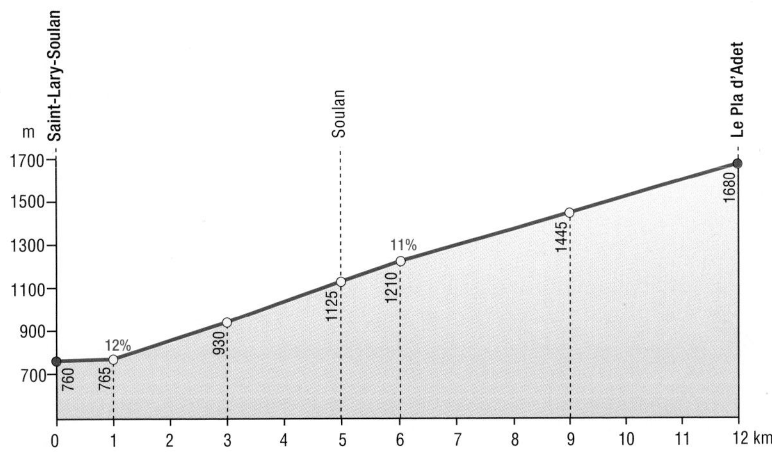

Racing fun for amateurs

The Pyrenees offers a number of fascinating cycling challenges. The 'L'Ariègeoise' was founded in 1994 and today is the most famous cyclosportive of the region. It offers three itineraries: La Passejade (shortest), La Mountagnole (around 100km) and the famous 'L'Ariègeoise'. In 2010 around 4000 cyclists from all over Europe took part. For the longest route they had to complete a distance of 165km and a total elevation of 3100m. Slightly more comfortable but still not exactly a stroll was the 'Mountagnole' route offered that day: a total elevation of 2580m over 117km. Advance registration on the website is recommended. As for all other cycling races in France a current doctor's certificate is required to participate if you don't have a licence from the French cycling club FFC.

Further information:
L'Ariègeoise Cyclo Club
Espace François Mitterrand
BP 70119
9401 Tarascon sur Ariege
Tel: 00 33/(0)561059494
www.cyclosport-ariegeoise.com

Soulan is a cosy Pyrenean village that does not seem to mind the mass tourism in the nearby ski resort.

You will now be rolling downhill and on a sweeping left-hand bend you'll change over to the opposite slope. There you'll head left (signposted) uphill to Pla d'Adet. Here too there are many Basque daubings, unfortunately also frequently among them *'Gora ETA'*, or 'Long Live ETA'.

Ski resort and descent

Next a long straight ramp leads towards the ski resort. The gradient reduces slightly and after a while you'll find yourself on a slope among a dense forest of birches.

After 11km you will reach a place with many lifts and big hotels. A very wide and densely graffiti-ridden road now leads through Pla d'Adet. At around 8 per cent you will need to push strongly on the pedals once more, no doubt looking forward to the descent. The rush downhill is pure delight!

The Tour de France for the collector

The passion of the fans of the Tour de France does not always restrict itself to just its athletic aspects. Especially in France, collecting objects associated with the Tour is popular. From a stamp via old autograph cards, from colourful woollen jerseys to rusty metal signs: once you have started collecting, you come across countless fascinating objects. How about, for example, a feeding bag or 'musette' from 1935, or a selection of drinking bottles from several decades of the Tour? An older bottle with a cork cap can go for €200. The history of the Tour is also reflected in many lovingly created objects. Historic Tour-themed card games, colourful posters or metal figures can be incredibly fascinating to nostalgia fans.

The relief car belongs in every collection.

Historically correct: An old timer in front of a bakery.

Those who have experienced the Tour from the side of the road know that the cars are also central to the race. Small miniature cars from the Tour de France publicity caravan are among the most popular collector's items. While older models change hands for several thousand euros, current new releases are available for around €10. A true enthusiast has several hundred model cars in his cupboard, and anything that's no longer available is reconstructed. It sounds elaborate but is understandable in view of the prices of rarer items: a metal car from the 50s can fetch €600, even if it is dented. And if you want to have a little figure next to the wheel, it will cost another €2 to €15. These little figures, for example from Salza, hold a bag of provisions in their hand, push-start the riders or observe the riders from the car of the Tour director.

Those in Lyons or Paris should look in on Aux Collections du Sport. This little shop is stuffed to the rafters with paraphernalia relating to past sporting events. For enthusiasts it's a real treasure trove!

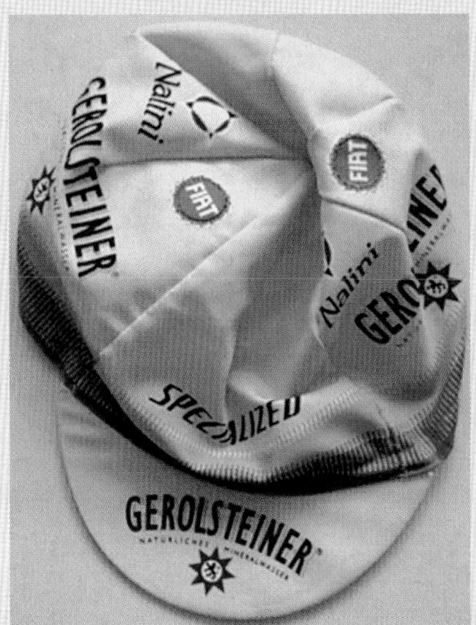

The past: Team Gerolsteiner only lives on among collectors.

7 Athletic tour on a perfect road
COL DE PEYRESOURDE

There are no secrets on the ascent to Peyresourde, the road is visible all the way up to the summit.

CLIMB TOP: 1493m
TOTAL ELEVATION: 900m
DISTANCE: 13.5km
MAX GRADIENT: 10%
AVERAGE GRADIENT: 6.8%
STARTING POINT:
Bagnères-de-Luchon (3040 inhab.), Département Haute-Garonne (31)
APPROACH:
From Saint-Gaudens initially on D8 to Saint-Bertrand-de-Comminges and on D33 and then D125 to Luchon
PARKING:
In Luchon follow the signs for Col de Peyresourde, then turn left into a small sign posted car park shortly before leaving town
ROAD CONDITION: Very good
MOUNTAIN PASS OPENINGS:
June to October

During the summer, holiday business is brisk in Luchon, because the little town has developed into one of the most prominent tourist centres in the whole region thanks to its thermal baths. Luchon reports up to 28,000 visitors annually to its thermal baths. These mineral springs have reportedly been in use since Roman times. Directly in the centre of town, *Les Thermes* are surrounded by a little park. A visit is naturally recommended, to pamper your tormented leg muscles after the ride. The springs offer a wide choice of treatments, which are supposed to alleviate rheumatism as well as lung disease. Among the latest programmes is a course to give up smoking. But in Luchon you don't just have to while away the time in the springs. A walk in the town centre is also rewarding. There are many historical buildings all around the Allées d'Étigny and the Musée du Pays de Luchon.

Immediately strenuously uphill

But to make the relaxing evening bath worthwhile, you will first have to push strenuously on the pedals. From the car park, take a left on to the road which immediately takes you out of the town. The ascent begins immediately, a ramp with up to 7 per cent gradient leads upwards. The valley becomes increasingly narrower and on the left there's a rushing stream. After around 3km a hairpin bend goes past a small chapel. Next you'll go along by a stone wall with a steep slope behind. The opposite slope is thickly overgrown with deciduous forest.

Beauty in stone

The way leads steeply through Saint-Aventin, a small town with gorgeous old stone houses and a 12th century church. After you

In high summer, the sun burns straight down – there is no shade here!

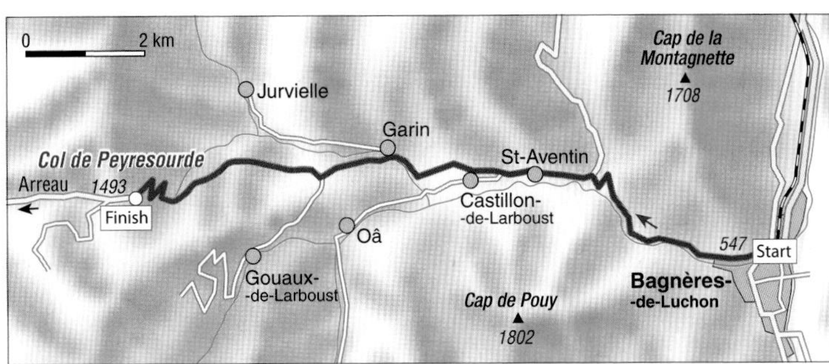

have left the town behind, you'll see the slate roofs that are typical of this region. Another beautiful stone church follows, and shortly afterwards you'll reach the next town via a road with unfortunately heavy traffic. At Garin you will have covered more than half the distance, but there are still around 450m of total elevation ahead of you. Beside the road on the left is a stone chapel from the 11th century, a little later you'll pass two stone water troughs. Next you'll go through the last of the trees, then you'll be exposed to the sun. The view widens and you'll be able to see past steep meadows to the mountain pass. To your right, beautiful wooded slopes stretch into the valley and you'll see little houses down below.

Last reserves of strength

You'll ride along a slope on your left and be able to see the mountain pass straight ahead and above you. The road winds upwards on the right around two hairpin bends. You should enjoy the view across the valley in the following two hairpin bends. A long straight bit takes you to your destination. On the crest the Département Haute-Garonne ends and the Département Haute-Pyrénées begins. On the last few metres to the top there is a lot of Tour de France graffiti on the road which will motivate you to step on it. Many professional cyclists have dug into their last reserves of strength here.

Arduous even for professionals

"Man, the Sunday stage was extremely hard. The speed, the six ascents, the heat – all leave you totally drained. On the first three mountains I could still keep up, on the fourth, Col de Peyresourde, I had to let them break away. I rode to the end together with Sebastian Lang and Georg Totschnig – at perhaps 13 or 14kph – just couldn't go any faster", confided Fabian Wegmann after the day's stage 15 of the 2005 Tour.

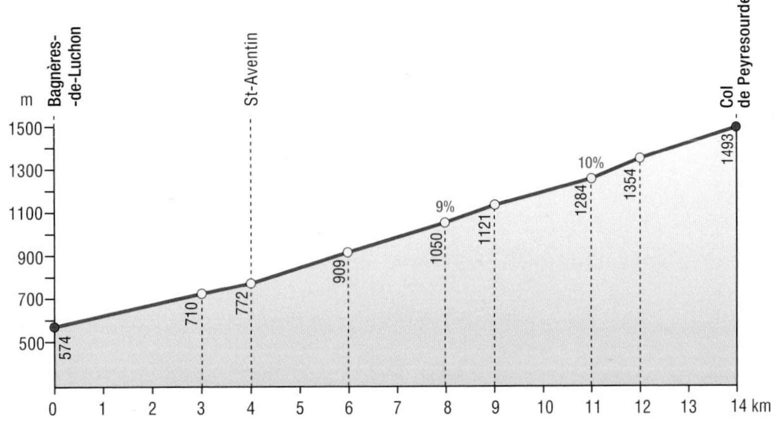

Steep bends

The mountain pass is characterised by very sparse landscape. A deforested slope begins on the right, otherwise you'll only see meadows and grazing sheep. There is nowhere to get provisions! Therefore, be sure to pack sufficient food and drink in advance.

After riding over the pass you will begin a descent rich in speed changes; the condition of the road leaves nothing to be desired. However, you should not model yourself on Jan Ullrich, who came off the designated route here (see 'Tour history', page 37). The bend where he disappeared into the bushes is the first steep bend on the descent and appears approximately 4km after the summit.

Unassuming veteran of the Tour

Despite its comparatively harmless ascents, Col de Peyresourde has made nearly 60 Tour appearances. But the height of 1563m is often not enough to create a decisive break away from the peloton. In spite of this, motorhomes assemble in the car park of the summit plateau on a Tour day since the place is made for it, as the wide slopes and partially flat meadows are ideally suited for parking and camping. The sparse vegetation also allows a wide view over the slope so that viewers should be able to follow the column of riders for some distance. For these reasons, compared to other ascents, it is very easy to be part of a live stage here. On the day of the Tour visit, the flat car park turns into a huge campsite with an international audience.

Rewarding all round

Similar to the ascent described here, the approach from the west has an average gradient in the region of 6 per cent. Those planning a round trip need to be prepared for a long ride (110km, 1800m elevation) because even the shortest route leads to Arreau and through the Aure Valley in the direction of La-Barthe-de-Neste. Just before the town the D938 leads off towards the east. Following the D33 and then D125 towards the south, you will reach Bagnères-de-Luchon again after around 100km.

Reserved! The motorhomes show that the race is making an appearance in Peyresourde today.

The Tour gets bogged down in the doping mire

June 30, 2006 was a black day for Germany's cycle sport fans. For weeks they had been eagerly awaiting the Tour – Jan Ullrich was expected to finally attain a second victory. Instead, Ullrich was suspended from his team and the Fuentes Affair was gathering momentum. Over the following month, the sport of cycling was overrun by an endless chain of scandals. The pattern was always the same: initially all professionals would sign up for the fight against doping, which would be followed by positive doping tests and ingenious excuses.

Tour de France 2006

Ivan Basso and Jan Ullrich, both customers of gynaecologist Fuentes, had to leave the Tour with other riders. It only became clear later on that doping had been organised for the T-Mobile team by doctors from the University-Clinic in Freiburg. Jörg Jaksche reported systematic doping in all of the teams he had been part of in his career. "Jan Ullrich did dope," was the verdict of the Public Prosecutor's Office in Bonn in 2008. Floyd Landis won the Tour but a few days after his celebrated victory, a positive doping sample appeared. He had drunk too much whisky before the stage, said Landis, in an attempt to explain the conspicuous testosterone levels. In 2010 Landis admitted a career of doping and accused Lance Armstrong of systematic doping.

Tour de France 2007

While the Tour was still in progress, Alexander Vinokourov was convicted of blood transfusion doping, and Christian Moreni of testosterone doping. Shortly afterwards, a positive doping sample from T-Mobile rider Patrick Sinkewitz became public knowledge. Sinkewitz as well as Matthias Kessler (Astana) who tested positive, was dismissed. The Tour was dominated by Michael Rasmussen, who had missed doping tests and concealed his training locations. When this became known his team withdrew him. Afterwards a doping sample established that his blood contained Dynepo during the 2007 Tour. Iban Mayo's sample also showed EPO abuse. The Tour was won by Alberto Contador, whose name was mentioned in connection with the Fuentes Affair.

Tour de France 2008

In 2008 pressure on the riders from sponsors and fans was growing. In vain: Manuel Beltran, Moisés Duenas, Ricardo Ricco and Leonardo Piepoli tested positive for EPO. TV viewing figures reached a new low. After the Tour, the German bomb exploded: the Gerolsteiner riders Stefan Schumacher and Bernhard Kohl both tested positive.

Tour de France 2009

Team Rabobank rider Thomas Dekker tested on Dynepo, Euskaltel rider Mikel Astarloza on EPO and Team LPR rider Danilo Di Luca on CERA before the Tour. Belgian racer Tom Boonen tested positive twice for the use of cocaine and was banned from the Tour by the organising ASO.

Tour de France 2010

Alessandro Petacchi winner of the green jersey was under investigation in Italy for doping. Weeks after the party on the Champs Elysees came the news that Alberto Contador winner of the Tour de France 2010 had tested positive for Clenbuterol.

8 Surrounded by 3000m peaks
SUPERBAGNÈRES

Dark clouds on the border with Spain – now cycling turns into soggy enjoyable fun.

CLIMB TOP: 1800m
TOTAL ELEVATION: 1150m
DISTANCE: 17km
MAX GRADIENT: 12%
AVERAGE GRADIENT: 6.8%
STARTING POINT:
Bagnères-de-Luchon (3040 inhab.), Département Haute-Garonne (31)
APPROACH:
From Saint-Gaudens on D8 to Saint-Bertrand-de-Comminges and on D33 and then D125 to Luchon
PARKING:
Into the town centre, park next to the town park, near the thermal spa
ROAD CONDITION: Perfect
MOUNTAIN PASS OPENINGS:
Open all year

Luchon is a very busy place. On market day, the whole region turns up and during the season it can really fill up. Although Luchon only has around 3000 inhabitants, the reputation of the thermal spa extends throughout the whole country. But on this route there's not much indication of the busy stream of visitors. Superbagnères doesn't attract so many summer visitors. In winter, it's completely different, because you are then able to reach Superbagnères directly from Luchon by cable car.

Idyllic mountain excursion

Although there is usually a lot of hustle and bustle in Luchon, this cycling trip is a relatively lonely mountain excursion. Past the thermal spa you will roll along the D125 (signposted) to Superbagnères. Immediately after the town it's stoutly uphill. Along a wooded slope you will initially cycle up a 9 per cent then a 7 per cent gradient along the Pique Valley. The view ahead is a view upwards: with a two-digit per cent incline you will be heading in the direction of Spain. In front of you lies an idyllic mountain landscape, with lots of interlocking valleys. It's especially picturesque when the tendrils of mist make their escape between the mountain slopes.

Through a cool valley

A small stream runs along the right side of the road. You'll still be on the Route de L'Hospice de France. The road leads directly to Spain, but you will be staying within France. After a short climb you'll turn right on to the D46 into a side valley. You will then ride downhill over a bridge and again along a stream (Lys).

Accompanied by the rushing sound of the stream you should be able to savour the ride along wooded slopes in a beautiful and lonesome valley. Created by a glacier, the Vallée du Lys shields you from the sun and is pleasant to ride even in high summer. At 6 per cent the road follows the stream and a formidable Pyrenean summit rears up in front of you.

During the first few kilometres after Luchon you'll roll along the wooded Pique Valley.

3000m view

After 7km the gradient increases to 11 per cent, the valley opens up and you get a wide view of an imposing mountain massif around the Pic des Crabioules (3116m) and the Pic de Maupas (3109m). Shortly afterwards you'll reach L'Ourson (the little bear). You'll escape upwards because the road branches off to the right and immediately starts the ascent on the D46 with a huge hairpin bend. Time and again you'll go past little, rushing streams. Compared to the other routes in the vicinity, there are relatively few cyclists about here.

After 11km a steep hairpin bend goes to the left and uphill on an extended ramp. After a quarry, you'll slowly work your way up the mountain, zig-zag fashion. The steepest part of the route is found here. The distance between individual bends is approximately 1km. In the bends you'll be rewarded with a beautiful view across the valley which you've already left behind. The view widens with increasing altitude and you get a good view of the 3000m peaks which string themselves impressively along the border.

What a pass!

After 14km you'll be able to see the first ski lifts and the end is not far away. You'll now find yourself surrounded by sparse grassy slopes, without a tree in sight. Numerous hairpin bends follow, and every one is accompanied by a change of direction which will present you with different scenery every time. Both sides are beautiful to look at and riding is now a special treat. You'll particularly enjoy looking at the snow-covered granite mountains. The distance between the hairpins becomes increasingly smaller and after a bend you will discover a large building at the head of the pass.

Over a long drawn-out straight you'll ride directly towards the Grand Hotel. On the right you can look into the depths as far as Luchon, which appears a long way away. During the winter 130 snow cannons ensure undiluted joy on the piste, but with its 24 pistes this ski resort is among the smaller winter sports destinations in the Pyrenees. On arrival in Superbagnères an agreeable little ski resort awaits you – without the ubiquitous concrete castles. A snack bar, a small pass sign – that's it. You'll no doubt enjoy the quiet and look forward to the descent. Superbagnères – really super!

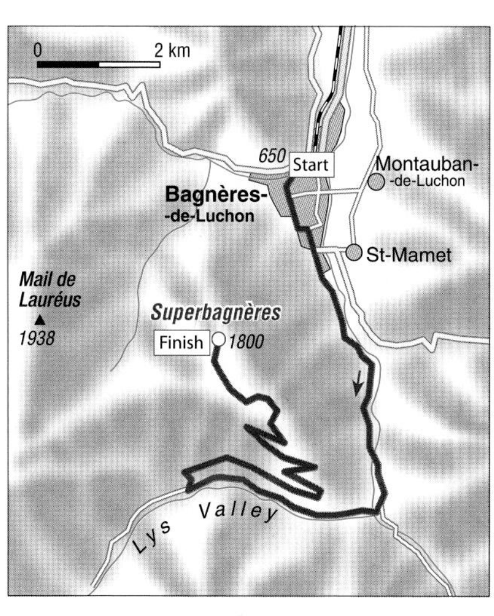

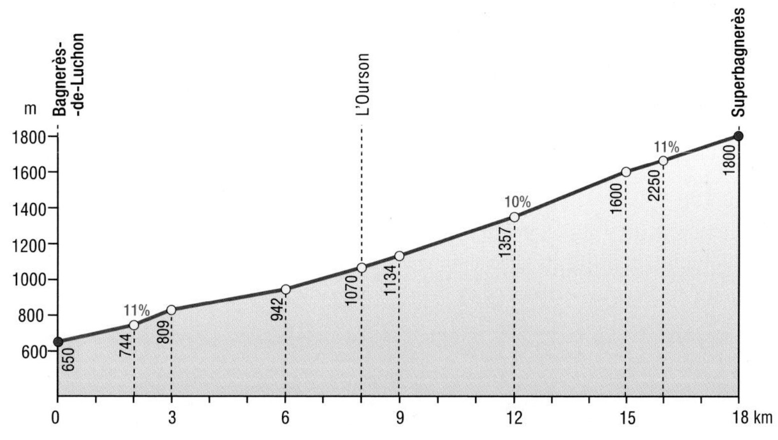

Greg LeMond defeats the Badger

In the history of the Tour de France, team mates are often among the greatest adversaries, which was also the case in 1985 in the team La Vie Claire: initially everything pointed to a confident fifth victory by the Breton Bernard Hinault. He had already slipped into the yellow jersey in the prologue. But shortly before the end of the 14th stage, he fell heavily and sustained a broken nose. With a blood-smeared face he rode on to the end after a few minutes' treatment. The Pyrenees were next and his injury was further aggravated by a loss of form. His teammate Greg LeMond, however, was in top form and could only be held back with repeated persuasion. In return for his restraint he was assured of Hinault's full support for the following year. Hinault unequivocally owed his fifth Tour success to LeMond's assistance; without him his reign would most likely have ended.

But in 1986 the 'Badger' suddenly exhibited signs of a poor memory, he had long since forgotten his promise of support. Hinault wanted to ride to his sixth Tour victory and therefore he attacked his teammate on the first day. During the following days he also showed no consideration and soon found himself in the yellow jersey. His teammate seemed to have fewer chances of a Tour victory with every new day. Therefore everyone was spellbound during the 13th stage from Luchon to Superbagnères, waiting for a preliminary decision. The overall lead of the Breton already amounted to 5 minutes. If Hinault won that day, a sixth Tour victory seemed within reach. But Hinault raised the stakes during the ascent and looked weak for the first time. On Peyresourde he got the bonk (sudden drop in performance when carbohydrate reserves are exhausted) and LeMond finally saw that his moment had come. He revved up for the big attack and crossed the line in Superbagnères with a clear margin. Although Hinault still wore the

A road loaded with history: Bernard Hinault began to struggle on the way to Superbagnères.

yellow jersey, his lead was significantly diminished.

Although the psychological battle between the two teammates continued, a page had clearly been turned. From Col du Glandon the American wore the jersey of the overall leader and in Paris he stood at the top of the winners' podium for the first time. Even at the finish in Paris, LeMond couldn't suppress his rage about his teammate Hinault. He was still bitterly disappointed at the betrayal by the Frenchman. "I won the Tour alone, without his help," he stressed during interviews. But his grudge was forgotten at last when he was received in the White House by the American president. Ronald Reagan outed himself as a cycle sports fan and LeMond was thrilled, since the Tour de France was still mostly unknown to most Americans then.

A new Tour favourite seemed to be born, but a horrific accident brought the American to his knees. During a hunting trip his brother-in-law accidentally discharged a load of shot into his lung. Seriously injured, he was delivered to hospital where the doctors fought for his life. Although he survived, his sporting career appeared to be in jeopardy. Only a few weeks after the tragic accident his team cancelled his contract. The Dutch PDM-Team looked optimistically to the future and offered LeMond a well-paid contract. In 1988 the American tried his luck at minor races but he was still severely affected and to add insult to injury, he was also plagued by injuries sustained in falls.

But in 1989 he actually surprised everyone with a comeback. He still had 36 shot fragments lodged in his lung when he lined up at the start for the Belgian ADR team. To all intents and purposes he only wanted to land among the top 20, but things worked out better as the race continued. The previous year's victor, Pedro Delgado, arrived two and a half minutes late at the start and thereby forfeited all chances. LeMond took over the yellow jersey during the 5th stage – a sensation! As with his first Tour victory the ascent to Superbagnères also seemed to play a significant role this time. Laurent Fignon assumed the overall lead and looked like a sure winner at last after his show of strength on Alpe d'Huez. On the last day of the Tour his lead over LeMond had increased to 50 seconds. The Tour ended with a time trial in Paris and it looked certain that Fignon would bring home the spoils that day. Defending a 50-second lead over a distance of 24.5km wasn't too difficult for a strong figure like Fignon. But LeMond had one trump card left – a special time trial bike with triathlon handlebars. The handlebars were a new invention and offered a decisive aerodynamic advantage. LeMond triumphed with a lead of 58 seconds and had therefore won the Tour with a lead of exactly 8 seconds. Afterwards, experts calculated what time advantage LeMond gained from the aerodynamic body posture. One thesis maintains that Fignon would have won if he had worn a streamlined helmet, because his long hair trailing in the wind had cost valuable seconds. Totally exhausted and with tears in his eyes, Fignon lay on the ground on the other side of the finish line. Greg LeMond on the other hand celebrated his victory, richly deserved after the knock-backs of the previous two years. His great achievement was that at long last the Tour de France had finally received recognition in America. With that he lay the foundations for a growing American fan base that travels to the Tour year after year.

Thanks to Greg LeMond, the American colours were represented on the Champs Elysées.

9 Athletic challenge
COL DE MENTÉ VIA PORTET

CLIMB TOP: 1349m
TOTAL ELEVATION:
Aspet: 580m, Menté: 750m
DISTANCE: 34km
MAX GRADIENT:
11% (return journey 17%)
AVERAGE GRADIENT:
Aspet: 3.5%, Menté: 7%
STARTING POINT:
Audressein (100 inhab.), Département Ariège (09)
APPROACH:
From Saint-Girons on the D618 to Audressein
PARKING:
Immediately on entering town, on the right opposite a restaurant
ROAD CONDITION:
Good condition on Aspet and many repairs on Menté
DANGERS: Extremely steep descent
MOUNTAIN PASS OPENINGS:
February to November

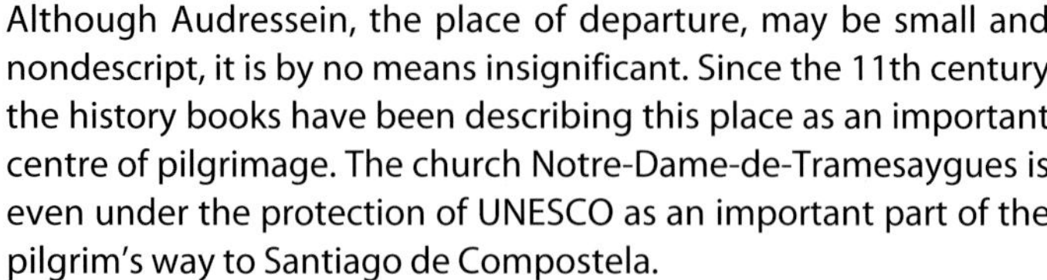

Although Audressein, the place of departure, may be small and nondescript, it is by no means insignificant. Since the 11th century the history books have been describing this place as an important centre of pilgrimage. The church Notre-Dame-de-Tramesaygues is even under the protection of UNESCO as an important part of the pilgrim's way to Santiago de Compostela.

Dark past

But a dark shadow lies over this ascent. The tragic death of the Italian cycling professional Fabio Casartelli (see 'Tour history', page 46) is inextricably linked with Portet d'Aspet. It's hard to suppress thoughts of the deadly fall, but a bit of reflection doesn't do any harm. In spite of this, combining the two Pyrenean passes is a beautiful day trip. If you also ride back over the ascent, you will have cycled over a total elevation of 1800m uphill. The fact that this also includes a short stretch with a gradient of over 17 per cent makes this stage an insider's secret.

A plus point for cycle sport fans

Visitors to the Tour de France also hold Portet d'Aspet and Col de Menté in high regard. The steep ramps of Aspet in particular offer spectacular scenery on the approach from the west. Inevitably the field is slowed down here and the view of the cyclists is therefore more prolonged than usual. But the steep hairpin bends of the Col de Menté also present an exciting backdrop for a Tour visit. However, since parking spaces are very limited, spectators first have to earn their place. Making the journey on your own racing bike is the most obvious solution.

Through a multifaceted valley

At the start it's hard to imagine gradient percentages in two figures, since the way leads initially along the very flat Bellongue Valley. Meadows, little villages, beautiful churches and stone houses along the way help pass the time. One village follows the next, all idyllic mountain villages with a lot of atmosphere and stone houses in the local style.

After 6.5km you will ride uphill for the first time in this very wide valley. Even after 10km the way continues mainly on the flat, but that soon changes: after a cow pasture the road leads into a bend with a 4 per cent gradient. After you may have almost forgotten how to ride uphill you'll be delighted that the road finally delivers. In

Steep slate roofs and unadorned stone houses: The local building style dominates the route.

D'ASPET

Saint-Lary the road leads you between a little bridge which crosses a stream and a beautiful stone church.

In the midst of partly rather worn stone houses the gradient picks up once again.

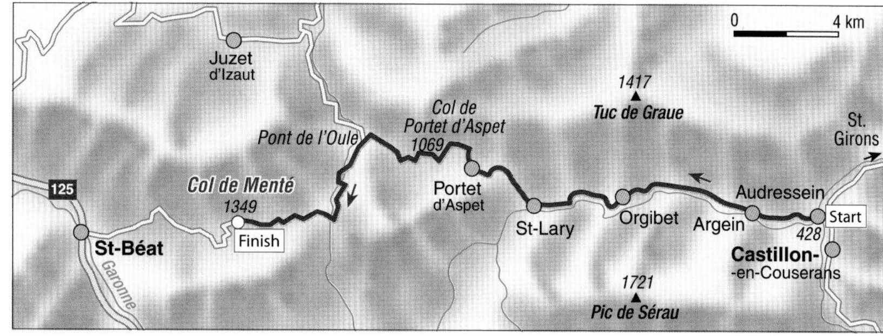

At the mountain pass

On a gradient of 4 per cent you'll leave the Département de l'Ariège and reach the Département Haute-Garonne. You'll now be cycling constantly uphill on a road in optimal condition. After 15km you'll reach Portet d'Aspet, and the view opens up. You'll already be able to see the route ahead and foresee the pass. The road winds upwards at 7 per cent through Portet d'Aspet.

Two hairpins later and you'll already be looking down on to the roofs of the place you just rode through. At a sweat inducing 9 per cent you'll be working steadily towards the mountain pass. At the third hairpin bend you'll be rewarded on the right with a wide view over the valley which you've already left behind, and you'll arrive rather unspectacularly at the summit. A small café and a drinking water fountain invite you to rest.

Steeply downhill

But naturally this is just the beginning and you'll need to prepare for the descent to Col de Menté. The descent is downhill and in shady well-tarred snaking lines. The extremely steep and winding road demands total concentration. Shortly before you finish the descent you'll reach the memorial to Fabio Casartelli and his deadly accident in 1995. A commemorative stone was set on the bend below the memorial. At this point he smashed against the barrier which has since been changed. Originally there were concrete blocks here as along the previous bends.

At the following junction, you won't turn right and downhill, but instead

Because of the lower altitude the pass is also accessible outside of the summer months.

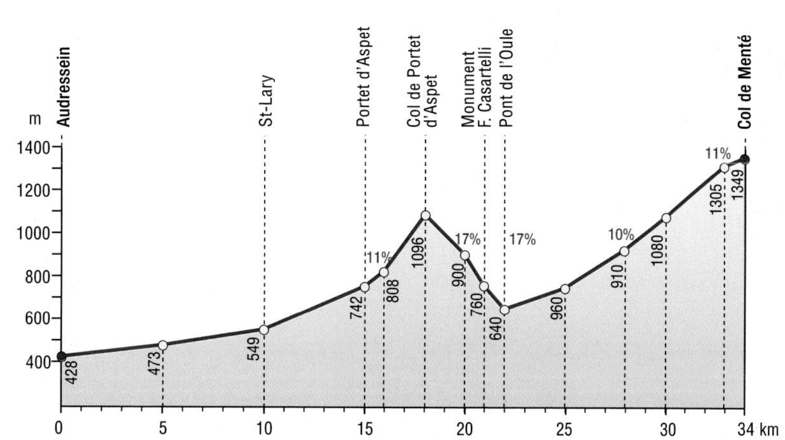

you'll go straight on and immediately uphill again. When I was on this stretch, after I had been concentrating hard on the descent, mindful of the fatal plunge, there was suddenly a loud bang on the level stretch – my tyre had burst. Fortunately it had been the most convenient spot of the whole route, but it had given me the creeps a little as it was so soon after I had passed the commemorative stone.

The view is worth a photo break.

The simple solution to the mysterious flat: the rim tape had first deformed and then developed holes.

Alternative route

Those who want to avoid the brace of Aspet and Menté can begin their tour at this junction instead. The start is at Pont de l'Oule, on the bridge exactly in the middle between the two mountains. However, there is no official parking space here. Next the route follows the incised Ger Valley along a stream. Only after you have crossed a bridge will you start to pedal uphill again. Information signs warn you that you are in bear country. Few would wish for an encounter and therefore you'll trust that any bears will hear your puffing from a great distance!

After Ger de Boutx the way leads constantly uphill at over 8 per cent, initially in a long extended straight, then again in bends.

Several hairpin bends follow during the final kilometres and the gradient climbs to 8 per cent. But a deciduous forest compensates for the no-doubt growing demands on your strength by creating shade. Between the trees on the right emerges a peak riddled with limestone and you'll already be imagining the location of the mountain pass. But contrary to expectations the last few metres to the charmless mountain pass drag on.

On Col de Menté there is a recommended restaurant with accommodation. Since the pass is

After rainfall special care is required because the slope at Portet d'Aspet goes far beyond the usual.

The hairpin bends on Col de Menté are a delight for the eyes and a treat for the legs.

surrounded by forest you'll have to forego the panorama.

And the whole thing again, backwards

Those who choose the descent in the direction of of St-Béat can rush downhill along steep bends. But the memory of Luis Ocana's painful fall urges caution here too.

In 1971 he created a sensation by beating Eddy Merckx. He had hardly donned the yellow jersey before he fell during rain and a thunderstorm and had to abandon the Tour.

In any case it's worth turning the bike around and going back the same way. The steep ascent to Aspet especially is a real joy. With gradients of up to 17 per cent the pulse rate will increase once again. You will have barely experienced the following 8 per cent as such a relief!

Massive choice of routes

Those who want to turn one or both ascents into a round trip have a large number of little, hardly used country roads to choose from. The simplest choice is obviously to ride to Col de Menté as described above. You'll cross the pass and ride north for 3km on the N125, before turning right on to the D618 which leads back to Col de Portet d'Aspet over the little Col des Ares (797m). Back in Audressein you will have over 100km and gradients of up to 17 per cent in your legs, something to boast about back home.

Those who like it a bit shorter can naturally go for Col de Menté on its own. Then you'll start in St-Béat and follow the N125 and D618 as described above up to the Pont de l'Oule. Here you'll take the right and continue to Col de Menté. A beautiful round trip that does not overtax at barely 60km.

Fabio – end of a cycling hopeful

There was no hectic racing in the bunch, when on Tuesday 18 July, 1995, the Tour de France began climbing the Portet d'Aspet. The 16th stage of the Tour was to go from Saint-Girons to Cretes du Lys and the field crossed the pass as a unit. Riders who had performed splendid feats on the mountain had already began to assemble at the bottom of the field. Most wanted to get the 206km stage over and done with, no one in particular had ambitions for a special performance on the day. Aspet is only the opener for a strenuous daily schedule with a total elevation of over 5000m, and therefore the race favourites were just cruising along in the bunch.

But an incident on the steep descent from Portet d'Aspet abruptly changed the mood. A group of riders took a fall on the last steep bend of the descent. There were no crash barriers, only low concrete blocks marking the road. The German Dirk Baldinger broke his pelvis, his Italian colleague Dante Rezze fell down the embankment. But one rider had taken a really bad hit: Fabio Casartelli lay curled up, his legs pulled up, on the tarmac and was not moving. Large quantities of blood were flowing from his head on to the road and he was already unconscious. Tour medic Dr Gerard Porte succeeded three times in resuscitating the Italian; a blood transfusion was planned to replace the blood loss. He was taken to the hospital in Tarbes by helicopter, but his life couldn't be saved.

This was also the case for the death of Tom Simpson in 1967. The Tour directors in 1995 reacted in an unemotional way. The victor's ceremony on the podium at the end of the stage was performed as usual; the two hostesses were simply advised not to kiss the stage winner quite so enthusiastically. Many riders only found out about the tragic accident at the finishing line and were, of course, shocked. Richard Virenque, who won the stage, enjoyed his win initially without a care. The following day the riders honoured their dead colleague. They rode the whole stage in a group, Fabio's teammates crossed the finishing line together.

Lance Armstrong, Casartelli's colleague in the Motorola team paid the dead man his respects a few days later. With a show of strength he won the stage which Casartelli had ear-marked for a break-away attempt. When he rode over the line he pointed towards heaven, a gesture he has repeated many times since as a testimony to Fabio Casartelli.

At the place of the accident a commemorative plaque has been set into the stone. A few metres further up a monument is a reminder of the hopeful newcomer whose career ended abruptly at the age of 24.

The accident led to fierce discussions regarding the compulsory wearing of helmets. A few years prior to the accident, the World Cycling Federation (UCI) had introduced compulsory helmets. But after a riders' strike in 1991 the federation had revoked this again. The Tour management went to the trouble to quickly explain that a helmet would not have made any difference in this accident. The Tour medic explained that the injuries had been mainly to the facial area. A helmet would therefore not have offered improved protection.

However, Michel Disteldorf, the French doctor who examined Casartelli's body in hospital disagreed with this interpretation. In his opinion, facial injuries had definitely not been the cause of death. Rather he regarded an injury to the cranium as the primary reason for the demise of the young cyclist. He was convinced that a helmet "would have made it possible to avoid certain injuries".

A small commemorative plaque marks the place where Fabio Casartelli met his death. A tragic accident – of all places on the last bend of the descent.

10 An idyllic bike ride with a grand finale GUZET

CLIMB TOP: 1520m

TOTAL ELEVATION: 990m

DISTANCE: 23.5km

MAX GRADIENT: 10%

AVERAGE GRADIENT: 4.2%

STARTING POINT:
Seix (720 inhab.), Département Ariège (09)

APPROACH:
From Saint-Girons on the D618 to Seix

PARKING:
Immediately on the left on entering town, signposted in front of the Office de Tourisme

ROAD CONDITION: Very good

MOUNTAIN PASS OPENINGS:
All year

Rarely is an ascent so clearly divided into two parts. The first part leads through a level side valley along cosy Pyrenean villages. But the great finale awaits with a final ascent that stretches over 10km.

Declining population

Seix has been losing inhabitants for years: only 720 people now live in the community. This is a surprising development, since Seix is ideally served by transport and gorgeous at the same time. However, neither a well-preserved old town nor the beautiful surrounding landscape secures its income. Only on market days, when the town is busy and bustling, is the economic hardship of its inhabitants alleviated. As is so often the case, tourism could be its salvation, since the advantages of the place are slowly becoming public knowledge. Activity tourism in particular has grown in significance over the last few years.

Through the water sports place

You probably won't want to leave Seix, since the place, with its old town along the river, seems so cosy. Among the high points are the medieval church of Saint-Etienne and the decorative town centre. But you'll ride out of Seix along the river Salat, where you'll be able to cast a last look back. You'll then continue over a level stretch between a rock wall and along the river.

Then it's past a canoe hire place and shortly afterwards along a narrow road between houses. In the last few years Seix has evolved into a centre for water sports. Canoe, kayak and raft tours are designed to attract the tourists to the area even in summer. But

The isolated Ustou Valley radiates an idyllic calm in summer.

you'll, of course, want to decline the offer with thanks and instead use your legs for the onward journey in the direction of Pont de la Taule.

We reach the place after approximately 4.5km and make a sharp left turn.

A mountain view into the Pyrenean village

You'll then change over into the Ustou Valley and the surroundings take on an increasingly more attractive shape. Since the road sees only little use, you'll really be able to enjoy the scenery. Along the road there are initially only gentle grass slopes. You'll ride over a bridge where soon afterwards the slopes change and begin to look a little wilder as they are interspersed with rocks, ragged but nevertheless covered in trees.

Past a beautiful stone house you'll continue on the flat. After 7km the view will open up and you'll see in front of you far distant peaks like Pic de Certascan (2840m) or Cap de Ruhos (2618m). You'll still be rolling effortlessly along, waiting for the promised climb. After 10km you'll reach Le Train d'Ustou, a little cosy Pyrenean village.

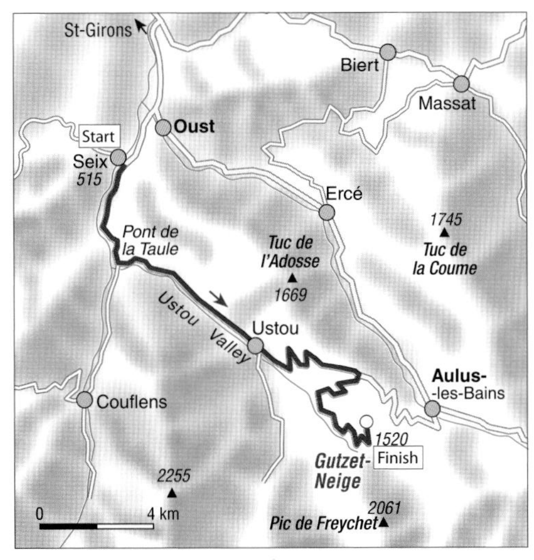

No more slacking

After Le Train d'Ustou you'll reach a junction where Guzet isn't signposted. Here you'll be at a loss without a map. (Note that on maps and in books the place is sometimes also referred to as Guzet-Neige, but never on signposts.) But even though the long, flat stretch strikes you as odd, you'll need to head straight ahead again, rather than right and up the mountain! Only Sérac d'Ustou is signposted here. Next you'll reach the place on the D8f where the Station de Guzet is signposted here once again. Here, there won't be any more dawdling, because you'll finally get to go uphill. Even the first bend will get you going and with a gradient of over 6 per cent the following ramp will also be no slouch.

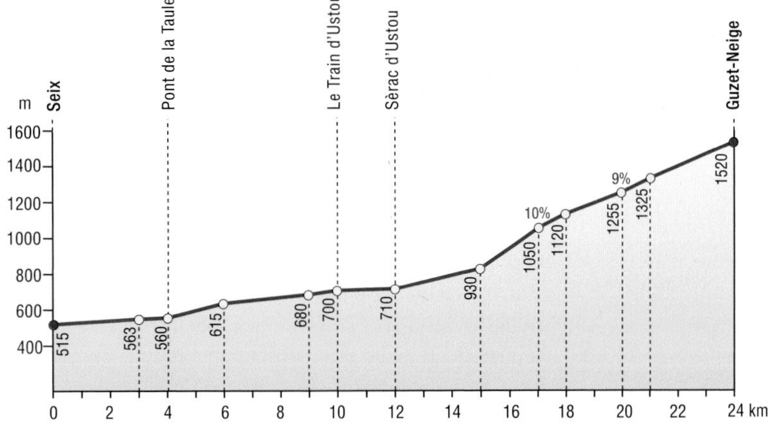

Towards the water

You'll then reach the junction to Col de Latrape, where you need to follow the signposts to the right. Your view ranges in the other direction over the whole of the valley through which you have cycled. Steep bends that wind upwards follow and confront you with up to 10 per cent. In between times you will repeatedly dive back into the shade of the forest. Alongside birches, beeches and oak trees it flattens out a little again.

During the first kilometres the route remains flat and you'll approach Guzet quite relaxed.

In the distance the first ski lifts will already be recognisable, so it won't be far at this point. After nearly 20km you'll reach a grand projecting bend that offers you a beautiful view of the surrounding peaks. The gradient picks up again and you'll already come up to the signs '*Bienvenue en Guzet*'. But you should save the pleasant anticipation until a bit later, because you won't be at the end. Get on to the left-hand bend and then you'll once more be riding sturdily uphill. You'll then ride along a slope covered in holiday homes. Past the Chalet de Edelweiss you'll reach a car park and will have finally arrived. Here you'll be presented with a wonderful view of steep mountain peaks in all directions and the Garbet Valley far below you. Sweaty and hot, you'll no doubt remember the little river on the outward journey – how lovely it would be to cool your legs in it! But first the descent on the perfect road awaits. However, you shouldn't forget that there is a very steep bend after around 9km. Onwards, towards the water!

Opposite: Jersey unzipped, eyes shut and go for it: Even the professionals fear the Pyrenean ascents – in this case Andreas Klöden.

Happy all round

A dense network of routes makes several variations possible on little-used roads. The most obvious possibility is a tour through the Vallée du Garbet back to Seix. This doesn't take much longer than the route described above and can be managed in half a day. In the neighbourhood nearby there are also two lesser-known passes of the Tour de France to discover. The Col de la Core and the Col de Port are among the prehistoric rocks of the round trip. Admittedly, on its own the ascent of Col de Port (1249m) and its total elevation of 600m and a length of nearly 12km is a very short pleasure. Those planning more than an afternoon's excursion however could build the pass into a round trip. In that case you would continue after the mountain pass of the Col de Port onwards to Tarascon and via the D8 and D18 back to Massat. The region is worth it for the landscape and for those interested in history the pass is unmissable. This is, after all, the first Pyrenean pass to be integrated into the Tour de France. The area around Massat is superbly suited to charming circular tours. The richly wooded area is criss-crossed by many little roads and in addition offers many possibilities to collect elevation gains. Although you won't be travelling through high mountains here, the tours are guaranteed to be attractive.

T··Mobile·
GIANT

The Tour as a stage for advertising

In the 20th century, the Département Ariège experienced cataclysmic changes. While it was still densely populated in 1910 at the time of the first Pyrenean stage, it was losing inhabitants decade upon decade. Above all the mountains were increasingly less populated and the wooded areas were increasing more and more rapidly. The greatest problem for the region was however the exodus of industry and the decline of agriculture. Sources of income were increasingly lacking. Only tourism seemed to offer a great opportunity. Naturally the Tour de France was particularly important for making the region better known. Many communities therefore go to extremes in using the public stage of the Tour to increase their degree of popularity.

While the little Alpine ski resorts have long since etched themselves into the holiday makers' consciousness many little places in the Pyrenean court attention. The relatively young ski station Guzet-Neige propelled itself into the limelight in 1984 via the Tour de France. The community of Saint-Girons paid 3 per cent of its total annual budget to host the stage finish. Failure to make it a success was not an option as investment in the tourist infrastructure also trebled. So the community and its inhabitants threw themselves into the preparations which resulted in an extravagant celebration.

Over 150 million grilled sausages and 60kg of cheese were fed to the visitors and 2001 wine bottles are intended to show off the best of the region. This seems to have

The '*Caravane Publicitaire*' comprises around 200 vehicles. Especially popular with the spectators are the promotional freebies, of which around 15 million are distributed along the route.

In the age of advertising logos even the Tour devil became a brand.

worked to a degree as the ski resort and its surroundings became widely known over night and continue to attract tourists.

The 2007 Tour de France began in London. The two main objectives of the Grand Depart 2007 were to promote cycling in the capital and to market London on a world stage. Social Research Associates published a research summary, The Tour de France: The Grand Depart 2007 (Social Research Associates). This summary revealed that the Tour de France directly generated £73 million in London and £15 million in Kent. There is evidence that the associated events of the Tour encouraged people from outside the UK to spend longer in London. Estimated attendance was around three million or more in London and Kent. More than half came from outside London, and 10 per cent came from overseas. Survey results indicated that just over half of those attending said they were more likely to cycle as a result of the Tour de France in particular for leisure. The research reported extensive media coverage months before the start of the Tour. An estimated £35 million worth of free publicity was generated from the articles and news items in the period 1 January, 2006 to 31 August, 2007. The conclusion of the research is clear but in terms of the economic gain, attendance numbers and positive media coverage, the Tour de France proved to be an extremely successful UK event. For further information go to www.tfl.gov.uk/assets/downloads/businessandpartners/tour-de-france-research-summary.pdf.

A vehicle in the advertising caravan costs between €200,000 and €500,000. This ensures that 15 million spectators along the route get to see the adverts. Even the French police is represented and advertises for new recruits with a caravan vehicle.

11 Steadily uphill
PLATEAU DE BEILLE

The elevation explains why the Plateau de Beille is also described as the Alpe d'Huez of the Pyrenees.

CLIMB TOP: 1785m
TOTAL ELEVATION: 1129m
DISTANCE: 16km
MAX GRADIENT: 11%
AVERAGE GRADIENT: 7.7%
STARTING POINT:
Les Cabannes (380 inhab.), Département Ariège (09)
APPROACH:
From Foix on the N20 to Les Cabannes
PARKING:
In Les Cabannes by the junction to Plateau de Beille, parking spaces opposite the post office and town hall
ROAD CONDITION:
Good condition but rough road surface in places
MOUNTAIN PASS OPENINGS:
All year

On many maps the Plateau de Beille isn't even marked and that's a good thing. As a result you'll share the route with only a few cars and will be able to concentrate fully on the surroundings. The stage has only been part of the Tour since the year 1998 and the climbing genius Marco Pantani, no less, rewarded the Tour Premiere with a stage victory. Back then Jan Ullrich climbed the mountain in the yellow jersey.

Conquered grazing grounds

The history of the Plateau de Beille has really only just begun. That's because until the start of the 1990s absolute mountain solitude dominated here. For hundreds of years only the shepherds came to visit. Year after year they crossed the high plateau with their herds; sheep and horses had the plateau to themselves. Development only began in 1990 and with that the construction of a road suitable for cyclists. The opening was in 1995 as part of a local cycle race and, coincidentally, Tour director Jean-Marie Leblanc was visiting. His interest was aroused when he flew over the stage during his outward journey. Those responsible on the ground dreamed of the Tour and were even contemplating a mountain time trial. When it was finally ready in 1998 and the Tour visited the Plateau de Beille, the locals fell over themselves. With a stage victory by Marco Pantani and two victories by Lance Armstrong it was immediately clear: this ascent was a real challenge where only the best could win. Comparisons with the Alpe d'Huez has been made many times, but here there is an ascent up many hairpin bends with almost no level stretches. You also have to gain a similar total elevation, so the comparison with the Alpe d'Huez is appropriate.

Steady gradient

Immediately after the car park the road incline is steep. It bears the name Rue de la Rampe and you'll understand this even without any

Hairpin bend upon hairpin bend allow you to wind your way up the wooded slope.

knowledge of French. On the D522 you'll ride past on the right of the imposing Chateau de Gudanes.

A sign beside the road will get you in the mood for the impending 8 per cent gradient. The road surface is very rough in parts but without serious damage. For a long time you'll ride along bends up the same massif. There are hardly any level interim stretches; from now on you'll go uphill all the way to the end apart from a few metres. The gradient fluctuates then between 6 and 10 per cent so that you'll be asked to pedal at a relatively constant rate.

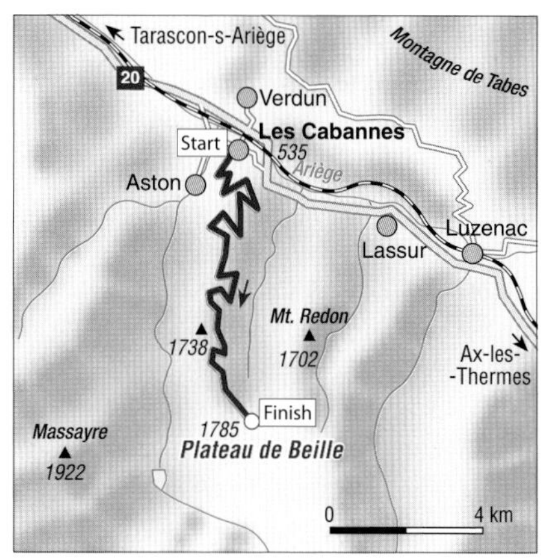

No fear of bears

Further up you'll be able to look back repeatedly into the valley which is bordered on the opposite side by the mighty massif of the Pic de Saint-Barthélemy (2348m). You will continue to ride along the wooded slope. On the left a beautiful panorama of a bare mountain range beckons. Time and again you'll have alternating shade and sun – depending on the direction and time of day. On the road you'll repeatedly find graffiti protesting against the reintroduction of the bear ('Ours = Danger'). After 4km you'll ride up a ramp with a gradient of up to 10 per cent. After a short relaxing stretch it's upwards again at 6 per cent along a birch forest. Now among birches and shortly afterwards in a mixed forest you'll wind your way up the mountain. One bend follows another and you'll have already covered half the distance. A large drawn-out loop takes you around the mountain which is on your right. After 10km you'll already be able to guess where it's going.

Shadowless expanse

Shortly afterwards you'll go round a bend and you'll get the impression that you've made it, but the speedometer will prove your optimism wrong. Chirping crickets and brooding heat in the height of summer increase the longing for the mountain plateau. There is no more shade, but instead

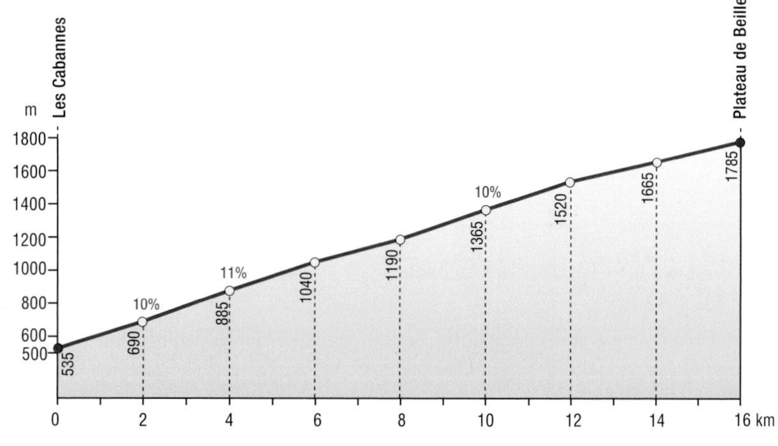

you'll get a very wide view. You'll cycle over a little interim plateau on which stands a little mountain hut (Cabane de Pierrefitte). The vegetation now changes markedly. There are hardly any trees, but instead many alpine flowers and shrubs. The course of the road ahead is visible for a long way, first it goes around an elevation where you'll have a panoramic view of the Pyrenean chain on the right. Then the road goes upwards in steep hairpins.

And we've won!

Since there don't seem to be any higher points, you'll suspect it already: after going round a relatively level bend you will have reached the end.

In order to follow the official Tour finish you'll need to ride left along the car park and in a wide circle along the right in front of a restaurant. Then you will have reached the official finish. In 2005 the official finish markings were still faintly visible. So smile, raise your arms, you've won!

The route of the Tour de France has so far led twice from Lannemézan and once from Luchon to the Plateau de Beille. In 2004 the riders already had 205.5km in their legs when they rode over the finish line at Plateau de Beille. In the process they had already cycled over two mountains in category one and four easier ones.

Mountain adventure

You'll probably now wish you had brought walking shoes but you can also enjoy the plateau without: a gorgeous panorama presents itself with a long chain of rocky mountain peaks. It is so peaceful that it's hard to imagine that all hell breaks loose here in winter. But the choice of slopes on the Plateau de Beille is professional and extensive. Over 70km of prepared cross-country skiing pistes are available during winter.

Anyone who isn't comfortable on skis can leave their trail in the snow with snow shoes instead. To ensure that no one can get lost there are 30km of signposted routes especially for walkers. Even lazy walkers don't have to go without snow adventures – there is now a route specially designed for dog sledges.

But you shouldn't think too much about the frosty time of year because it gets cold enough already during the steep descent into the valley!

The view of massive chalk-like cliffs of the Pic de Saint-Barthélemy.

The devil conquers the Tour

By now it's a well-known image: when the riders of the Tour de France approach the last few metres of the end of a mountain stage the devil breathes down their necks. But in this case he was quite human and even came from Germany. Didi Senft with his beard, devil's costume and trident had long been the Tour de France mascot. Didi was not only one of the greatest and best-known cycle sport fans but could himself demonstrate success on a racing bike. During the times of the GDR the amateur cyclist won several victories in the regional championships.

The loner from Koplin feels especially at home in the mountain stages – and that is also where he began his Tour de France career. The devil made his first appearance in 1992 during the stage to Andorra. Even then he combined his passion for cycling with being a self publicist; a company in the automotive industry sponsored the fuel for his tour of France. Equipped with a small backpack, he stuffed his VW van with gherkins from the Spree forest and canned sausages. The bus naturally also served as his bedroom and some even claimed that one could smell Didi even before seeing him!

But soon Didi was very popular with both the riders and spectators. After he had been included in the official programme booklet of the 2002 Tour he was even allowed to sign autographs. But it is by no means the case that 'El Diablo' doesn't strive for records – in fact, he delivers some of his own. For years he has been a single-minded bike tinkerer. His contraptions are mentioned several times in *The Guinness Book of Records.* He also invented the world's biggest and smallest bikes.

His fame has also improved his comfort levels during his travels. Frequently he has a sponsor for his overnight accommodation, and the well-known Tour devil is engaged for a fee at many events. This makes him the only professional cycle sports fan in the world. The devil does not only make mischief during the French round trip. He also appears regularly at the Giro d'Italia, the Tour de Suisse or the Bayern-Rundfahrt (Bavarian circuit). In his capacity as devil the family man is on the go for around 180 days a year. In 1995 he even visited the World Championships in Colombo and in 2000 the Olympic Games in Sydney. However, he hasn't always had positive experiences. In Poland he was robbed at night during the Course de la Paix and during the Tour de la Suisse the police fined him. While he was decorating the road between Litzirüti and Arosa with his paintings, the Canton police turned up. Because of forbidden foreign advertising and misleading markings they stung him with a substantial fine. Senft had to pay 900 francs on the spot and was threatened with a larger bill. In desperation he tried to remove the paint again but he laboured in vain.

Where the mountains reach for the sky the representative of the underworld is present. Didi Senft in his devil's costume raises hell for the riders.

In his spare time Didi prefers to dedicate himself to his passion for handicrafts. Finally he fulfilled his lifetime's dream a few years ago: a bicycle museum for his 200-plus handcrafted artworks. The Museum für Fahrradkuriositäten (Museum for Cycling Curiosities) in the Neu-Boston part of Storkow is also home to all 17 bikes with which he appears in *The Guinness Book of Records.*

12 In the paradise of passes
COL DU CHIOULA

Ax-les-Thermes is surrounded by well-know passes, here one doesn't easily run out of routes.

CLIMB TOP: 1431m
TOTAL ELEVATION: 700m
DISTANCE: 10.3km
MAX GRADIENT: 8.5%
AVERAGE GRADIENT: 6%
STARTING POINT:
Ax-les-Thermes (1500 inhab.), Département Ariège (09)
APPROACH:
On N20 from Foix to Ax-les-Thermes
PARKING:
In the centre of town pay car park in front of the casino or free parking next to it
ROAD CONDITION: Very good
MOUNTAIN PASS OPENINGS:
All year

The infrastructure for tourism is perfect in Ax and shops and hotels in the popular spa town are open all year round. The town lies at the intersection of the Ariège, Lauze and Oriège valleys and has been known as a thermal spa since the Middle Ages. Many tourists find their way here in peak season every year.

Those who want to avoid the hustle and bustle in high summer look for accommodation in the vicinity. A stay is always worthwhile because there are many rewarding destinations all around Ax. One of these is Col du Chioula which offers opportunities for climbing without difficulties on a wide good road.

Leisurely introduction

The pass is already signposted at the roundabout in front of the church. A few metres later at a bridge a cyclists' sign informs of pass details. You'll ride through Ax-les-Thermes, where the gradient begins to increase near the last few houses.

A steep bend leads you out of the town on the A613. Initially there are still relatively many cars en route, the road is in good condition throughout. A little waterfall bubbles on the left and on the right you'll already be able to catch a glimpse of Ax-les-Thermes lying below you.

Over bends you'll grind your way up the mountain. The lush slopes are still populated. You'll then ride along a rock wall and after 3.7km you'll reach the junction to Pailhères. However, you'll need to go left and push more strongly into the pedals at around 7 per cent. The road continues along between trees and the gradient reduces markedly which will provide you with a bit of respite. Now and then you'll pass small meadows, often with grazing sheep.

When leaving Ax-les-Thermes the road begins to climb.

At the wall

The tarmac now becomes noticeably rougher and on the right of the road there is jagged red-brown rock. You'll reach a level stretch ideal for a slight recuperation where you'll be riding along gentle wooded slopes in a narrow valley.

After 7.5km a slope will appear in front of you like a wall which seems to stand in your way. Does the way lead to the right or the left around the wall? After 1km you'll know more: it actually goes directly up the 'wall'! You'll conquer the steep slope in several ramps and on closer inspection it isn't nearly so frightening.

Alongside beech forests you'll corkscrew upwards one bend at a time. You will have crossed the 'wall' without significant increases in gradient, reaching a high plateau with grazing cows and many ferns. The end of the climb is within reach. A restaurant in a modern concrete building is all that awaits you at the summit.

Big wide world

The panorama on the Col is known throughout the region because it is absolutely peerless. In the distance you'll see the Andorran peaks and those of the Département Ariège.

Directly opposite lie the Plateau de Beille and the Plateau de Bonascre. Those with time on their hands can go to the Signal du Chioula over a gravel piste. Around 20 minutes away from the pass on foot, visitors can get a geography lesson here. All peaks in the vicinity are recorded and named on a chart.

You should not only enjoy the view of the Pyrenees, the nearby Massif d'Aston is also beautiful. It is indeed worth lingering here for a while.

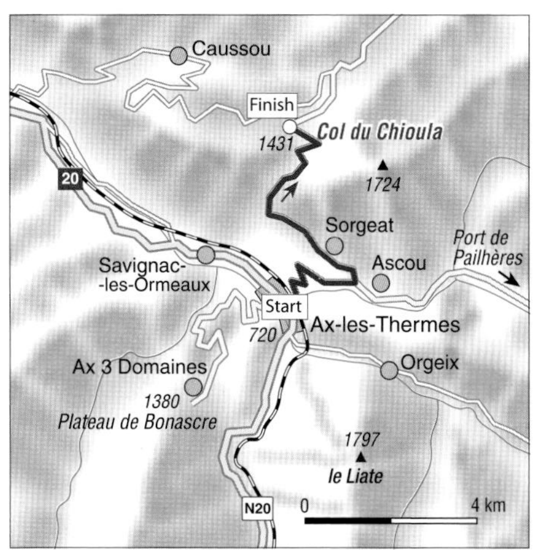

Rare building block in the Tour plan

The Col du Chioula is a rarely used building block in the stage plan. It has been crossed four times so far and each time from another starting point. In 1955 the stage started in Narbonne,

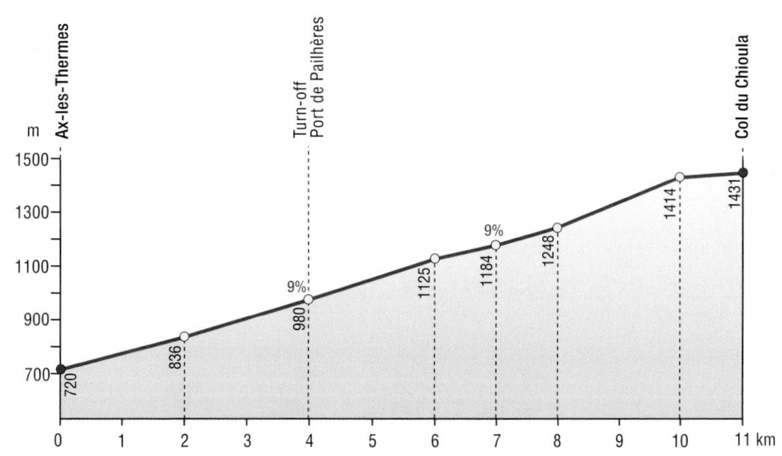

in 1965 in Bagnières-de-Bigorre, in 1997 in Andorra and in 2001 in Perpignan.

During the last visit the Col de Jau and the Col des Sept Frères had previously been on the programme. The finish was 166km later in Ax-3-Domaines. The riders appeared to regard the ride as a day of recuperation because on the next day things began for real.

The 222km-long stage went over Col de Port, Portet d'Aspet, Col de Menté, Col du Portillon and Col de Peyresourde.

As if that wasn't enough, the end of the stage was in Pla d'Adet. A programme hard as nails, and therefore it wasn't a surprise who finished this stage in pole position: Lance Armstrong, for whom – as ever – no mountain was too steep.

Finale at the thermal spa

Those who want to can integrate Chioula into a day-long and very athletic round trip to Pailhères. To do so you will need to cross the Col du Chioula on the D613 and ride past Belcaire to Espezel.

Those who want to collect kilometres now should choose the easy-to-find road to Axat. Shorter, however, is the variant over the D29 and then D20 via Aunat to the D118. The roads become increasingly smaller and even with a map you'll be constantly on the lookout. In exchange you'll experience the landscape in a unique way, because you'll move into an area that is almost devoid of people and partly on adventurously narrow roads. The road isn't always in good condition and the signposting is very complicated; be sure to bring a map along! The spectacular landscape is however sufficient reward for the complications in finding the route on this round trip. In the evening a visit to the thermal spa in Ax is worthwhile. The healing waters have been flowing in the Bassin des Ladres since 1260 – your legs will surely be delighted at this dive into history.

Gentle meadows on Col du Chioula

Jan Ullrich on the way to Tour victory

After two tough Pyrenean stages things were a bit quieter during the 11th stage of the 1997 Tour. It was the day on which an acceptable altitude profile allowed the teams to dictate the tempo and attempt to play to the gallery. At the end of the stage there was a mass sprint and the field crossed the line with an 18-second deficit. So a totally normal stage? Not entirely, because when the main field crossed Col du Chioula on the 16 July, 1997, Jan Ullrich wore the yellow jersey. His first day as overall leader was rather unspectacular, but that would have more than suited him after the stresses and strains of the previous 24 hours.

The previous day, the whole world had witnessed a new cycling genius placing himself at the head of the Tour de France. Only a few kilometres before the end of the stage from Luchon to Andorra the team rankings had been clear. Jan Ullrich was the helper and therefore had to wait for Bjarne Riis, the captain of Team Telekom, when he weakened again. But 13km before the end the team's chief, Walter Godefroot, lifted the team order with the words "Go for it, Jan, ride on" and gave Ullrich the green light to take off. The then 23-year-old man from Rostock didn't need to be told twice. He virtually flew up the mountain and Richard Virenque, his most important rival, kept repeatedly looking behind him to Marco Pantani for help. But despite mutual support they had no chance. "When I speeded up, only a few could follow me, then even fewer and at the end I was alone," Jan Ullrich said about his tour de force.

Three kilometres before the end Virenque and Pantani were already 1 minute behind and could no longer manage to catch up. In the white jersey of the German champion Ullrich wound himself upwards hairpin by hairpin, pushing powerfully on the pedals and riding in a seated position. He maintained the distance to his pursuers with an expression of concentration and everyone felt at the end that they had witnessed more than just a stage victory. And this despite the number one at the start, Bjarne Riis, beginning a desperate hunt to catch up, riding the last few kilometres with the large chain ring. But with nearly 5 minutes' deficit in the overall rankings he had lost the Tour conclusively. Even the French television reporters spoke of a new chapter in the history of cycling after Jan Ullrich's impressive performance. From the hands of the cycling legend Bernard Hinault Jan Ullrich received his first *maillot jaune*. Jan Ullrich acted modestly at the end and was delighted that "his dream had come true".

The Fuentes Affair plunged Ulle and the T-Mobile Team into the depths.

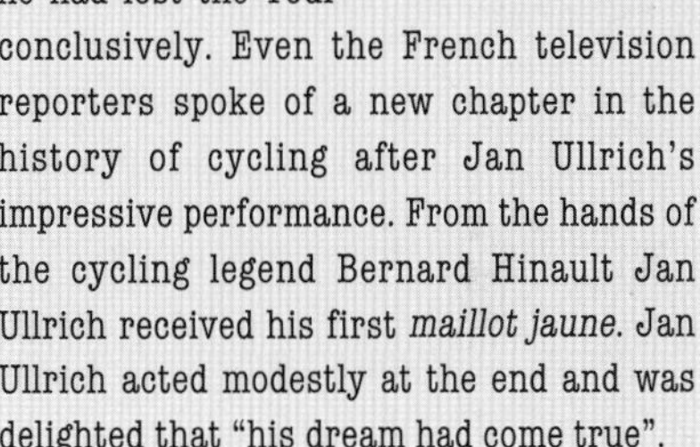

Jan Ullrich did not only carry the yellow jersey safely over the Col du Chioula, he also wore it to Paris as the winner. This sealed the first German Tour victory in history and started an unprecedented enthusiasm for cycle racing. But the prognoses were a bit premature: Spanish media compared him with Indurain, others with Merckx and prophesied a boring future. Ullrich would win one Tour after another and would hardly be thrilling.

Lance Armstrong made similar noises but in the following years he himself managed to disprove his own prognosis through hard work.

13 Perhaps the most beautiful pass of the Tour
COL DE PAILHÈRES

A personal favourite: The hairpin bends on Pailhères are a dream!

CLIMB TOP: 2001m
TOTAL ELEVATION: 1216m
DISTANCE: 15.5km
MAX GRADIENT: 12%
AVERAGE GRADIENT: 7.8%
STARTING POINT:
Ussons les Bains near Rouze (90 inhab.), Département Ariège (09)
APPROACH:
From Carcassone on D118 via Axat and then D16 to Ussons les Bains
PARKING:
Drive through Ussons les Bains (so small it's hardly recognisable as a place), turn right towards Rouze (D16) and left after 500m towards walkers' car park.
ROAD CONDITION: Good
MOUNTAIN PASS OPENINGS:
June to October

Even though this tour has only twice been included in the Tour planners' programme, one should definitely not omit it. Because what the pass is lacking in historical significance it makes up for with an impressive and lightly used road. Undoubtedly one should however approach it from the east, because the more beautiful side is located here. It also makes it worth putting up with the circuitous approach.

High point of Ariège

The Port or Col de Pailhères forms a direct road link between Ariège and Cerdagne. In spite of this it is hardly used because the narrow road is fortunately not suitable as a main road. It is actually the highest pass road of Ariège, which renders it unusable for many months. The varied landscape is unique and the altitude profile impressive.

Full steam ahead

The kick-off begins with a thunder clap: the toughest kilometres of today's programme start immediately after the car park. Many a cyclist has pulled on the handlebars with all their strength, while others work upwards in wavy lines. Getting into up to 10 per cent gradients almost immediately with cold muscles is not everyone's cup of tea.

Alongside relatively flat, wooded hilly mountains and with a view of the imposing ruins of a castle the route goes along a river. You will reach Rouze after 2km, where you'll ride over a bridge and follow a left-hand bend out of the little place again. It becomes a bit flatter for a short while and you'll be able to regain your breath. At the next road junction, the signposts are initially confusing. The Col

The closer the mountain pass, the narrower the road. Cars can barely get past each other.

de Pailhères is not signposted yet, so you'll need to go right on the D116 towards *'Ax les T'*.

The abbreviated signpost stands for Ax-les-Thermes – they were obviously economising on long signs here!

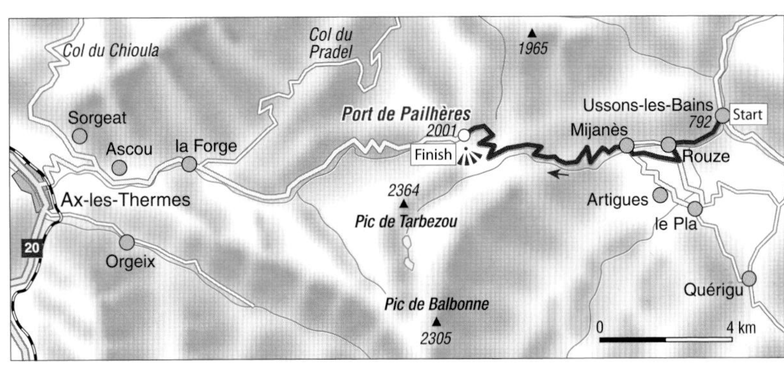

Hilly mountainscape

You'll then cycle uphill over rough tarmac, and on the right houses are arranged in steps along the slope. Here it's signposted right on the D25 to Col de Pailhères and again to *'Ax les T'*. The whole area, including the road, is covered in a colourful maple leaf. After seeing how the cycling fans were bringing tourism to the area, the local tourist association decided to paint the official logo of the region – the maple leaf – on to the roads.

You'll then ride past the last houses, where the road is in perfect condition. A beautiful mountainscape spreads out before you: wooded hills as far as the eye can see. One steep bend follows another up the wooded slope. You won't see any houses for miles, only unspoilt mountain idyll. You'll get a wide view of wooded hills and grassy slopes interspersed with rocks. After approximately 8.5km the valley opens and a small plateau with grazing horses appears. You'll continue on the right past the cattle herders' huts in the direction of Ax-les-Thermes.

Good exercise for heart and circulation

The road narrows perceptibly now and is only 3m wide. This is quite uncomfortable for the race field and also for the numerous spectators. During the 2005 Tour the fans found ingenious ways to use the remaining centimetres. Even at the narrowest places veterans of the Tour managed to park their cars along the slope.

However, when the Tour isn't in town, this area is impregnated with a deep silence. It continues under the shadows of trees, where the road stays flat. It's a beautiful section where you'll get peace and quiet with your fitness training thrown in – this should be

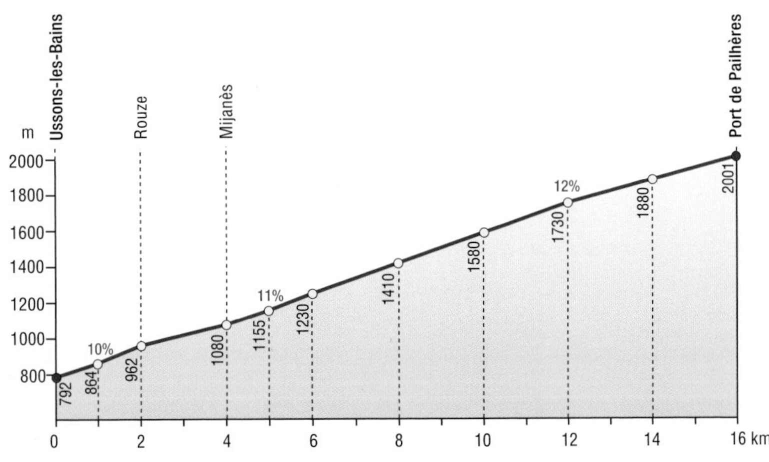

available on the NHS! But after a few metres you'll leave the relaxing stretch behind and climb upwards again, directly past craggy rocks.

Bends upon bends

In front you'll see 11 varied kilometres worth of technical climbing of the absolute finest order.

You'll wind your way up the hill on short hairpin bends that are densely pressed together.

The whole slope is covered in little snaking lines and the view down on to the bends you've already conquered is outstanding. It is doubtful if there is anywhere else with such a beautiful tangle of bends in such a small space. Sometimes the distance between the bends is only 10m long and with such delightful scenery the 10 per cent gradient is quite manageable.

Endless vastness

You might be a bit disappointed when you leave this hairpin bend section behind and start working your way along wide bends towards the pass. The landscape is mostly alpine and there is hardly any vegetation, with only broad meadows. You'll have a wonderful, comprehensive view in all directions as you strive higher. After a bend the road ahead becomes visible. The slope tumbles steeply downhill into emptiness on your right and the end of the climb will seem within reach.

But don't celebrate just yet: you'll have one more uphill bend to climb before it's downhill and straight towards the mountain pass. On Col de Pailhères another view into the Ariège Valley beckons. Those who cross the pass and continue on to Ax-les-Thermes do so on a good, wide road. The only problem with the descent is the very rough tarmac in places. But in comparison with the eastern side it's almost a disappointment. Although it is beautiful here, the other side is a real delight.

Those who nevertheless want to ride up from the west must master a total elevation of around 1281m in around 18.6km. With an average gradient of barely 7 per cent the ascent from the west is a little easier.

Traces of the Tour visit on the road to Pailhères cannot be ignored. The density of road markings increases the closer you get to the mountain pass.

Ulle returns

The pass, which is sometimes also described as Port de Pailhères, has only a very recent history. It made its debut in the year of the 100th anniversary of the Tour and immediately created an impression. During the stage from Toulouse to A-3-Domaines the cycle sports world experienced a thriller that increased in drama from one stage to the next. Only the day before, Jan Ullrich had reasserted himself with a thunderclap during the time trial. With a head start of 1:36 he outclassed Lance Armstrong. The cycling world was experiencing something akin to a resurrection.

In 2002 Ullrich reached the absolute nadir of his career. That year he started extremely early with preparations, in spring his weight was already at Tour level, but then his knee failed. It was a problem he was repeatedly plagued by. Instead of continuing with his training schedule, he regenerated himself with aqua jogging. The frustration was great and his stupidity even greater: while drunk he trashed a bicycle rack with his Porsche and did a runner. The affair was discovered and Ullrich was in trouble.

A knee operation followed and then Ullrich tested positive for amphetamines. According to his own admission he had taken a recreational drug. The doping offence lead to the termination of his contract with Team Telekom. Ullrich was at rock bottom. Then a new sponsor seemed to emerge in December 2002. A private financier wanted to put together Team Coast with Ullrich. But the whole thing turned into a fiasco. Payments weren't flowing and in March the World Cycling Federation withdrew the team's licence. Despite the continuing troubles Ullrich continued to train with his colleague Tobias Steinhauser and was in good shape. For the first time in 14 months he was at the starting line, at the Sarthe circuit. However, even on that morning everything was still on the cusp. The previous sponsor had no money available and Ullrich only succeeded at the last minute to secure Bianchi as a new sponsor.

With the uncertainties over for a while, a Tour start for Ullrich seemed possible. He regarded the 2003 Tour merely as a trial run to familiarise himself once more with cycle racing. But it turned out much better than he himself and the experts expected. Ullrich was in unusually good form. It was a real miracle that Jan Ullrich could start with his new sponsor after all. The rank outsider had transformed himself over night into a serious competitor for Lance Armstrong.

A heated duel flared up over the following stages and despite a gastrointestinal infection Ullrich managed to keep the time lost within bounds even in the Alps. When he took 1 minute 36 seconds off the Texan in extreme heat during the time trial on 18 July, 2003, the Tour turned into a thriller. Everyone was asking themselves: “Would Ullrich finally succeed with his second Tour win?”

On 19 July, 2003 the tension could have hardly been greater. Ullrich was only 34 seconds behind Armstrong. Ullrich and Armstrong eyed each other critically on Pailhères. They rode at the head of a small group and Armstrong showed clear signs of strain. At the end of the stage Ullrich even succeeded in leaving Armstrong behind. He rode a short distance ahead to the point where he lay only 15 seconds behind the Texan. Even though it wasn't enough at the end and Ullrich could not overcome Armstrong, it had been a while since the Tour had been that thrilling!

14 The athletic challenge
AX 3 DOMAINES

Challenging ramps lead from Ax-les-Thermes to Ax 3 Domaines.

1 ***

CLIMB TOP: 1375m
TOTAL ELEVATION: 670m
DISTANCE: 8.35km
MAX GRADIENT: 11%
AVERAGE GRADIENT: 8.2%
STARTING POINT:
Ax-les-Thermes (1500 inhab.), Département Ariège (09)
APPROACH:
On N20 from Foix to Ax-les-Thermes
PARKING:
Immediately left on entering village depart in direction of Plateau de Bonascre/Ax 3 Domaines, parking spaces after a bridge.
ROAD CONDITION: Very good
MOUNTAIN PASS OPENINGS:
Open all year

To begin with cycle sport fans can get confused here: although the ascent to Ax 3 Domaines is familiar from the reports, the town is often signposted as Plateau de Bonascre and also appears like this on maps. But there is further confusion, because the third variation is Ax-3-Domaines, with two hyphens.

On this route it's either steeply uphill or very steeply uphill. Although there are only 670m of total elevation to cope with the high average gradient reflects the character of the ascent.

Regional magnet

The starting point Ax-les-Thermes is the biggest tourist magnet in the surrounding area. The approximately 80 hot springs attract tourists from all age groups all year round. But this is by no means a sleepy spa town, because the place is also popular with the younger generation and there is quite a buzzing nightlife. The many sporting attractions have contributed to the broad appeal. Walking, mountain biking, canoeing and climbing – tourists here are spoilt for choice.

Ax-les-Thermes lies at the confluence of the Ariège, Oriège and Lauze and is surrounded by mountains in all directions. The nearby Vallée d'Orlu owes its name to the French word *or*, gold. For decades gold prospectors searched for the glittering precious metal in the little river Oriège. Today it is worth a visit because of the beautiful landscape. In the Réserve National d'Orlu, you'll find chamois, vultures and other inhabitants of the mountains. Many demanding walks are worth a day trip without a bicycle.

Steep ramps

Before you can get stuck into this attractive stage there is initially a challenging climb. You'll pedal along the river and after 300m, signposted right on the D820, up to Ax 3 Domaines. The road winds in steep bends out of the village. Right from the start there are many road markings. You will need to ride upwards along a rock wall, where you'll steadily gain altitude. After only a few bends you'll already be high up over Ax-les-Thermes and will have an overview of the town. Along wooded slopes, the road goes steadily uphill without any relaxing stretches. The gradient increases significantly en route and time and again beautiful drawn-out bends give great views below you.

One turn follows another, interspersed with steep ramps of between 8 and 9 per cent. The slope becomes increasingly rockier and the gradient decreases slightly. After 4.5km the steepest part of the trip awaits you at 10.5 per cent.

After a wide bend you'll have to cope with the gradient on a steep ramp.

Steep up to the end

The road leads upwards between trees and only after 6.5km will you have a short stretch for relaxation. But the gradient increases again immediately and you'll soon be riding beneath the first ski lifts. It goes upwards along a slope covered in birches and you'll soon anticipate the end. To make the conquest of the summit really appealing, the gradient once more exceeds the 10 per cent mark and the first hotels come into view. Again, you'll be dealing with a clinical-looking hotel, where the number of beds clearly won out over architectural creativity. In fact, there is not that much to see in Ax 3 Domaines and so you'll probably prefer to do a victory loop around the roundabout ahead, before riding back and once more plunging down into the deep.

Dirt on the jersey

Ax-les-Thermes also has its own Tour de France history which goes a long way back. It was used as a stage town as far back as 1933 but the local paper *La Dépêche* dedicated only a few lines to the event. A local cycle race appeared to be more important to the journalists. The local reporter was particularly impressed with the shiny aluminium wheels of the lead cyclist. But he couldn't resist a swipe at his totally sweaty and dirty jersey. The Tour was already attracting the first fans in 1933. The newspaper report noted the many cars from Spain which were following their countryman Vicente Trueba.

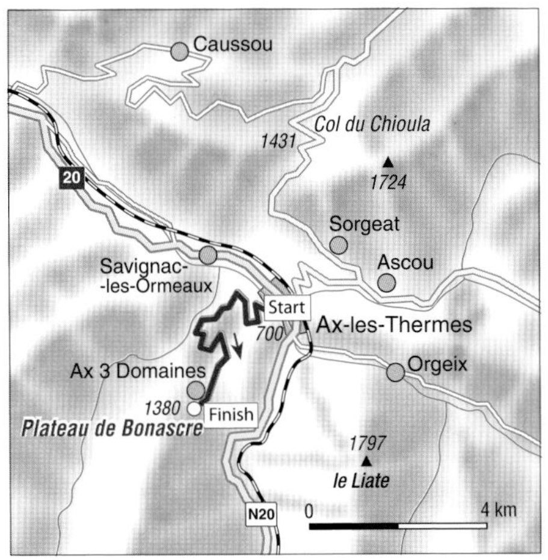

After the Ax-les-Thermes premiere in 1933, the Tour returned in 1934, 1937, 1955, 1957 and 1965. But since then the field has always cycled through Ax-les-Thermes at high speed and the end was moved to Ax 3 Domaines or the route went over one of the numerous passes in the region.

At the Tour Premiere in Ax 3 Domaines in 2001, the Colombian Felix Rafael Cardenas managed to secure the stage victory. After 100 years of the Tour de France the South American country achieved 12 stage victories and 3 mountain jerseys. They rode to most of their stage victories in the mountains – it is not without reason that Colombians have a reputation as excellent rock climbers.

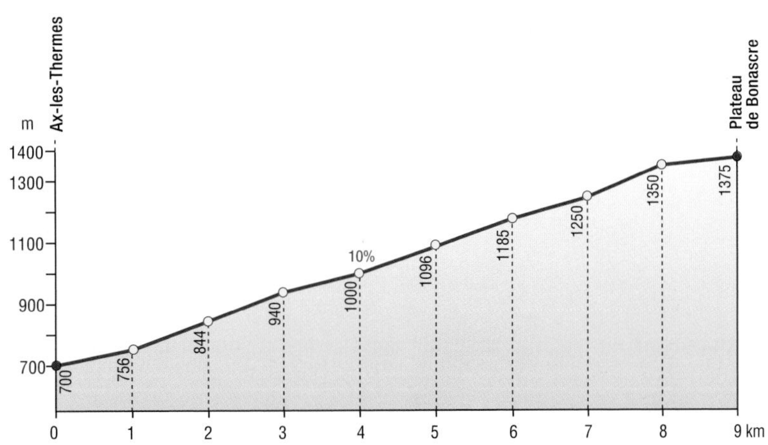

Racing bikes: Evolution instead of revolution

Since its infancy the Tour de France has been at the centre of bicycle manufacturing. Any material that is the centre of attention during the best-known cycle race in the whole world also attracts the interest of buyers. During the first Tour de France in 1903 the racing bike was already quite advanced. Diamond frames, racing bars and chain drives were already standard: only derailleur gears were a real novelty. Starting in 1928, the first derailleurs were mass produced and shortly afterwards they were used in the first races. As ever, the Tour directors once again resisted any kind of innovation. Jacques Goddet only gave up his resistance in 1937 and permitted the derailleur. Racing bikes were then already optimised for low weight which is why aluminium rims and components made from aluminium could already be purchased.

Critics claim that there have been decades of technological stagnation in the realm of the racing bike. Although this view is slightly exaggerated, the following years saw primarily changes in materials.

Bianchi and Colnago (right) belong to the most traditional racing bike brands.

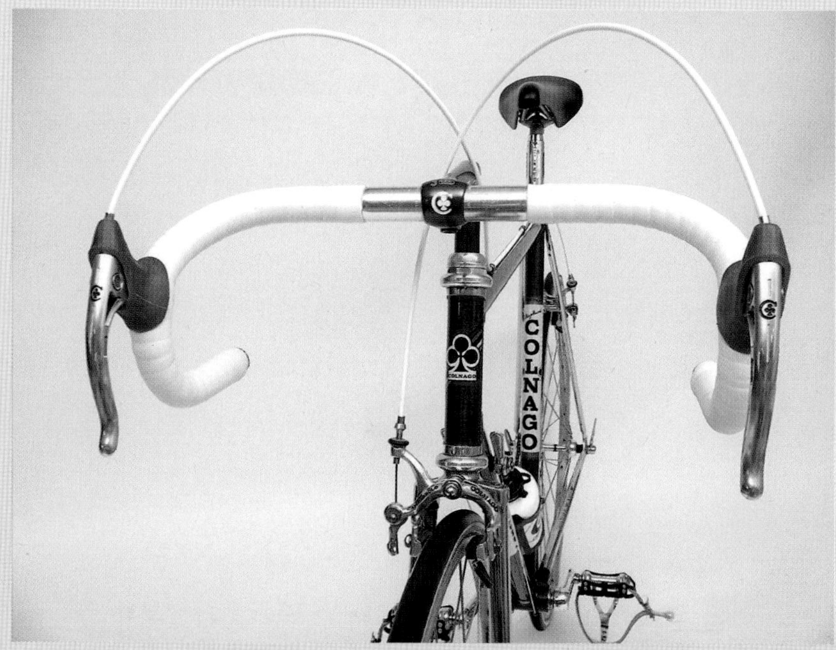

At the start of the 70s, Eddy Merckx was already riding a titanium bike that weighed around 6kg. However, steel frames remained the standard right into the 80s. But even then the first bikes with carbon tubes were being built and aluminium became all-encompassing.

Bianchi and Colnago are two traditional Italian brands without whom racing developments would long have been unthinkable. But the days of a Fausto Coppi, Marco Pantani or Eddy Merckx are over. Over recent years the variety of brands has grown and with that competition has also increased. The old racing bikes by Bianchi and Colnago still exude a beauty today against which even a carbon racer for €6000 cannot compete.

SOUTHERN ALPS

15 High point of all Tour de France stages
MONT VENTOUX FROM

Tree felling took place here many years ago, yet even today grass still does not grow.

CLIMB TOP: 1909m
TOTAL ELEVATION: 1560m
DISTANCE: 22km
MAX GRADIENT: 10.5%
AVERAGE GRADIENT: 7%
STARTING POINT:
Bédoin (2660 inhab.), Département Vaucluse (84)
APPROACH:
From Orange on D950 to Carpentras and D974 to Bédoin
PARKING:
Avenue of trees after village entrance
ROAD CONDITION: Perfect
SPECIAL FEATURE:
Velodateur at the Office de Tourisme
DANGERS:
Tight bends in the middle part of the descent
MOUNTAIN PASS OPENINGS:
Mid April to November

Previous double-page: A cyclist on tour in the French Alps.

Right: Here we go! Behind this bend awaits the most famous view that the Tour de France has to offer.

All racing cyclists dream of riding in Provence because, next to Alpe d'Huez, Ventoux is an absolute must in a racing cyclist's life. Ventoux is certainly most beautiful from this side. The ascent follows the classic direction of the Tour de France and fulfils the expectations created by television reporting and Tour photographs.

By the sweat of one's brow

Sweating cyclists in the foreground, flickering heat lying heavily on top of a chalky-white expanse of scree and, standing lonely behind it, the white observatory with its antenna – this is the familiar face of Ventoux. When you see photographs of Ventoux, you imagine that the mountain consists only of the southern slope of the peak. This distinctive scenery and historical tragedy come together here. The glowing heat in the stony desert of Mont Ventoux contribute much to the legend of the Tour de France. Nowhere else can the painful fight of the professional cyclists be so closely observed and captured in pictures. Mont Ventoux has become a place of pilgrimage for the cycle sports community and cycle racers from all over the world puff hard to storm the summit. The death of the British cyclist Tom Simpson has contributed significantly to the sad publicity of the mountain. Stage victories by Charly Gaul, Raymond Poulidor, Eddy Merckx or Marco Pantani transformed Ventoux into a living myth.

Windy mountain

But the mountain has always been special and that is revealed in its name. 'Vent' stands for the wind that regularly sweeps around the summit. A gentle breeze is a blessing and provides refreshment, but that all changes when the mistral strikes on the day of an ascent. The record measured for this wind streaming in from the north is around 250km/h. The wind continues to make a cyclist's life a misery the following day, as after a windy night, the roads are often covered with stones.

BÉDOIN

It can turn uncomfortably cold and foggy on Ventoux even when it's still cosy in the valley.

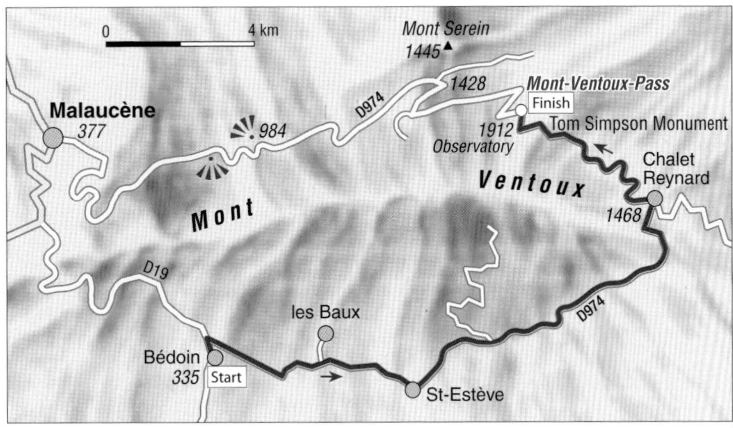

Warming up slowly

The landscape of this mountain definitely offers an experience of special quality. Little Bédoin with its shady avenue exudes the typical charm of Provence. Shortly after entering the town, the D974 to Ventoux branches off on the left of the roundabout. You'll ride gently uphill past vineyards and a few brick buildings. That's the special feature of this ascent: you can warm up slowly during the first few kilometres. You should definitely resist the invitation to a wine tasting on the right, but a bottle of Côtes du Mont Ventoux is a fine way to celebrate later.

Tight bends

After around 3km you'll ride through Sainte Colombe, a beautiful cosy place with many cafés. Shortly afterwards you will pass through Les Drous, the last place on the route. Now it's noticeably steeper uphill and you'll plunge into a pine-covered slope. This remains unchanged over the following kilometres. Thick crash barriers secure the road and tight bends wind their way through the rocks. Mont Ventoux has been used for car races since 1902, and even in recent years there have been races. During the descent it is particularly dangerous on the tight bends in the lower part of the ascent, if oncoming motorists cut corners in the bends.

Tail wind or head wind

Along the road you will find signs regarding distance and gradient so that you can follow the steadily increasing gradient. You'll initially be climbing at 8, then 9 and finally at over 10 per cent. It's steeply uphill and as a trained racing cyclist you will pull past many a gasping colleague. At around 8km in one go with a gradient of around 9 per cent, there will be no time to preserve your strength.

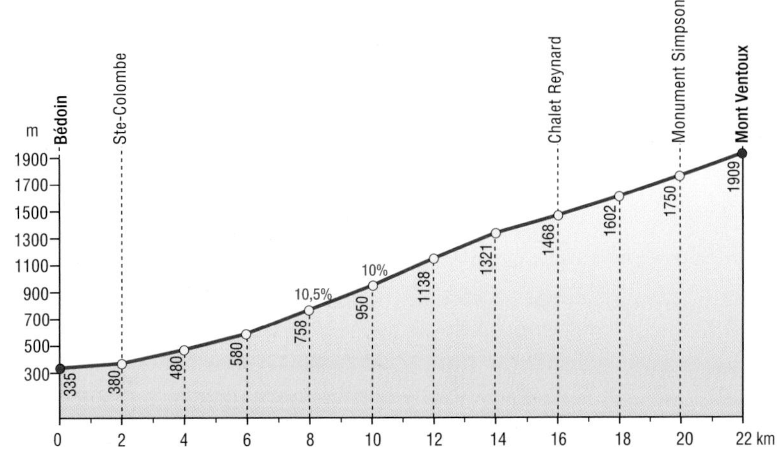

Initially you will have been riding along a thick mountain forest, and you'll later think longingly of this shade-dispensing valley. After around 10km the oak forest begins to thin out and the road now widens again. But the gradient continues on. Only near Chalet Reynard will you get a short respite in a large bend.

From here it's a total elevation of 500m to the summit which means hard labour, particularly in high summer. Those in luck will catch a light wind that blows here often, which is cooling. Those who draw the short straw face an unpleasant headwind in addition to a steep road.

On the moon

You'll then ride along a wall of rubble and after a bend the observatory and the huge antenna in front of the 'moonscape' of this stony mountain region finally comes into view. Only a few amateur cyclists will now have enough strength to use a higher gear. Those who remember the television broadcasts of previous years can only regard the speeds of the professionals as alien. Joseba Beloki commented on Lance Armstrong's 2002 stage victory with the words: "Today we landed on the moon and saw the astronaut."

Tom Simpson's memorial

Spurred on by the attractive landscape, the last few kilometres will be twice as much fun. With all that enthusiasm however you should not forget to make a stop at the memorial to Tom Simpson. In the midst of all that stone and the rush of climbing it is easy to overlook the commemorative plaque to the right of the road, after around 20km (see 'Tour history', page 76).

After the commemorative plaque the road goes via a long bend along the left of the slope to a restaurant and into a right-hand bend up a very steep slope. There you should keep to the left to ride on to the summit station. The gradient climbs once more to a tortuous 10 per cent before you arrive at the observatory. Usually in summer it is bustling with tourist traffic and the awestruck glances from tourists on the buses are balm for the cyclist's soul. As always, you shouldn't compare your time with the professionals. Iban Mayo flew up Ventoux in only 55 minutes and therefore holds the record. Those who accomplish it in two hours should be content, one and a half hours are a hard fought tour de force.

Dauphiné Libéré

While the Tour has criminally neglected Ventoux, the Dauphiné Libéré regularly heads for the mountain. On several occasions time trials were even held on Ventoux. The race is traditionally regarded as the dress rehearsal for the Tour de France, so it's no wonder that Lance Armstrong won the round trip several times. But the Texan was denied a victory on Ventoux. In 2004, during the mountain time trial over 21.6km between Bédoin and Mont Ventoux, Iban Mayo rode into first place with a new record time. In 2005 Alexander Vinokourov was first to the summit of Mont Ventoux; in both cases Armstrong could not keep up with the speed. "To win here is once again surely something special: that doesn't happen every day," rejoiced Vinokourov.

Round trip

Those who want to kill two birds with one stone should ride back to the starting point via Malaucène. This side with its wide road is clearly the better descent. What's more, you'll also gets a beautiful part of the hilly Provençal landscape thrown in for free. In Malaucène you'll turn left and roll along the vineyards in the direction of Carpentras. After around 3km at the end of a small descent the main road goes into a right-hand bend and you should head straight on to the D19 towards Bédoin. A narrow road between pine tress will lead you back to the starting point. This variant results in a beautiful round trip of around 57km and offers all the high points of Ventoux and its surroundings.

On the moon at last: The final kilometres to the summit leads you through the famous stony desert of Ventoux.

Death on Ventoux

Mont Ventoux is inextricably connected with the tragic death from the overuse of performance-enhancing drugs of the British professional cyclist Tom Simpson. Many see Simpson as an unscrupulous cheat who tried to force a victory by illegal means. Others see him as the victim of a system, because it is an open secret that he wasn't the only rider who availed himself of assistance.

Simpson was the first successful British cycling superstar. The youngest son of a mining family, he began his career as a track cyclist. In 1959 he dared to make the jump into professional road cycle racing, where he placed quickly and impressively. In 1962 he rode the Tour de France and wore the yellow jersey for several days. In subsequent years he won the Milan to San Remo race, became world road cycling champion and won the Paris to Nice race. He was therefore by no means an unknown by 1967 and even fancied his chances for the Tour victory.

It was the 13th stage and, bizarrely, 13 July, 1967. There are many reasons for the tragedy that was to follow. Tom Simpson started the race in an already weakened state because of stomach problems. In addition it was already clear in the morning that this would be an especially hard day's racing. At the start in Marseilles the thermometer already stood at over 30°C and would climb up to 40°C during the course of the day. Simpson knew therefore that he would have to give his all on that day if he wanted to stand on the podium. Before the ascent he had already taken a cocktail of alcohol and amphetamines. Witnesses reported that Simpson had gone into a bar at the foot of Ventoux together with the Frenchman Jean-Pierre Genet. Throughout the ascent one could see that the 29-year-old was fighting a desperate battle. While he had attacked powerfully at the start, he was soon forced to fall back. But it only became obvious that something was wrong 3km before the end. Simpson could no longer ride straight. In zig-zagging lines, and with glassily crazy eyes, he lurched from one side of the road to the other. Finally he fell over and couldn't even get his feet off the pedals. Spectators helped him up and put him back on the bike. But only a few metres further on he fell over again and was caught by spectators.

"The lanky man in the British jersey is obviously no longer master of his senses or muscles. He needs the whole width of the road and his zig-zags are fatally reminiscent of those of a drunk. He manages perhaps another hundred metres. Then he seems to tread on the spot before he begins to list very slowly, as though in a slow motion film, to the right," described Hans Blickensdörfer at the scene.

This time it was clearly serious and a policeman desperately called for the Tour's medic Dr Dumas. He found the Brit lying by the side of the road and immediately recognised the seriousness of the situation. Although Tom Simpson was already dead; the desperate resuscitation attempts continued for over 40 minutes. Finally he was flown by helicopter to the hospital in Avignon but it was already too late for any help. The much quoted saying, "put me back on my bike," therefore appears never to have been spoken by Simpson, but was said to be dreamed up by a British cycle racing journalist.

Dr Dumas, the Tour de France medic, found three little bottles of amphetamines in the back pocket of Simpson's jersey. The substances weaken signals of physical exhaustion and thereby disable all warning signals. Simpson died of a heart attack brought on by dehydration and exhaustion. The autopsy revealed the presence of alcohol and amphetamines in the athlete's body. In those days mixing amphetamines with alcohol was credited among cycling professionals as being especially effective.

But the drama on Ventoux had long been looming on the horizon. In 1955 on Ventoux the Swiss Ferdi Kübler suddenly fell into a zig-zag course and started to yell incoherently. It looked even worse for Jean Malléjac. Just 10km before the summit he fell off his bike, unconscious. Although Dr Dumas succeeded in stabilising his condition with artificial respiration, the Tour medic understood the situation and used the incident to issue a warning against doping.

It is beyond dispute that doping was the standard practice among cyclists back then. During an unannounced drugs test in 1962 during the amateur cycling championships amphetamines were detected in almost half the riders.

France introduced its first anti-doping legislation in 1965 and one year later the World Cycling Federation also issued the first anti-doping directives. The first tests, however, caused discontent among the riders and in 1966 even led to a 'go-slow strike'. It was therefore already obvious to the public before the death of Tom Simpson that doping was a burning issue for the sport. Five years earlier Simpson had openly addressed the issue when he admitted as such in an interview: "Only a super-athlete can bear the stresses and strains of cycling without chemical means. I can't."

The cult surrounding his commemorative plaque on the mountainside takes on some bizarre traits at times. There were not only inner tubes and drinking bottles placed by it on my visit, but also a little glass with pills. A form of worship that should provoke thought, because the site is certainly not intended to be a temple to doping.

Idol worship: The memorial stone for Tom Simpson is covered with drinking bottles, jerseys, photos and other memorabilia. The increasingly mythological status of the mountain is particularly highlighted here.

16 Relaxing on the mythical mountain
MONT VENTOUX FROM

Even Lance Armstrong has proper respect for Ventoux.

CLIMB TOP: 1909m

TOTAL ELEVATION: 1530m

DISTANCE: 21km

MAX GRADIENT: 10.9%

AVERAGE GRADIENT: 7.3%

STARTING POINT:
Malaucène (2600 inhab.), Département Vaucluse (84)

APPROACH:
From Orange on D950 to Carpentras and D938 to Malaucène

PARKING:
Immediately after the turnoff to Mont Ventoux

ROAD CONDITION:
Perfect throughout

SPECIAL FEATURE:
Velodateur at the Office de Tourisme

MOUNTAIN PASS OPENINGS:
Mid April to November

Those riding up Mont Ventoux for the first time should do so from Bédoin to experience the classic ride through the scree desert. But the ascent from Malaucène is also a worthwhile experience. You should therefore go for both ascents! Where total gradient and total elevation are concerned both sides are very similar. But on the ascent via the western side from Malaucène there are repeated sections with a lower gradient, and most importantly the sun doesn't beat down so mercilessly on the road. In high summer it is therefore definitely the easier side, but 'easier' doesn't signify much where a height difference of over 1500m is concerned!

Pure Provence!

The starting point of Malaucène is a typical Provençal place. The main street is bordered by a beautiful avenue of plane trees and old fountains and houses from the 16th and 17th centuries adorn the centre. The focal point of the town, the chateau mountain, offers a beautiful view over the maze of little lanes. Those who want to find out more about the history of the place can take part in a historical guided tour offered by the tourist office. But from our perspective the most important historical date goes a long way back: in 1336 Mont Ventoux was first climbed by the Italian scholar and poet Francesco Petrarch.

Through exotic growth

There is definitely no hanging around on this side. It's uphill from the very first metre. On a gradient of around 4 per cent you'll ride past a chapel from the 13th century and shortly afterwards past a restaurant and picnic place. Immediately after the bend the road goes slightly steeper uphill and from then on it continues along uninhabited wooded slopes. The road runs along a rock wall and the 7 per cent gradient offers a taster of the day's programme.

On the approach from the west, you'll get a view of the rocky summit during the final kilometres.

MALAUCÈNE

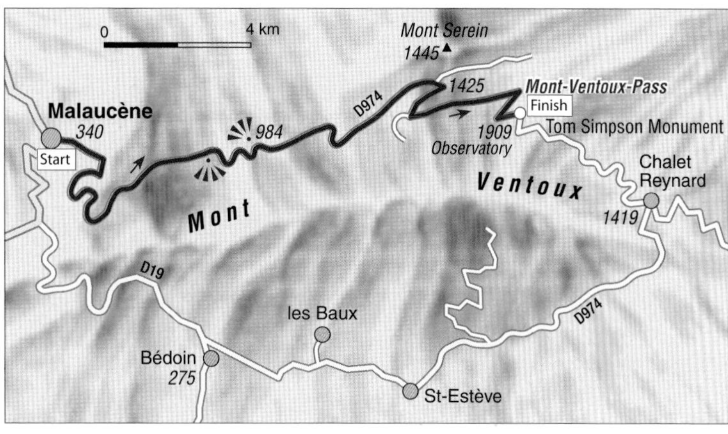

Along the road regular per cent indicators provide motivation, and you won't always feel the increasing numbers in your legs. You'll wind upwards over long bends through light pine cover. After 5km the gradient reduces briefly and offers you an opportunity to catch your breath. You'll pass many car parks for walkers. Large displays also provide information on the special characteristics of the local flora and fauna. Nowhere else in France is there such a concentration of special and diverse plants. Among them are cedars, firs, pines and even exotic plants like an alpine poppy which can only be found in Greenland.

On the panoramic route

You will then ride along three beautiful panoramic bends, each of which offers you a broad view below into the valley. This is another difference to the ascent from the Bédoin. Many places offer views down into the valley. While tight bends snake through the forest on the other side, it is mostly very light here; there are only a few conifers by the side of the road and, assuming the weather plays ball, all in all it proves a nice ride. Ventoux is by no means a guarantee for good weather. While there is only light cloud cover in the valley, it can get uncomfortable on Ventoux. Thick fog and a cold wind are common on Ventoux. After the last wide bend, 10km and around 600m of altitude, you'll get a beautiful view of the slope on the right. The road will lead on to this northern stretch of the Ventoux, which you'll follow up to the summit from then on. At this point, if not sooner, it becomes obvious that the ascent from here is also not just a Sunday outing. In front of you is the steepest part of the route that ascends at up to 10.9 per cent. The wide road is in immaculate condition and this turns the steep road into a pleasure.

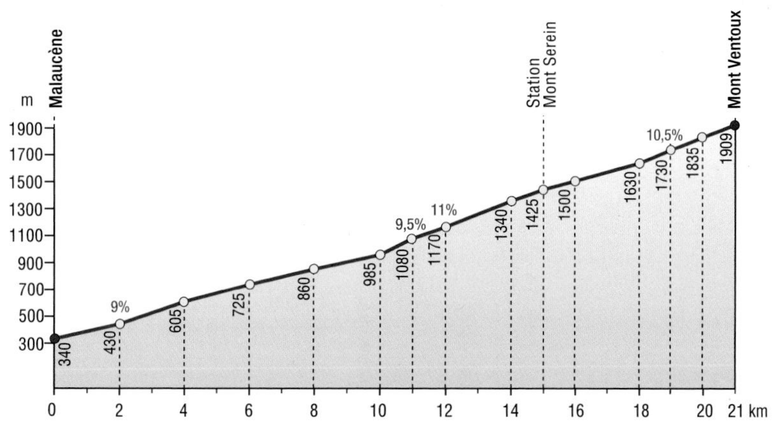

Cycle racing on Ventoux

The cycle race La Ventoux Beaume de Venise takes place every year at the beginning of June. Several different distances are on offer; the range extends from 21km over 102km up to 170km. Participants in the long round trip climb Ventoux right at the start and afterwards ride on as far as Chalet Reynard. Altogether this circuit comprises an impressive 3500m of altitude. But as is customary on Ventoux, it's neither the altitude nor the kilometres that present a challenge. In the past few years the greatest problem for the participants has been the murderous heat. Many a cyclist battles with last reserves of strength to the nearest feeding station. Those who are too slow are either scooped up by the police and deposited in the relief van, or persuaded to turn off into a shorter round trip. Further information is available from www.sportcommunication.com.

Into the stony desert

But you still have a long way to go. First you'll come unexpectedly upon a roundabout where you'll need to turn right.

You'll then cycle around a wide bend past a restaurant and immediately uphill on a ramp. You should take note of this next bend well and take care on your descent as it is surprisingly steep!

Between pine trees you'll continue ever upwards along the slope. Although it initially goes uphill at a comfortable 6 per cent, now the gradient increases steadily. Two bends with long visible ramps ring in the final ascent on the northern side. Those here for the first time will then be confused, because the summit doesn't conform to the familiar image at all. But those who beat the last few very steep metres at over 10 per cent will soon solve the riddle. A bend leads around the mountain and the landscape changes abruptly. In front of you lies the light brown stony desert blanketed by flickering heat. On the right it's only another few metres of altitude to the summit station, which means you'll need to put your foot down for the last time.

A flickering heat surrounds the giant of Provence, below the summit offering an extraordinary panoramic view.

Once you've arrived at the top, you'll be able to enjoy the wide panoramic view – and of course the respectful glances of the tourists.

Tough philosophy

Even those who have never taken an interest in philosophy will savour the words of the French philosopher Roland Barthes: "Mont Ventoux is the king of pain to whom one must submit. A despotic demon to cyclists who doesn't forgive anything and to whom the weakest must pay heavy tribute in pain."

Agonising journey to the moon

Ventoux has many nicknames and 'the alien' aptly describes the impression that the summit conveys. For many athletes, however, the 'moon landing' turned into a crash landing, since they had underestimated the ascent. There is hardly another mountain that is as representative of the suffering and pain in cyclists' lives as Ventoux. This is not just down to the percentage gradients and metres of altitude, but those factors that cannot be expressed in numbers, like the partly desert-like climatic conditions or the merciless gusts of wind. Next to fitness, the weather conditions are therefore decisive in determining when to tackle the stage.

The 'chalk mountain's debut in the Tour was in 1951, when the western approach from Malaucène was chosen, which became a rare occurrence in following years. In total, the mountain was crossed six times and served eight times as a stage destination. The conversation between Ferdi Kübler and Raphaël Géminiani in 1955 is legendary: "Watch out Ferdi, Ventoux is no ordinary mountain." Whereupon Kübler countered: "Ferdi is also no ordinary cyclist. Ferdi is a great champion," a cheeky speech which he bitterly regretted only a few kilometres later. Fortified by performance-enhancing drugs he thought himself invincible, but instead he lost control of his body. Just a few kilometres below the summit he had difficulty cycling in a straight line and could barely stay on the bike. When his athletics coach, Alex Burtin, rushed to his aid, Kübler could not understand him and was unable to respond. During the descent to Malaucène he began hallucinating and yelling incoherently. At the end of the descent he poured a beer down his throat and, full of energy, jumped back onto the bike. Unfortunately he rode off in the wrong direction. He yelled loudly: "Ferdi has gone mad, Ferdi is going to explode." The following morning he announced that he was pulling out of the race and that he was to retire from cycling.

The death of Tom Simpson heightens the riders' fear of Ventoux. Nevertheless, time and again the mountain becomes the stage for gripping attacks. In 1970, Eddy Merckx made an audacious attack on the ascent. He was surrounded by the great names of his era. Raymond Poulidor, Joop Zoetemelk, Lucien Van Impe and Joaquin Agostinho eventually had to concede victory to Merckx. Over the final 4km he fought a lonely battle. The pain had overwhelmed him, his face was distorted into a grimace. With a final surge he won the stage, but a few minutes later he collapsed and had to be given oxygen.

Even Eddy Merckx made a poor decision on Mont Ventoux.

During the 2000 Tour a gripping finale between Lance Armstrong and Marco Pantani took place on Ventoux. Approximately 5km before the summit Marco Pantani started a breakaway attempt. The leading group fell apart – Jan Ullrich, Joseba Beloki, Roberto Heras and Richard Virenque could no longer keep up. Only Lance Armstrong countered and succeeded in closing the gap with Pantani again. They took turns for the remainder of the breakaway and quickly established a 30 second lead over their pursuers. They maintained the lead until the end and Armstrong relinquished the stage victory to Pantani.

The 2009 drama can hardly be surpassed: Mont Ventoux was the mountain destination on the last stage before Paris – it couldn't get any more exciting!

17 Scenic delight
COL D'ALLOS

Almost throughout, the ascent to Col d'Allos runs over barely used roads.

CLIMB TOP: 2247m
TOTAL ELEVATION: 1108m
DISTANCE: 19.5km
MAX GRADIENT: 10%
AVERAGE GRADIENT: 5.6%
STARTING POINT:
Barcelonnette (inhab. 3310), Département Alpes-de-Haute-Provence (04)
APPROACH:
From Gap on D900 to Barcelonnette
PARKING:
Parking Centre Ville in Barcelonnette
ROAD CONDITION: Very good
DANGERS:
Occasionally narrow roads (descent!)
MOUNTAIN PASS OPENINGS:
Mid May to November

Col d'Allos with its minor gradients does not offer any superlatives but that is exactly why you can enjoy the wild and varied landscape to the full. The first 4km are identical to the arrival at the mountain in Pra-Loup. While there the way goes off to the right, you'll need to continue straight ahead. It's steadily uphill for the next 16km. Although there are a few very short gradient increases, you should be able to easily find your rhythm at between 5 to 7 per cent.

Through alpine landscape

The mostly very narrow road winds around a very rocky mountain slope. You'll frequently ride directly alongside a rock wall. The landscape is characterised by its southerly aspect: on a hot summer's day you'll sizzle in the sun. Although many pines and deciduous trees adorn the slopes, they are too light to provide shade. On the left you'll see the impressive rocky peak of Pain de Sucre (2560m) which accompanies you almost all the way. Savour the alpine surroundings to the left of the road. The rocky wall on the right opens every now and again and a little stream channels its way into the deep. You'll continue to ride upwards on a beautiful bridge. Climbing evenly at around 5 per cent, the road goes straight along the valley for quite a long time.

Backdrop like the Dolomites

The gradient increases to up to 10 per cent and in a right-hand bend you'll turn into a side valley where an impressive mountain panorama spreads out before you. Directly in front of you is the outline of the mountain's massive alpenstock of Grande-Séolane, which is reminiscent of the Dolomites.

From here you'll be able to see the course of the road because it goes straight ahead and then takes a wide left-hand bend upwards on the opposite slope.

On your left there is an almost vertical drop without road barriers; the way to Col de la Cayolle snakes through the valley far below.

Above you on the right a little chapel is enthroned on the slope and you'll also ride past a lift.

Shortly afterwards you'll want to dive into the shade-dispensing forest of larches where the road goes uphill along little streams. In the small hairpin bends, the gradient increases to 7 per cent. There are no houses here for many miles, only an idyllic mountain slope. Through the deciduous trees you'll have a wonderful view on your left of the opposite slope. Like a grey snake, your approach is outlined deep below you.

Next the road winds itself around the mountain in a right-hand bend. Wherever you look, you are presented with a formidable mountainscape – you'll realise that you have already left the steep rocky crags of the Pain de Sucre behind you.

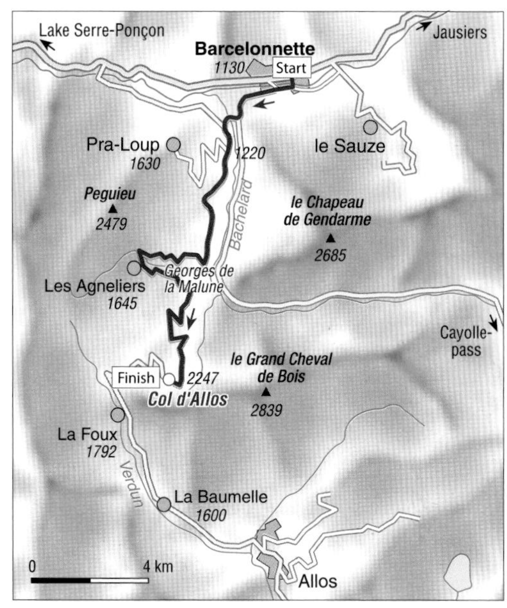

Reward at the pass

The gradient now reverts to around 4 per cent and the road goes straight up again. Plant cover becomes markedly more sparse and while the road is constantly rising to snake upwards you'll now be exposed to the sun again. On a grassy slope the road goes uphill in hairpin bends. It's only another 200m of elevation to the summit and over beautiful big bends you'll climb upwards at 7 per cent.

Next you'll cycle upwards along a larch-covered mountain flank, where the gradient drops to 3 per cent. Time and again little streams run down from the side. You'll then reach the Refuge du Col d'Allos on the right, and you'll no doubt wonder where the end of the pass is. However, shortly afterwards you'll arrive at the pass of Col d'Allos. A small, unassuming sign is tucked away on the left behind the summit.

The summit itself is just a small car park surrounded by meadows, but the panorama is a magnificent compensation for this: a whole chain of proud, scree-covered 2000m giants is strung out in front you.

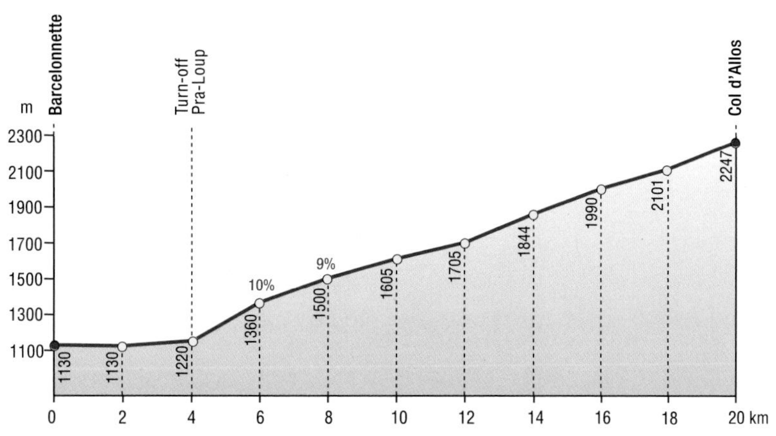

The end of the Merckx era

Eddy Merckx is still venerated today as the most successful rider in the history of competitive cycling. At his first Tour victory in 1969 he had a lead of 17 minutes over Roger Pingeon, in second place. At no other time has there been a rider who has dominated cycling so completely. Because, unlike Lance Armstrong, Merckx did not content himself with just the Tour. He also won the most important stage races from Giro d'Italia via Vuelta a España to the Tour de Suisse, and still had enough energy for victories in one-day races. He established the world hour record and dominated six-day racing, an uncanny reign that only came to an end after five Tour victories.

In 1975 everything seemed to be going according to plan again. Eddy Merckx appeared confident as ever after the first two weeks and naturally rode in the yellow jersey. He had already won both time trials and no one doubted the sixth Tour victory for the Belgian. But his downfall began with one of the most unsporting incidents in the history of the Tour. During the 14th stage to Puy de Dôme a French fan punched him in the kidneys. Tormented by pain and psychologically shaken, Merckx dragged himself over the line.

But the progress of the race during the 15th stage initially corresponded completely with the Belgian's expectations. His keenest competitor was the Frenchman Bernard Thévenet , who still lagged 1 minute behind him. The stage went over five ascents and on the descent from Col de Champs Thévenet actually lost contact because of a flat tyre. On the ascent of Col d'Allos he caught up again with the leading group around Merckx. The 'cannibal' lived up to his name and climbed up at a hellish pace. On Col d'Allos he was in the lead and on the descent he even broke away. He threw himself into the narrow bends, holding nothing back, and reached such a speed that accompanying vehicles could barely keep up. Thévenet, Gimondi and Zoetemelk took

Bridge to success: For Thévenet the stage over Col d'Allos turned into the ride on to the winner's podium.

Eddy Merckx was the best-known cycling athlete of his time. Anyone who ended up in second place behind him could chalk this up as a success.

up the pursuit and were forced to risk all, but they could not follow.

The narrow road hugs the rock wall, on the right there is a vertical drop of several hundred metres into the valley. But Eddy had his eye on his sixth Tour victory and knew no fear. Even the accompanying vehicles had to be careful not to lose contact at such a hellish pace. With squealing tyres they went in pursuit of the Belgian when the accident happened: the team car of the Italian Bianchi team overshot the bend and plunged 100m into the deep. Seconds later the helicopter transmitted pictures of the crashed car and the fear mounted. But, miraculously, Giancarlo Ferretti, the athletics coach, and a mechanic escaped with only minor injuries.

At that point Thévenet appeared to have already lost the Tour. He rode the descent with concentration and caution which earned him a deficit of one and a half minutes over a few kilometres. But when the road branched left to Pra-Loup he threw himself with wild resolve into the ascent. After only a few minutes he was surprised to see Merckx ahead of him, who was experiencing a serious drop in energy. The chance was too good for Thévenet to miss. He overtook Merckx, kept on fighting upwards and even overtook the Italian Gimondi, who himself had overtaken Merckx. Thévenet eventually reached the end of the stage almost two minutes ahead of the Belgian. On the eve of the French national holiday he offered France a reason to celebrate. He had won the yellow jersey and immediately proved on the following day that the object was dear to his heart. The stage went over Col d'Izoard and Thévenet again succeeded in reaching the end two minutes ahead of the Belgian cycling legend.

Towards the end of the Tour Eddy had even worse luck. On the way to the start he fell awkwardly and broke both his upper jaw and cheekbone. The doctor's advice was unambiguous: with such an injury, pulling out of the race was the only possibility. But the King of Cycling didn't relinquish his sceptre so easily. With a bloody face he nevertheless went to the start and attempted to prevent Thévenet's victory. Despite his serious facial injury he attacked on Col de Madeleine and Col de la Colombière – a truly brave rally which Thévenet only managed to fight off with strong support from other riders. Therefore Thévenet kept the yellow jersey to the end of the Tour and rode as the victor along the Champs Elysèes amid French jubilations.

18 Beautiful road to an over-developed resort
PRA-LOUP

Everything a cyclist needs: Details of height, distance and gradient.

CLIMB TOP: 1630m
TOTAL ELEVATION: 500m
DISTANCE: 10.5km
MAX GRADIENT: 10%
AVERAGE GRADIENT: 4.8%
STARTING POINT:
Barcelonnette (inhab. 3310), Département Alpes-de-Haute-Provence (04)
APPROACH:
From Gap on D 900 to Barcelonnette
PARKING:
Parking Centre Ville in Barcelonnette
ROAD CONDITION:
Average with rough patches
MOUNTAIN PASS OPENINGS:
All year

Pra-Loup is one of those little ascents that you can almost collect in passing and is a nice detour from the main road that makes an ideal combination with Col d'Allos. The Tour of 1975 also offered the combination of Col d'Allos and Pra-Loup for the legendary fight between Merckx and Thévenet.

With the mountains in sight

The start is Barcelonnette, which owes its name to an immigrant from Barcelona. It is in the Ubaye Valley and was designed on the drawing board in the 13th century. The impressive construction of the place and its beautiful buildings was mentioned in medieval documents. The right-angled roads are still recognisable today, although nothing remains of its fortifications. It also has close links with Mexico. For decades Mexico played a significant role as a destination for emigrants and at the start of the 20th century as a business partner to the local textile industry. Mexican culture is still evident even today: Mexican fiestas and concerts take place on a regular basis and in addition Barcelonnette has entered into a twinning agreement with a Mexican town.

Signposting is perfect from the start, and you'll ride in a westerly direction and then left over a bridge. You'll then be on the D908 and will leave Barcelonnette on a long, straight but still flat stretch of road, passing houses as you go. You'll already be able to see the mountain chain in front of you and the ski resort high above you. This is naturally motivating since it doesn't look very far. For the first kilometres you will ride along the road for Col d'Allos and you'll already see imposing mountain peaks in this direction. But after around 4km the paths diverge. While it continues straight on to Col d'Allos, the turn-off to Pra-Loup is signposted right.

The vegetation has strong southern characteristics, totally different from nearby Galibier.

Route with gradient indicators

You'll then we change over on to the D109, a small country road with minor traffic. Immediately after branching off you'll pedal north and thus gain impressions of a completely different landscape. You'll be confronted by the chain of mountains over the way which was previously behind you.

At the roadside there are kilometre markers with perfect height, distance and (especially for us cyclists) gradient indicators. At the start the gradient stays within bounds. But after the first bend it increases up to 8 per cent. On the right you'll get a view over the built-up valley which is not particularly beautiful from above. The slope is overgrown with larches, pines and deciduous trees but these offer hardly any shade. At the height of summer the sun beats down strongly on the slope.

Flying visit to Pra-Loup

Next you'll have a short relaxing section and soon the first houses will appear on the right. But you won't have reached the actual place itself. In between you'll go downhill for a short while before you reach Pra-Loup after around 8km. Straight on through the town, you'll now ride on a better road. After the bend you'll have to breathe deeply because the usual construction sins of a French ski resort will take your breath away. Everything that skiers could want is

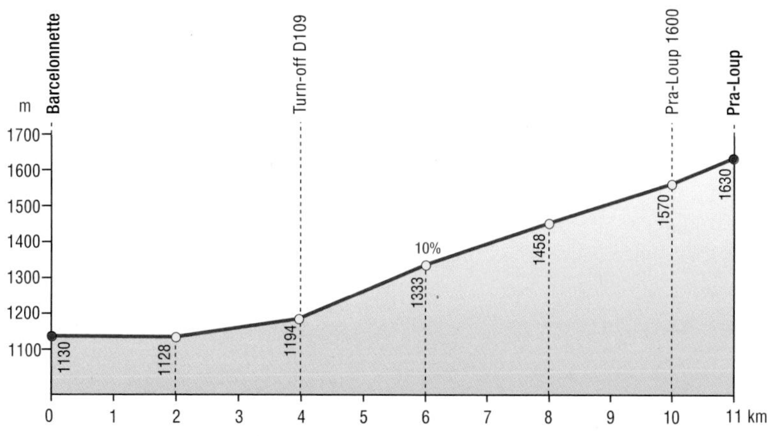

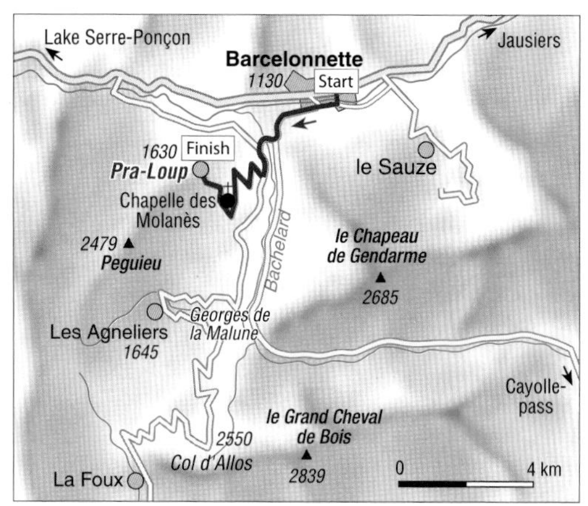

on offer here: hotels, sports shops, lifts, ski hire and bars are lined up along the road.

A one-way street leads through Pra-Loup so you'll simply carry on uphill and will then return to downhill to the road out of town via a long left-hand loop. The place doesn't exactly invite you to linger – so enjoy the descent instead!

Big plans

After such a small detour there is enough time to make big plans, because there is an abundance of beautiful routes and particularly impressive ascents. To the north, Col de Larche and Col de Vars are within reach. The Col de la Bonette and Col de la Cayolle are also accessible. At 2802m, the Col de la Bonette is the highest pass to be traversed in the history of the Tour. The risk of bad weather however, has become too great for the Tour planners to include it as a regular Tour climb. Be sure to obtain a weather report for your own ascent.

You'll want to do without the joy of cycling 1660m in the rain or snow. Col de la Bonette is not a true pass but a mountain road around the Cime de la Bonette. Regardless of the direction from which you approach Bonette, you'll first have to go over the Restefond Pass. A maximum gradient of 14 per cent over the last few kilometres is a tough assignment even for the professionals.

Sprinters' nightmare

When the pass was climbed by the Tour in 1993, Robert Millar crossed it in front of Miguel Indurain, Claudio Chiappucci and Tony Rominger. As always on such stages, the sprinters had to suffer the most because, in spite of the demanding height profile, a very high speed was imposed at the front since the fight for the yellow jersey had not been decided yet.

At the end of the day 15 riders were thrown out of the rankings because they had exceeded the time limit. Miguel Indurain confirmed his dominance and strengthened his claim to the Tour victory. But the tough stage over the Restefond Pass had claimed a particularly prominent victim: Laurent Fignon was out of the race. Although nobody knew it yet, this would be Fignon's last Tour de France. The Tour winner of 1983 and 1984 fell apart during the ascents of this stage and never attempted a comeback.

Alternative close at hand

Although Col de la Cayolle isn't as challenging as Restefond it is no less worthwhile. You can combine the pass with the ascent of Pra-Loup because if you have any strength left on the way back from Cayolle, you can simply turn left towards Allos/Pra-Loup. Seen from Barcelonnette, the D902 leads directly to Col de la Cayolle. Deep in the Bachelard Canyon, the very narrow road winds along for around 30km up to the mountain pass. The 1200m of total elevation are not too great a challenge but over the last few kilometres there are gradients of up to 10 per cent. Those in the mood can even plan a round trip and ride over Col des Champs and Col d'Allos back to the starting point. Then you'll have a day-long excursion which you'll certainly feel in your legs!

Welcome to the test tube town: No need to cycle up here for the architecture.

Late victory of the 'eternal second'

During the 1980 Tour Joop Zoetemelk was already an old hand in the peloton. It was already his tenth Tour de France and he had become lumbered with the image of the 'eternal second'. In 1970, 1971, 1976, 1978 and 1979 he had already occupied this thankless position. It was his misfortune to start his sporting career at the same time as cycling geniuses like Merckx and Hinault. He had already spent 12 days cycling in the yellow jersey but he would always have to hand it over again at the end. Everyone in 1980 expected another victory from Bernard Hinault, who had already won the prologue. Zoetemelk appeared already too old to land the big coup. But on the evening before the first Pyrenean stage Hinault announced his withdrawal due to knee problems. Zoetemelk sensed his chance and made known his ambition for a Tour victory in the Pyrenees. The little Dutchman had a great talent for climbing and had twice won the stage to Alpe d'Huez. His successes in the mountains were no coincidence because he felt most at home there: "The harder the better. Ascents that hurt most of the riders, for example Puy de Dome... those I used to love."

Thus after the first Pyrenean stage on 11 July, 1980 he took the yellow jersey. But unlike in previous years he did not give it back. When he was still riding in the yellow jersey on 13 July on the 208km-long stage from Trets to Pra-Loup, his countrymen believed in his victory. There was also another reason for them to celebrate: fellow countryman Hennie Kuiper was in second place. This running order continued until Paris and everyone delighted in the first victory for the Dutchman.

Even after his first success Zoetemelk didn't lose his taste for cycling. In total he can look back on a proud 16 participations in the Tour – an unbroken record even today. Even so he had to digest quite a few lows during his career. He sustained an almost unbelievable injury in 1974. Shortly before the end of the first stage of the Midi Libre race, a spectator's car caused a mass fall in which the Dutchman was also involved. However, the outcome of the hospital examination was positive, as he appeared to have survived the crash landing on the tarmac without injury. With his bad headache he got back into his car and drove 100km home. But in the meantime the pain had become unbearable and he decided to go to hospital back home. Doctors there diagnosed a basal scull fracture! This life-threatening injury was diagnosed far too late and his recovery extended over several months. One year later, however, he returned to the cycling stage, ready to fight. What luck for the sport that this story had such a positive ending!

Zoetemelk also rode in the legendary Flandria team.

19 Wild start, fantastic central stages, grand finale
COL D'IZOARD

Every metre on the way to the summit of the Col d'Izoard has seen its share of cyclists' sweat.

CLIMB TOP: 2360m
TOTAL ELEVATION: 1300m
DISTANCE: 31.5km
MAX GRADIENT: 11%
AVERAGE GRADIENT: 4.1%
APPROACH:
On the N94 from Briançon to Guillestre
PARKING:
In the centre of town in front of the Tourist Information Office
ROAD CONDITION:
Good but some rough patches
AREAS OF RISK:
Partially narrow roads and in the last stage wet and dark tunnels (lack of lighting)
MOUNTAIN PASS OPENINGS:
June to middle/end of October

The Col d'Izoard is an impressive mountain pass between the Northern and Southern Alps. Its two ascents differ greatly but the southern ramp is definitely more desirable. It starts as a harmless and gentle excursion but suddenly changes into a trial of strength in a hostile environment. The mountain is a wonderful synthesis of art and nature and it is regrettable that in recent years it has rarely been chosen for the Tour. The pass has become less important as the race hardly ever goes via Nice. Indeed, the pass belongs to one of the classic thrills of the Grande Boucle. In 2006 the Tour showed how well Col d'Izoard could be integrated into the alpine climbs.

Tough, tougher EmbrunMan

If you asked which was the toughest triathlon in the world, the answer would probably be the Ironman Triathlon in Hawaii. But only insiders know that Hawaii is a stroll in the park in comparison to the gruelling EmbrunMan in France. This long-distance triathlon has a bike course which poses a genuine challenge: the course is 188km long and has integrated the Izoard Pass in the circuit. It therefore challenges the competitors to an impressive 3800m in altitude. This figure indicates that the Izoard is not the only ascent in this circuit. The planners took special trouble to integrate a stage with a 20 per cent gradient. But whoever is able to survive this should not cheer too soon. While you're over the swimming and cycling circuits, the marathon is as nasty as the rest. As conventional marathon distances seemed too easy to master, gradients up to 10 per cent were incorporated into the circuit. This is why some competitors hanker back to the ascent of the Izoard, where at least they could change to the small gear ratio.

The view of the northern climb to the pass is a feast for the eyes.

Col d'Izoard

"The swim circuit?" sums up 12-time Ironman-finisher Ulrich Fluhme, "Well, it is flat but if they could put in a mountain, they would do it!" A fellow trainee concluded: "You can compete in races such as Ironman Lanzarote every year. It is tough but in 365 days you will have easily forgotten the pain. Embrun is different. It brands you. Only a maximum of two-year cycles is possible. You could not forget these aches and pains quickly during the winter break."

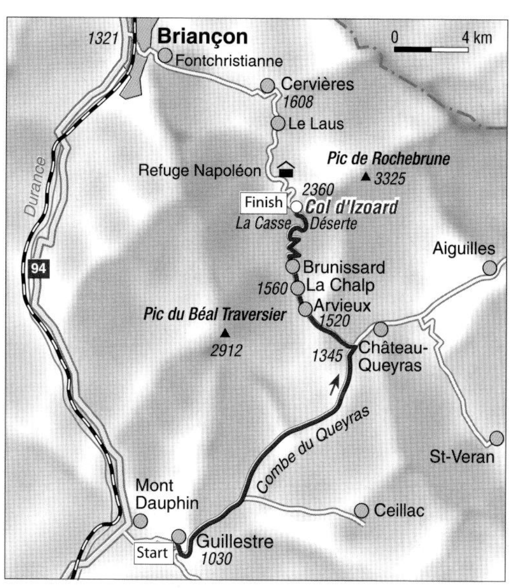

In the southern part of the Alps

In comparison to these agonies, this pass is a mere walk in the park. You'll leave Guillestre going uphill past the supermarket towards the next roundabout where only the Col d'Izoard is signposted. After 2km you'll speed downhill for a while. This road is very bumpy and goes along spectacularly long overhanging rocks. They are so close that you feel like ducking. You'll then trundle down the hairpin bends, which are followed by a number of partially unlit and unfortunately also wet tunnels. You'll emerge into an extremely wild and rocky landscape which makes a grand setting. It will also be obvious that you are in the southern part of the Alps. Chirping crickets, summery pines and shimmering heat on brownish rocks escort you. It is impossible to imagine that the Col du Galibier is in reach.

So far, so good

Parallel to the road is a very deep creek bed and straight ahead, you will be met by a very small gap in the rocks. Going through it, you're accompanied by the loud babbling of water and thankfully only a few cars will be around. You'll then cycle along a long and straight path along the brook, and having cycled for 7km you won't have gained in elevation at all. As yet, you will have

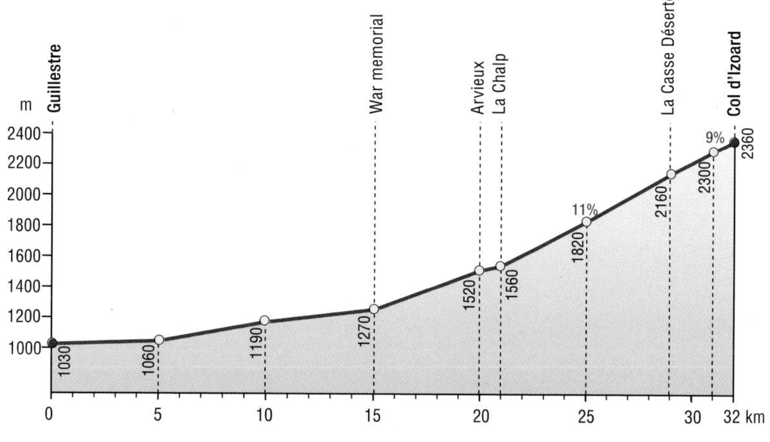

been on a harmless family excursion and not on a dreaded stage of the Tour de France. After another unlit tunnel the road goes slightly downhill and then along a long flat stretch. You'll find that there is still no incline in sight.

Continuing to Arvieux

After 15km the road leaves the brookside and your wish comes true. Finally, the fun part of the climb begins! You'll cycle on small hairpin bends past a war memorial and ahead you'll be able to make out the Château Queyras on the horizon. But you won't be journeying towards the Italian yonder to which the road leads; instead you'll lunge towards the left into the next incline. The road goes noticeably uphill and opens up onto a tremendous mountain panorama. On the way to the small village Arvieux there are short level sections here and there. On the way into the village is the 16th-century gothic stone church St-Laurent. You'll speed through a tight passage past restaurants and shops through the village.

The steepest stage

Sign posted vie ferrate ('iron roads', or iron ladders on mountain walls) indicate that alpinists enjoy themselves greatly here too. You will be in a wide valley with several little villages which blend beautifully into the landscape. The gradient increases after 25km and after a bend you'll climb the steepest stage of the route. The very narrow road winds up the pine-covered slopes with a gradient of up to 11 per cent. Hairpin bends follow each other one after another you'll get a beautiful view into the distance. Sublime mountain tops appear on the horizon and on a stunning summer day gliders populate the sky.

Unique landscape

After some bends you'll suddenly reach the Casse Déserte. After the experience of forested slopes with a calm, Mediterranean flair the contrast with this wild alpine rock and boulder desert is tremendous. Nowhere else in France can you find a similar landscape. The view across the eroded cliffs is fascinating. Rockfall is a daily occurrence and it is advisable not to stop in the wrong place when taking your photos. A memorial to Fausto Coppi and Louison Bobet is placed on a rock to the left at the end of the 300m-long downhill section. Shortly afterwards, you'll be able to see the top of the pass. The last bends follow and the incline increases quite noticeably.

Opposite: It could not get more stunning: The last kilometres of the southern slope to the Izoard.

Below: In Casse Déserte, a memorial was erected in honour of Fausto Coppi and Louison Bobet. The marble plates were installed on behalf of the readers of the sports newspaper L'Équipe.

Like a playful earth worm

At the summit a grand monument commemorates the builders of the road. Nestled just beneath the top of the pass is the Chalet d'Izoard. On both sides of the summit, the roads meander downhill like a playful earthworm. If you wish to return on the same route, you have to be careful on the descent. The upper section of the road is extremely narrow and the unlit and wet tunnels at the end of the descent pose a considerable risk. Still, before the return you should savour the words of the Tour founder Henri Desgrange: "The Izoard is like a never-ending bedtime story. The Izoard does not end, it is infinite: at times, it suggests that you have conquered it. But this is most definitely not the case. Just after a big sigh of relief, a bend is followed by a climb that would have a mule gasping."

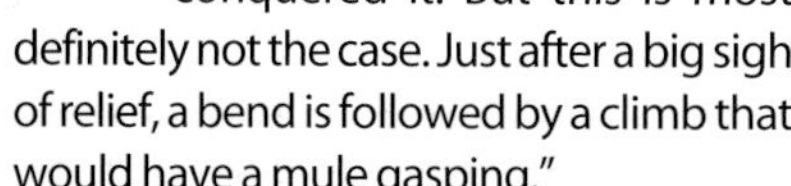

A monument commemorates the construction of the road.

Highest city in Europe

If, for practical reasons, you consider going up the Izoard from the north side, you forego these scenic highlights. But in regard to the athletic challenge, the north ascent is also a pleasure. Just about 1000m in altitude have to be mastered across 21km. The route starts in Briançon which prides itself on being the highest city in Europe. The road D902 leads with only a mild incline through the Valley of the High Cerveyrette. The incline increases only halfway through. You'll approach the top of the summit with a 12 per cent gradient. The roads also allow for a not too challenging round trip. The N94 connects Guillestre and Briançon and therefore makes a quick return possible. Unfortunately, this main road carries heavy traffic. After the beautiful surroundings at the Izoard, the traffic can be a real shock.

You should not stop for photographs in the Casse Déserte as falling rocks are a frequent occurrence.

Alone in the desert

For a long time the Izoard was regarded as one of the most important mountain passes on the Tour. In most cases, the stages started at the coast in Nice or Cannes and ended in Briançon. The Col d'Izoard lost its importance from the 1980s onwards as the Tour did not extend to the Mediterranean Sea anymore. The first journey into the desert took place on 13 July, 1922, 11 years after the first crossing of the Col du Galibier. The stage led from Nice to Briançon and the Belgian Philippe Thys mastered the 274km in 12 hours 50 minutes.

Three names are inextricably linked to the Izoard: Gino Bartali, Louison Bobet and Fausto Coppi. In 1938 Bartali proved his superiority by cycling in a solo run across the pass. His support staff had already told him on the ascent that he had taken over the overall lead of the Tour. But Bartali was not able to enjoy this as his exhaustion was too great. He arrived at the goal of Briançon with an advantage of 17 minutes over the present champion and seized the yellow jersey.

World War I forced the Tour into a break, but Bartali accomplished great achievements: he used his training sessions to transport false documents saving the lives of many Italian jews. He used his position to bring information and documents to the Italian resistance movement. In 1948, 10 years after his first victory, Bartali returned to the starting line. Meanwhile, he had remained 'il Vecchio', the old timer. The Tour led again over the Izoard and Bartali had been given the honorable task to save his country from a Civil War: just before the start of the stage the Italian prime minister phoned Alcide De Gasperi to tell him that the leader of the Communists, Palmiro Togliatti, had been murdered. Gasperi appealed to Bartali to win this stage to distract the nation and prevent chaos.

The conditions on the day were atrocious. In freezing rain and snow storms, Bartali struggled up the pass. Unfortunately, he had not stocked up with food or drink. He dragged himself up another 10 grim kilometres and three bananas from a spectator saved him from collapse.

Fausto Coppi did not only dominate the front pages of the sports newspapers but involuntarily also featured on the broadsheets.

Bartali took his task from the prime minister very seriously; he won three stages in succession and arrived in Paris as the winner.

In the following year however, an Italian changing of the guards took place. Bartali and Fausto Coppi climbed up the Izoard side by side. Coppi was clearly superior and let his teammate win the stage as it was his birthday that day. Coppi achieved the victory of the whole Tour. The whole nation was split into supporters for the devout Bartali and supporters for the sober strategist and epicurean Coppi.

In 1950 Louison Bobet reached the summit first. Here, he profited from the absence of the Italians. In post-war France, anti-Italian sentiments gathered momentum. At the Col d'Aspin, a scuffle broke out and the Italians returned home furious.

In 1953 Bobet triumphed again at the Izoard – perhaps one of the spectators in particular motivated him. None other than Fausto Coppi cheered him on at the road side. Bobet won the yellow jersey with an advantage of 11 minutes over the then champion and kept it until Paris.

Over the following years, the list of stage leaders at the Izoard was filled with prominent names: Eddy Merckx, Bernard Thévenet, Lucien Van Impe, Claudio Chiappucci and Santiago Botero each crossed the pass as the winner.

20 Relaxing tour with an arduous start
COL DE VARS

CLIMB TOP: 2109m
TOTAL ELEVATION: 1057m
DISTANCE: 20km
MAX GRADIENT: 9%
AVERAGE GRADIENT: 5.3%
STARTING POINT:
Guillestre (2280 inhab.), Départment Hautes-Alpes (05)
APPROACH:
On the N94 from Briançon to Guillestre
PARKING:
In the centre of town in front of the Tourist Information Office
ROAD CONDITION: Perfect
MOUNTAIN PASS OPENINGS:
All year

Admittedly, if you cycled the Col d'Izoard on the previous day, you will not be impressed by this stage. The differences are obvious: there is more traffic on this route and the landscape, of course, is not as spectacular.

Colourful climb

Nevertheless, the route is worthwhile as the changes in altitude are taxing and the vista over the valley definitely noteworthy. The valley of the Durance is an important meeting point between Italy and France where cars and trucks from Italy as well as from the French Alps roar towards the south. The congestion on the route to Guillestre is therefore heavy. But luckily, the actual ascent is spared this. Already in the first kilometres will you recognise that this stage is by no means a walk in the park. The route from the car park on the D902 towards Vars starts with an uphill climb.

The first hairpin bends after around 2km will change your orientation and direct your view on to the pine-forested landscape. During the subsequent kilometres constant bends offer various views over the valley. The road then narrows and directly passes a rock with a constant gradient of 8 per cent.

More steep hairpin bends lead you uphill along beautiful meadows. After 8.5km you'll cross a small bridge and pass a water fountain to the left of the road inviting you to fill up your water bottles. Due to the constant gradient you will have already completed over half of the elevation and will be rewarded with a short descent.

After a few kilometres after Guillestre, tranquillity is restored.

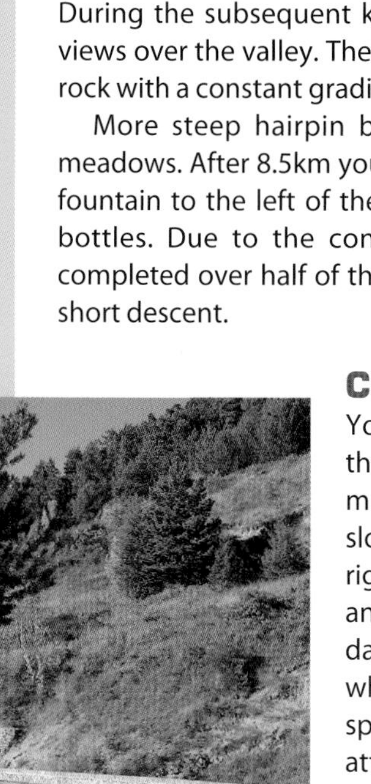

Courage to dare?

You'll reach Vars and trundle downhill through the village. Ahead of you will be a massive cornice which you'll approach slowly over the coming kilometres. To the right you'll see slopes with the first ski lifts and you'll cross another part of Vars. You'll dart up on the gentle incline, wondering whether it's really possible to adhere to the speed limit of 30km/h. However, this cocky attitude will be immediately punished by a very steep hill at the end of the village. You'll soon reach the next district of the skiing region.

Its ugly houses however won't invite you to stay and you'll continue for another 16km to finally enjoy the actual landscape, undisturbed by concrete. You'll pass through a larch forest and in front of you an austere alpine vegetation will appear.

You'll then cycle full of vim and vigour on to a plain past the Refuge de Napoléon which has been here since 1858. In front of the chalet lies a small mountain lake with a fantastic view on to the giant rocks just in front of you. The road goes steadily uphill until you reach the summit (bar/resto). The vista towards the south is magnificent. The steep hairpin bends which lead on the other side towards the valley are dizzying.

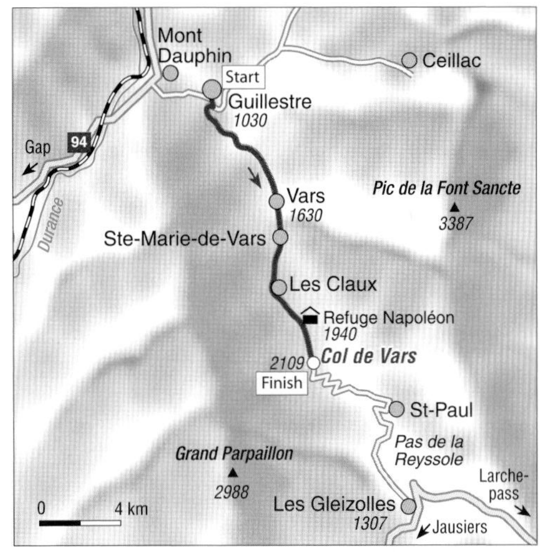

Steep grand finale

If you chose to approach Col de Vars via the south elevation of Les Gleizolles, you have to tackle a tamer climb. Even if you decide to choose the more remote Barcelonnette (1150m) as your point of departure, you have to cycle further but conquer less elevation. Nevertheless, the route is still not a walk in the park. While the first kilometres are an easy ride, the last section turns into a challenging affair. You'll only become aware of the gradient at the small village of Saint-Paul (1488m). But before the climb really gets going, another plain follows. In the last sections with gradients between 8 and 12 per cent you'll gain proper altitude for the pass.

Well connected

Ideally, you'll connect the Col de Vars with one of the other many mountain passes near by. An escort vehicle would be an advantage as you'll then get to dispense of the climb on the return. If you chose to climb the pass as described and head via the south side towards the valley, you could easily continue on to the Col D'Allos, Col de la Cayolle, Col de Restefond/Bonette or Col de Larche. The latter is directly on the Italian border and therefore has never been part of the Tour's route. If you take the descent of the Col de Vars into Les Gleizolles, you can easily follow the

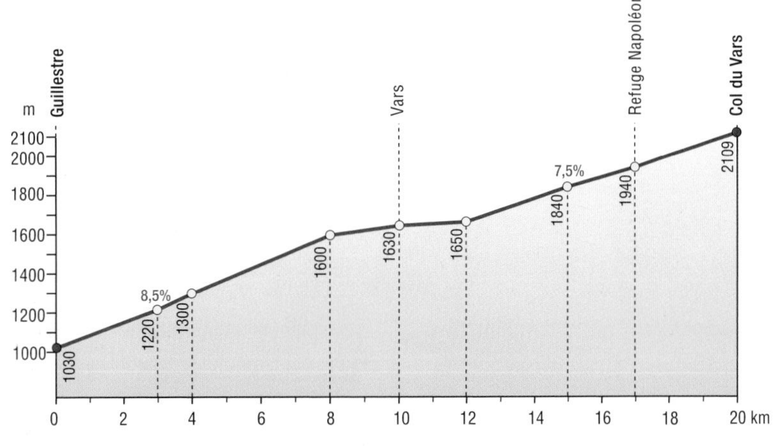

Under the Southern sun, the shadowless ascent to the Col de Vars is no walk in the park.

signs to Col de Larche on the D900. It is only 16.5km to the summit and you would not overextend yourself without an escort vehicle if you return on the same route.

But in order to conquer the summit, you have to master 1100m in altitude. The route however is one of the most beautiful mountain pass routes in the Alps. In addition to a sublime mountain setting it also offers a great road. Magnificent hairpin bends lead up the 1996m pass. Once you have arrived at the top, a view down towards the Italian Piedmont will reward you greatly. Such a worthwhile detour with these magnificent attractions will not make the return to Guillestre too difficult.

Rolf Aldag's ride in the mountain jersey was captured in the documentary Hell on Wheels *(NFP/Universal).*

German Kings of the Mountain

Climbs have never been the strength of the German cyclists and therefore it is not surprising that only three German riders have earned the right to wear the polka-dot jersey. All three seized the jersey under very unusual conditions.

Jens Voigt has become notorious for his break aways and has provided thrilling entertainment on numerous stages of the Tour. In 1998, when the 9th stage led from Montauban to Pau, he was relatively young and inexperienced. As the 210km long route passed his then home he was particularly motivated and wanted to show off to his neighbours. After 41km he cast himself to the wind to get some extra mountain points. With this dedicated attack, Voigt created a break away group within which three riders lead the way towards the finish. Voigt was clearly in the lead and gained points at three mountains Grade 4. As the former Peace Race winner, he was also the lead in Pau but had two experienced riders in tow. Therefore he did not win the stage but he was allowed to wear the mountain jersey the next day. The pleasure did not last long as he had to hand over the jersey to his former training partner Jan Ullrich, who was very pleased.

Marcel Wüst's pursuit of the polka dots was even more cunning. His Tour started with a 16.5km individual time trial. The only elevation during the stage was a small hill of 37m in altitude. The rider who climbed it the fastest would get the mountain jersey. Wüst took his normal bike to the hill and climbed it with great speed. On top of the hill he changed to his individual time trial machine. Although he was only placed 142nd on the stage, he had acquired the mountain jersey. This was a masterstroke by the sprinter, which brought him into the spotlight. He continued to wear the polka-dot jersey for another four days and, in the stage to Vitré, he won the mass sprint which only one other King of the Mountain has achieved.

All-round rider Rolf Aldag scored a coup in the anniversary year 2003 which he himself could not believe. On the 7th stage from Lyon to Morzine Richard Virenque pursued the mountain points. Aldag followed him closely and crossed the finishing line 2 minutes after Virenque. The Frenchman won the yellow and the polka-dot jersey. As he was not able to wear both, he relinquished the latter to Aldag. Aldag was third in the overall classification at the end of that stage and was celebrated by his roommate Erik Zabel. The wisecracking celebration by these two likeable veterans is recorded in the film *Hell on Wheels*. On the next day, Aldag had the honour to cycle across the Col du Galibier to Alpe d'Huez. He was the first German who raced up the 21 hairpin bends at the 'Dutch Mountain' wearing the mountain jersey. First, he felt uncomfortable wearing the jersey because he did not know if he would be able to do it justice on this very challenging stage. "I feel", he explained during an interview, "like a tramp in a smoking jacket at a reception at the Élysée Palace." He joked with his team manager to hide the jersey under his raincoat. Years after this run the mountain jersey had been given a place of honour in Aldag's collection. The former racer and Ironman-finisher is fondly remembered by Tour fans because of his constant and longstanding achievements.

Even a minor mountain pass can cause media-hype, in particular when it helps a German to the mountain jersey.

NORTHERN ALPS

21 Challenging excursion to the Chartreuse Mountains
COL DU GRANIER

On the way to the Col du Granier.

CLIMB TOP: 1134m
TOTAL ELEVATION: 840m
DISTANCE: 17.5km
MAX GRADIENT: 12%
AVERAGE GRADIENT: 5%

STARTING POINT:
Barberaz near Chambéry (4800 inhab.), Département Savoie (73)

APPROACH:
From Annecy (towards the motorway to Grenoble) via Chambéry, and then exit 19 La Ravoire. You will turn immediately left over the bridge, turn left towards the motorway, and after 50m you need to leave at exit Barberaz. You'll then go parallel to the two-lane motorway, after 200m under two bridges, you'll need to go left towards Barberaz Centre. Take the right exit at the roundabout to Centre Commercial parking

PARKING:
Parking Centre Commercial (shopping centre) in Barberaz

ROAD CONDITION:
Partially road repairs

DANGERS:
The upper part of the circuit has narrow hairpin bends; short and unlit tunnels

MOUNTAIN PASS OPENINGS:
April to October

The Col du Granier is a casual but sporty challenge. At first the level of difficulty leads you to believe that the route is easy and after a few metres, you are put right on that count. It is recommended that you join the route later: if you start in Chambéry, you have to squeeze through congested streets of a big city and you're liable to get lost due to the lack of clear signposting. From personal experience, despite a city map and several nerve-racking efforts, it was almost impossible for me to find my way around. It is therefore worth departing from the described parking space in Barberaz, even if you have difficulty finding it.

No signposting

There is no signposting at the start of the circuit and you'll have to pay close attention when riding the first few metres. From the car park you'll need to turn to the left and ride up a steep slope that leads through rows of houses. After a couple of hundred metres you should turn at the church to the right; again there isn't a sign to indicate the way. Your route will now go along a stone wall and on the right side you'll see the highrises in the centre of Chambéry. You'll reach the outskirts of Chambéry and after an approximately 200m-long descent you'll need to turn towards the left to the D912. This is where you'll finally come across the first traffic sign for the Col du Granier, pointing towards the Chartreuse Mountains. From herein the route is straight and you won't lose your bearings.

Through the wild and rocky scenery

After 3.5km you'll leave Chambéry and reach Jacob Bellecombette, from which you'll go straight on towards the Col du Granier (signposted). The first kilometres already take you uphill with an average gradient of 6 per cent, which will warm your muscles.

You'll then have to pass through several villages before the densely populated area decreases. After 6km you'll reach the steepest section of your stage which, with a 10 per cent gradient, will claim all your energy. On the left loom the perpendicular boulders which shape the scenery of the area. After 9km a hairpin bend starts the most beautiful section of the route. You'll cycle directly past brash rocks, safely secured with iron mesh as once in a while the crumbly rock lands on the road. The road goes through a tunnel to the left of the boulders. The approximately 80m-long tunnel is unlit and particularly unpleasant on the ascent. The road continues to the right uphill with perfect signposting. The surface repairs will significantly slow down your ascent and on the descent will demand your greatest attention. You'll now be face to face with a massive rock, the Chamechaude (2088m). The highest mountain of the Chartreuse Mountains remains directly in sight of you until you reach the summit. On your right, small mountain streams rush down and you'll continue on long straight stretches with a small incline towards the summit. You will have now reached the Parc Régional de Chartreuse.

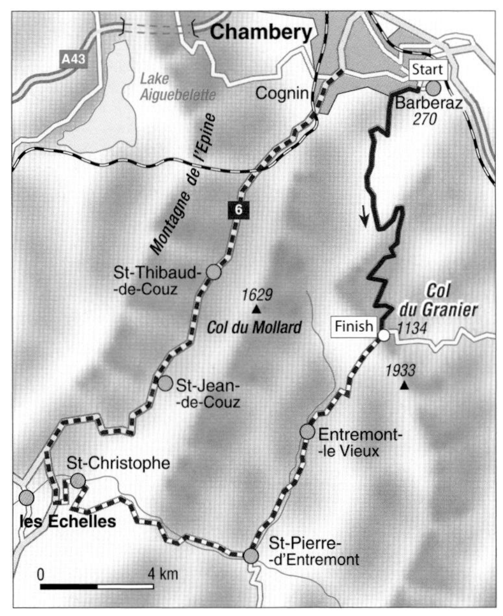

The circuit

After 15km you'll cycle across a bridge (Pont de Sauvière), past a waterfall and finally arrive at the Col du Granier. A wonderful view awaits you at the summit. In case you are hungry or thirsty, a restaurant will provide for you. I would recommend expanding this ascent into a circuit. If you follow the cycle route Circuit de Chartreuse number 26, you will cross the pass, and in Entrement-le-Vieux turn to the right to Corbel. Then you'll follow the signs back to Chambéry. If you follow the route, you have completed a wonderful excursion to the Chartreuse Mountains and won't have exhausted yourself on

Opposite: Towering over the Chambéry valley the road runs directly past the rocky landscape.

Previous double spread: You can find the saying: "Ulle [Jan Ullrich], push yourself!" at the Col de la Madeleine.*

* In 1997, Udo Bölts shouted at Jan Ullrich "Push yourself, you lazy bastard!" on the stage through the Vosges to Colmar and he did indeed win that stage.

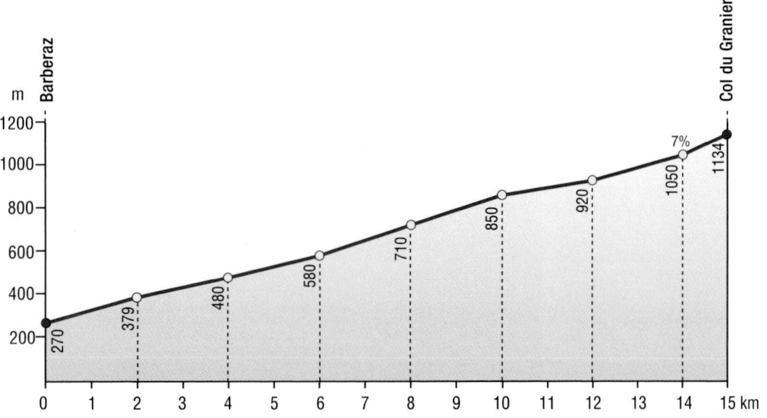

Planning routes with a GPS

Cycling in the alps has become more and more popular in the last few years. With the help of Internet resources cyclists are able to share their latest climbs and routes. One very helpful tool for planning a trip are websites using Google Maps. This easily allows you to map the elevation profile and assess the difficulty of your route. Travelling along a planned route can be even more comfortable when using a GPS-enabled cycling computer. Garmin Road Maps of Europe in the past have been the most common option for GPS mapping. Another alternative is to obtain free downloadable road maps available based on the Open Street Maps. You will be sure to find some amazing resources for planning your trip on the Internet. There are several websites offering tracks of challenging routes in the Alps and the Pyrenees. Even if you don't have a GPS-unit you can use those websites to plan your trip. Tracks are visualised on Google Maps and give you an idea of distances and altitude on any bike route.

Useful websites:
www.gpsies.com
www.bikemap.net
www.velomap.org

the 56km and 1180m in altitude. The only disadvantage of this particular route is that you return 1km off the point of departure and have to find your way back.

Although the sign posting here is very good, you can get lost easily on the return to Chambéry. Therefore, you'll need to memorise the way to the point of departure.

Opposite: The Col du Granier offers a varied climb.

Right: The massive rock of Chamechaude accompanies the cyclist on the climb to the summit.

Poupou's first stage victory

In 1962, everyone agreed: only the Frenchman Jacques Anquetil could be the winner of the Tour de France. Anquetil, the victor in 1957 and 1961, was again in top form during training. However, at the Col du Granier a new and serious contender emerged. Farmer's son Raymond Poulidor impressed everyone on his first Tour de France with outstanding achievements and showed that he would be a future title contender. Initially, though, it did not look good for him. He broke his hand and had to start the race with it in a plaster. Despite his wrist pain, he dared to attack on the 19th stage between Briançon and Aix-les-Bain. In a solo run he climbed the Chartreuse Mountains across the Col du Granier and secured his first stage victory. But despite this victory, Poulidor did not start a new epoch of the Tour as he seemed to have a monopoly on bad luck. Although he gave his best year in and year out, he never won the Tour. The challenge between him and Anquetil dominated the following years and 'Poupou', as he was nicknamed, always came off second best. But this did not damage his popularity: he was the darling of France.

Poulidor storms nearly to the top with a tight grip on the drops.

In 1964 the Tour de France was dominated by the fierce competition between Anquetil and Poulidor across the total distance of 4500km. Already at the start, the conditions for a thrilling duel were ideal. Jacques Anquetil had already won the Giro d'Italia for the second time and excelled in his performance. But Poulidor could also display his good form as he had just won Vuelta a España (the Tour de Spain). In the first two weeks both competitors scrutinised each other critically but none could yield the advantage. In 1964 Poupou was on the verge of triumph as never before. But he missed his chance to lead three times. In a sprint finish on the Monaco track he made the mistake of sprinting one lap too early. Anquetil won and took a valuable time bonus. Approaching the Pyrenees, it seemed as if Anquetil was too sure of his victory. The previous evening he ate as if he was celebrating his final victory. Photographers caught him at a party, drinking sangria and smoking cigarettes. It is therefore not surprising he suffered for his sins at the first 30km-long ascent. At the start he looked pale and his strongest competitors saw the ideal moment to defeat him. He struggled up the pass with heavy legs. Poulidor was so encouraged by his advantage that he already imagined himself in the yellow jersey. Anquetil had already lost 4 minutes on the summit of Port d'Envalira to his rival and was near collapse. His teammate and his trainer had to cheer him on as Anquetil was close to giving up the race completely.

The Tour de France lives on its myths and stories which often do not distinguish between fact and fiction. This is particularly apparent in the accounts of the 1964 Tour. Legend has it that on the last stretch of the pass Anquetil's manager, Raphaël Géminiani filled Anquetil's water bottle with the champagne reserved for the coming celebration. "Either this stuff will kill you," he was supposed to have said to the journalist Les Woodland, "or will get you back on your feet." Although the mountain was veiled in thick fog, Anquetil thrust himself down into the bends. This was particularly astonishing as in other legends a clairvoyant had predicted an accident on this stage. The fast ride into the valley brought Anquetil nearly to the lead, missing by 2 minutes. He managed to find allies in his race for the lead and at the end of the race the tables had turned. Anquetil won a 1-minute bonus. But it was not only his strategy of attack but also Poulidor's misfortune that helped his victory. A spoke broke on Poulidor's bike and he was devastated as he "won and lost the Tour on one day." Poulidor was ahead of Anquetil before he had the breakdown.

Also legendary was the duel between the two French men during the 20th stage. The finish was on the 1415m Puy de Dôme and Anquetil was exhausted. Nevertheless, he was able to distract his competitor with some tricks. The whole French nation trembled when both cyclists rode elbow to elbow. About half a million spectators watched the thrilling event, which was broadcast live on television and fascinated the whole nation. The racers climbed up the mountain kilometre by kilometre and at times their elbows even touched as they were so close. Anquetil was at the very limit of his strength and used psychological tricks. He chatted to Poulidor about the time bonus the Spanish racers ahead of them would gain. He therefore distracted Poulidor who thought that he had missed his chance of winning. Poulidor noticed too late that Anquetil was not at his best and chanced in the last kilometres an attack. He gained an advantage of 56 seconds but threw away his chance to achieve a decisive time advantage. At the finish, Anquetil asked how much his lead was. When he was told that it was 17 seconds he answered, "16 seconds more than necessary."

Follow the footsteps of Raymond Poulidor and ride the Col du Granier.

Just 48 hours later, the whole nation was watching the time trial between Versailles and Paris. The honest and brave Raymond Poulidor was the undisputed favourite. The spectators hoped that after all the mishaps, Poulidor would be favoured by fortune just once. Anquetil on the other hand sensed the hostility from the audience who practically longed for his defeat. The people were bored by his constant success and hoped for a sensation. But Anquetil was not only a level-headed strategist, but also a superb time trialist. He had a very characteristic posture; photographs of the race show him huddled over his bike, his body bent tightly over the crossbar, his head just above the handlebars and his combative expression betraying his determination. He easily won the battle against the clock and thus also the Tour de France. Poulidor again came second overall, he missed the victory by 56 seconds.

During the 15 years of his cycling career at the Tour de France, Poulidor was never able to sport the yellow jersey. But despite being an eternal runner-up at the Tour, we should not forget 'Poupou's' long list of victories. He won the Vuelta a España (1964), Milan–San Remo (1961), La Flèche Wallonne (1963), Paris–Nice (1971, 1973), Critérium du Dauphiné Libéré (1966, 1969), the French Championship and numerous other races. Only the Tour de France was jinxed for him, and he came second or third eight times in the race.

22 Start in lively Grenoble
COL DE PORTE

The road is not always as empty as this in the southern part of the Chartreuse Mountains.

CLIMB TOP: 1326m
TOTAL ELEVATION: 1100m
DISTANCE: 18km
MAX GRADIENT: 11%
AVERAGE GRADIENT: 6%
STARTING POINT:
Grenoble (157,000 inhab), Départment Isère (38)
APPROACH:
The Téléphérique opposite the Bastille in the city centre of Grenoble.
PARKING: City centre
ROAD CONDITION: Good
MOUNTAIN PASS OPENINGS:
April to October

Grenoble is a busy metropolis. Therefore this route is only recommended to city lovers. First, you have to struggle through the crowded streets of the city to find a parking space in the centre. Therefore, this tour is only really rewarding if you combine it with a city tour or continue to the Col du Granier. The city brings further disadvantages: on the weekends and holidays, many inhabitants of Grenoble are drawn to the mountains. Consequently, the road to the Chartreuse Mountains can be extremely busy. If you want to spare yourself the stress of finding a parking space, you could switch to your bike at La Tranche, reducing the climb to 15km. Although the climb is not all straight forward, the Tour de France has been a frequent guest in the Chartreuse Mountains. The Col de Porte is seen as the gateway to the Alps and is traditionally combined with a tour to the Col du Granier.

Olympic city of Grenoble

Boasting 157,000 inhabitants, Grenoble is the most elevated Hautes-Alpes city. Greater Grenoble accommodates approximately 532,000 people. This capital of the Départment Isère encompasses a long history which goes back to the Celts. From an athletic point of view, Grenoble is very interesting as it hosted the 1968 Winter Olympics. It was chosen because it is nestled between the Chartreuse, Vercors and the Belledonne mountain range. The writer Stendhal summarised his impression succinctly: "At the end of every street is a mountain." The city is famous for many nearby ski resorts nestled in the surrounding mountains with around 150 ski resorts in the vicinity of a 1.5-hour drive.

400 steps up the hill

Needless to say the city offers a lot of attractions during the summer, too. The buzzing life of the university city occurs around

The view from the south on to the Chamechaude is also impressive and cannot always be seen on the climb up the Col de Porte.

the central Place Grenette. Many historical buildings adorn the pedestrian area. Particularly important, in addition to the cathedral Notre Dame from the 12th century, the Eglise Saint-André from the 15th century is in the Quartier (Latin quarter) of Saint-Laurent. Art lovers are drawn to the Musée des Beaux Arts which houses the third biggest art collection in France with many important artifacts. If the challenge of a sightseeing tour is not testing enough, then you should visit the Bastille. It sits on the mountainside overlooking Grenoble. To enjoy the view, you either have to climb 400 steps or cheat by taking the Grenoble-Bastille cable car. On a clear day you can even see Mont Blanc from the fort. The Bastille was erected as a series of fortifications in the 16th century against attacks from the north and it houses a semi-underground defense network.

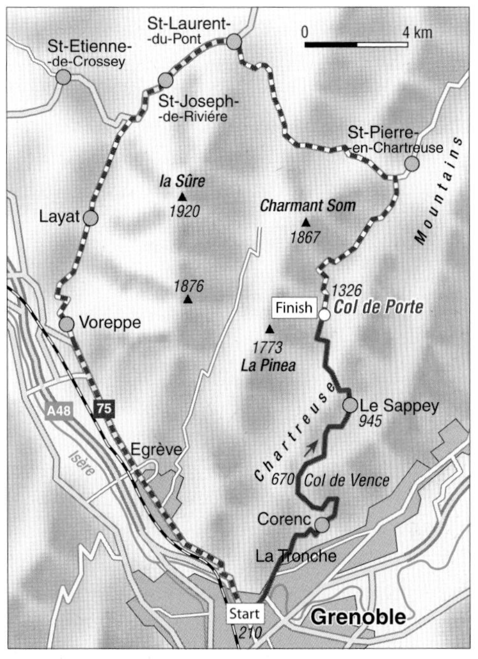

Full frontal towards the rock

At the valley station of the mountain railway in the centre of Grenoble you'll follow the signs to 'La Tranche'. After about 800m you'll need to change over to the left side of the river and continue towards Chartreuse. You will reach La Tranche after 2 km and there you'll turn on to the D512. This is the first time you'll see Col de Porte signposted and the road goes uphill immediately. The first kilometres will take you through the outlying suburbs of Grenoble. The road runs through neat houses and small gardens. In Corenc, a big rock will become visible which will look as though it is in your way. To the right, you'll have an expansive view across Grenoble and its highrise buildings. You'll start getting suspicious as the rock keeps closing in

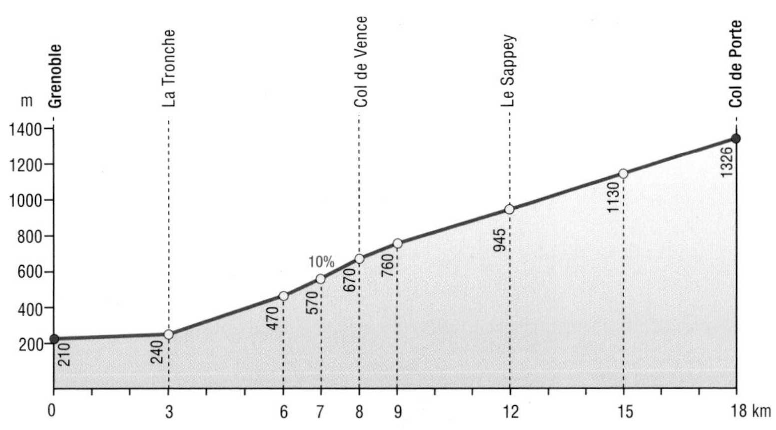

and it seems that you'll have to climb it by rope to conquer it. But soon the mystery unravels; a road takes you past the rock to the left in a big sweep.

You'll now be in the Parc Naturel de Chartreuse, high up from Grenoble. You'll cycle along rocky inclines and a long upward sloping curve continues to take you past that impressive rock.

All goes well

When you are on a hill, you'll have left the rock behind. You'll now be able to get a glimpse of the massive Chamechaude (2080m) which you'll have already spotted from the Col du Granier. You'll then cycle gently uphill along a creek towards Le Sapey-en-Chartreuse. The village is drawn out across several kilometres and the road continues with a left bend up the mountain pass. While you are doing alright, others are doing even better. Le Sapey-en-Chartreuse has made its name among runners in the vicinity for classy mountain running competitions. These tricky competitions take place on a regular basis. The Montée Pédestre des 3 commune goes along exactly the route that you will have taken. The fastest runner covered the 10.5km from La Tranche to Le Sappey in 2006 in 47 minutes. This is an average of 13km/h which even some cyclists cannot make.

Viewed in this light you are lucky that there are no other runners. Who wants to be overtaken by a 'pedestrian' while cycling with your extra-light carbon bike in full racing regalia?

Difficult decision

After 13km you'll arrive at the Col de Palaquit (1154m). On the final kilometres gentle bends will take you through the mountain forest to the top. There are restaurants on top of the mountain pass and you'll be able to spot the ski lifts. In the winter, this is a popular ski resort, in the summer, it serves as a general area for recreation. You will now be faced with a serious decision: are you strong enough to continue towards the Col du Granier or should you return to Grenoble?

The blossoming fruit trees reflect the mild climate of the Col de Porte.

Ultracycling: The Tour Direct

Cycling is developing rapidly. Extreme ranges of performance are now possible with new and modern training methods and sophisticated technology. The 'Tour Direct' needs to be seen in this light. In 2005 the 'Tour Direct' ran for the first time and cycled the 'Tour de France' circuit nonstop. The racers had to manage 4069km and 47,193m in altitude in total. It is based on the 'Race across America' (RAMM), a transcontinental bicycle race from the west to the east coast of the US. The competitors have to manage their own schedule and breaks and rarely sleep more than 2 hours per day. In 2005, the departure point of the 'Tour Direct' was the Dutch town Gilze-Rijen. The tour then led across the Alps, through Provence via the Pyrenees, back to Gilze-Rijen. The race crossed classic mountain passes such as Alpe d'Huez, Mont Ventoux, Col d'Aspin, Col de Menté, Col de la Madeleine, Col du Glandon, Col du Lautaret and the Col de Peyresourde. The winner Jure Robič reached the finishing line after seven days.

The extreme athlete and RAMM winner Wolfgang Fasching came second, even though he had to cycle with a hand in plaster after a fracture. In his book *Non Stop: Le Tour Direct* he records his battles with pain, tiredness and lack of motivation. He also recounts a spectacular accident. On the morning of the fifth day, he fell asleep during a descent, cycled into a rock and smashed his front wheel. Luckily, he was not injured and he certainly was awake after the accident! During the 8 days of the race, Wolfgang Fasching slept only 6 hours and 40 minutes! But the biggest challenge was navigation: "We already got lost at least 10 times. The other competitors have the same problem. I do hope that we will eventually manage these curious directions. The only good thing was that Wolfgang did not get tired and did not sleep as he was perturbed all night about the inadequate roadbook!" remembered a member of the Fasching crew from the first day.

'Le Tour Ultime', as it was renamed, was supposed to happen every year. But in 2008 it was cancelled as there were not enough sponsors available for a launch.

Sleepless nights: Extreme athlete Wolfgang Fasching is accustomed to cycling for days without a break.

The first mountain pass of the Tour

After the first successful attempts at the Ballon d'Alsace, the Col Bayard and the Côte de Laffrey, the journal *L'Auto*, which was the organiser of the Tour, extended the mountain section. In 1907 the cyclists were led for the first time across a mountain pass higher than 1000m in altitude. The Col de Porte was a real test which some cyclists did not pass. At the premiere on 16 July, 1907 the weather was hot and muggy. Tour-organiser Henri Desgrange has remembered this initiation for years: "I experienced my most brutal and intense moments of my athletic career at the Col de Porte. I felt that all cyclists went beyond their limits. This is when I became afraid; I was afraid to have gone too far."

The cyclists had already conquered a steep 250km and were appropriately struggling with the ascent. A small group was in the lead which finally lost Gustave Garrigou. He was overcome by the exertion, and stopped and laid down on the road in complete exhaustion. Only Émile Georget and François Faber were left. They crossed the pass together. The stage between Lyon and Grenoble spanned 311km. Georget reached the finishing line after exactly 11 hours and 17 minutes, followed by Faber after only 7 minutes. They were ahead of Lucien Petit-Breton by about half an hour. At the time, the points system was very complicated. With judging by elapsed time, time differences of several hours were not rare. This is why all was not lost for Petit-Breton, who in the end won the Tour. The achievement of Faber was astonishing as the Luxembourger weighed a hefty 91kg. In comparison, recent jersey-winner Michael Rasmussen weighed just 59kg. Faber's muscular body gave him an impressive appearance and the nickname 'the Giant of Colombes'. It was only at the second Tour across the Col de Porte that cyclists did not have to dismount to cross the pass.

Georges Passérieu is the brave one and, if you believe the historical documents, he fought against simply inhuman obstacles. The road, or better the path, was so muddy that his tyres sank into the mud several centimetres deep. When he arrived in Grenoble, 2kg of mud was stuck to his bike. Despite this obstacle and even with a fixed-gear bicycle, he was able to achieve a fantastic average of 27.87kph over the 311km.

In subsequent years, the Col de Porte went out of fashion. With the newly discovered alpine giant Col du Galibier, the interest declined in the Col de Porte. But it didn't take long for its time to come and many great names in cycling have since made history there. Charly Gaul has always felt at home in the Chartreuse Mountains and when he didn't encounter rain there, he was invincible. In 1958 he took a definite step towards final victory during the 219km stage between Briançon to Aix-les-Bains. Suffering sub-zero temperatures and lasting rain he kept warm by pedalling vigorously. At the end of the stage, he managed to get ahead of Géminiani, the holder of the yellow jersey, by 14 minutes and two stages later, he took over the overall lead.

Opposite: The eyes of a killer; the cannibal Eddy Merckx on the Col d'Izoard.

MIKO

23 In the shadow of monumental rock and ice giants
COL DE LA CROIX DE FER

At the beginning of the ascent to the Croix de Fer, you do not yet notice the hard 12 per cent incline.

CLIMB TOP: 2067m
TOTAL ELEVATION: 1340m
DISTANCE: 37km
MAX GRADIENT: 12%
AVERAGE GRADIENT: 4%
STARTING POINT:
Bourg d'Oisans, Départment Isère (38)
APPROACH:
From Grenoble on the N91 to Bourg d'Oisans
PARKING:
City centre in front of the Office de Tourisme
ROAD CONDITION: Generally good
MOUNTAIN PASS OPENINGS:
End of May to October

Bourg d'Oisans has developed into the cycling centre of France. Therefore, in the summer, the campsites transform into cycle racing camps. Most cyclists cycle up the Alpe d'Huez and most are also drawn to the Galibier. But you should certainly not miss the third highlight: the Col de la Croix de Fer offers a challenging ascent in an impressive landscape. You'll only encounter cars in the first few kilometres, so you'll be able to enjoy the majority of the route in peace and quiet. Although, the Col de la Croix de Fer links the Arc Valley to the Romanche en Isère Valley, it is insignificant for long-distance travel. Most of the time at the Tour de France, the Col de la Croix de Fer was approached from the Arc Valley from the north. The following tour has one distinct advantage: the point of departure is Bourg d'Oisans, which is so much more beautiful than Saint-Jean-de Maurienne.

Dubious example

Although he has generally been a bright star of cycling, nobody should enlist the method of Bernhard Hinault for his first climb up the mountain range: "On arrival at the bottom of the Croix de Fer I noticed the mountains. I was overwhelmed and it seemed impossible to me to be able to cross summits like these by bike. I pedalled like mad behind the main bunch. At the Télégraphe, my aide Maurice Champion gave me a water bottle filled with champagne. I emptied it and in a half-drunken state tackled my first big mountain pass."

The first kilometres will take you uphill on the busy N91 road towards Grenoble. After 7km, just before a restaurant, you'll turn to the right into a big bend towards the Col de la Croix de Fer (signposted). First, you'll trundle swiftly along but you'll encounter your first obstacle just after Allemont. Two impressive hairpin bends will take you up the walls of a reservoir. The iron chain bridge at the edge of the Lac du Verney Reservoir connects both sides of the road and especially on the descent you have to be extremely careful as the large gaps on the road are dangerous for small racing tyres.

A few kilometres after Allemont, the gentle wheeling turns into a steep uphill climb.

Through the garden of hairpin bends

Along the Lac du Verney Reservoir, the roads are relatively flat. As you leave the shore, the road goes uphill again. With an incline of 10 per cent, you'll start to break out in a sweat. The road goes steadily uphill along the following kilometres. To the right, you'll be able to see right into the valley, ahead of you lies Le Rocher Rissiou (2622m). After Rivier d'Allemont the road turns to the right and you'll roll downhill along hairpin bends to cross a creek. This is a wonderful vista, which may remind you of the narrow bends of the Col de Pailhères.

Steeply uphill

After 'the garden of hairpin bends', the road cuts along the other side of the valley. You'll continue straight ahead towards a recess that seems to obstruct your way like a wall. The incline of 12 per cent demands strong pedalling. But you'll be rewarded with a wonderful view over the Lac de Grand-Maison, glistening light blue in the sunshine. The just 5km-long lake is part of the biggest hydroelectric power station in France. The road continues along the left side of the lake and you won't know where to look first: to the right, the lake glistens, to the left, the rocks of the Casse de l'Argentière loom. These kilometres offer a scenic delight and are everything a mountain pass cyclist loves. The absence of difficult climbs provides the opportunity to trundle along nicely. After approximately 36km you'll reach the junction to the Col du Glandon. If you want to collect achievements of distinction, you could quickly take a detour here. After all, the Glandon is only some minutes away and you won't get such an opportunity again. Your actual route will take you to the Col de la Croix de Fer at the junction. You'll come across an inn with refreshments, but there are only 2km left to the final destination where there's another small inn. When you arrive at the summit, you will enjoy a tremendous panorama. If you look back on to your ascent you will see an astonishing route. The Aiguilles de l'Argentière provides a wonderful photo opportunity – provided that the weather plays along

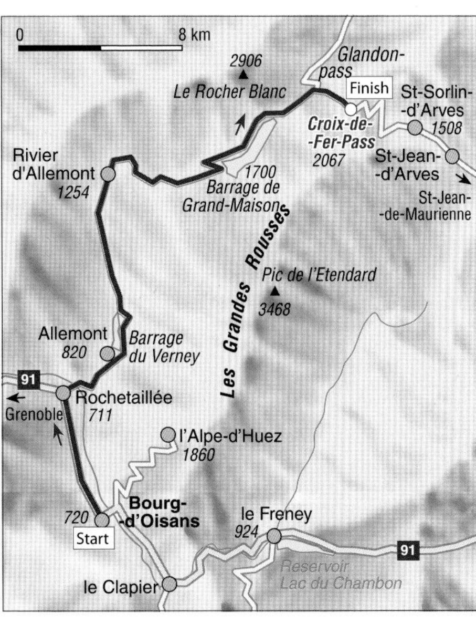

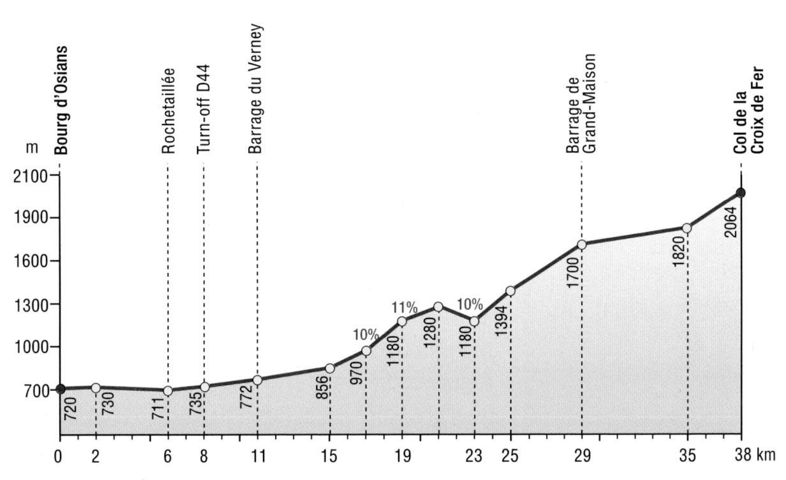

France's most famous amateur race

Every beginning of July, the campsites of Bourg d'Oisans overflow. Amateur cyclists from France and other parts of Europe make a pilgrimage to the most famous mountain race in France. Italy has the Maratona delle Dolomite, Austria the Ötztaler Cycle Marathon and France has the Marmotte. The route offered is 174km long and features 5000m of climbing. Since 1982 the route has always been the same except for one year when a building site in 1995 made a detour necessary. The event is inspired by the Tour de France, as it goes across four famous Tour climbs. The cyclists climb the Col de la Croix de Fer, the Col du Télégraphe, Col du Galibier and finishes at the top of one of the most famous Tour de France climbs, Alpe d'Huez. If you are not tired after this tour, you should quickly become a professional! The road is unfortunately only partially blocked and therefore serious accidents, even deaths, have occurred. Caution should, of course, be exercised. Registration for this event is possible online.

Bourg d'Oisans also offers a range of other cycling events for mountain bikers as well as racers. The newest highlight in the diary is a triathlon (www.alpetriathlon.com). You should ask at tourist information in order not to miss this exciting race.

Further information can be found at www.sportcommunication.com.

and reveals the view on to snowcapped giants. The iron cross that gives the mountain pass its name is placed at the summit.

For the inexhaustible ones

The Col de la Croix de Fer can be integrated into several different circuits. The standard tour takes you to the Col du Glandon (1924m), downhill to La Chambre (436m) to Saint-Jean-de-Maurienne (546m). Then another climb starts at the end of the village with an incline of 8 per cent over 4km. The landscape is impressive: green mountain meadows surround you, a creek guides you while, at the same time, you'll see the silhouette of the rocks of the Aiguilles d'Arve (3510m) on the horizon. You'll cycle through four tunnels, but only one of them is longer than 200m and as a reward, the road flattens. The road will take you from the east towards the Col de la Croix de Fer via Saint-Sorlin-d'Arves (1508m). The last kilometres demand a bit more effort with their 8 to 10 per cent incline, but once you have reached the summit, the memory of the pain will be quickly replaced by the wonderful panorama. You've managed most of the challenges and you'll roll down into the valley, revitalised. The whole circuit is 130km long and if this is too short for you, I recommend the following, bigger circuit. Start at Bourg d'Oisans (720m), cycle as described above to Allemont (730m), over the Col de la Croix de Fer (2067m) and downhill to Saint-Jean-de-Maurienne (546m). There the fun really begins as the route will take you over the Télégraphe (1566m) and the Galibier (2646m). If you then return to the point of departure you have managed 163km and certainly got your money's worth.

Self-marketing: Cows and goats advertise their own milk.

Long, longer, longest

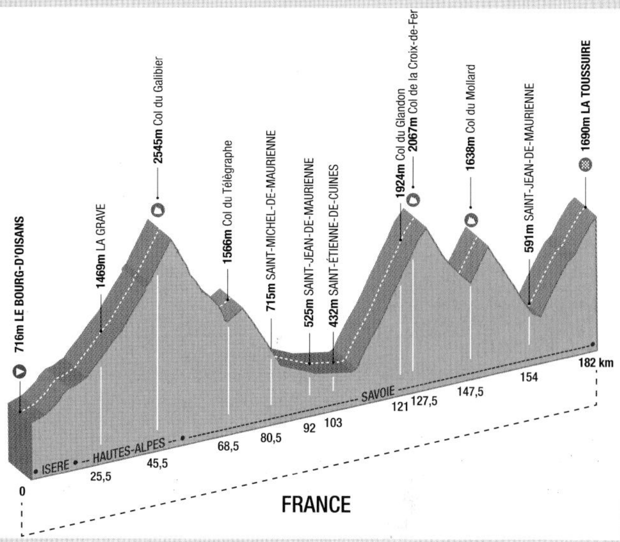

A typical stage at the Col de la Croix de Fer: As you can see, there are enough mountains in the vicinity that can block your path.

The Col de la Croix de Fer was only integrated into the programme of the Tour after World War II. In the first years after the war, the Col was part of the stages between Briançon to Aix-les-Bains. In addition to the metres in altitude, cyclists had to struggle along over 200km. But if you remember the 'heroic days' of the Tour, this distance is not very impressive. The length of the stages and the overall distance of the Tour de France were, in comparison to today, often longer. Stages of 200, 300 and even 400km were not rare. For instance, the stage from Les Sable to Bayonne was a favourite in the programme of the Tour de France – with a daily distance of 482km.

But at the Col de la Croix de Fer, most strong mountain riders shone. If you look at the list of winners over the last decades, you will find great cyclists such as Gino Bartali, Fausto Coppi, Federico Bahamontes and Bernard Hinault who were all overall winners. Old photographs document that the road conditions after the War were miserable. Thus, the thrilling duel between the Italian Gino Bartali and the Frenchman Louison Bobet took place under very difficult conditions. Heavy rain pelted down on the cyclists and the roads turned into muddy obstacles. Bobet and Bartali fought side by side along the muddy roads of the mountain pass. "It looked more like a cyclo-cross when both rivals ploughed through the 'quagmire'," described the journalist Peter Leissl the race. "Splashed with dirt, both Bartali and Bobet reached the summit first. Bartali sprinted over the summit as you could still get time advantage points. This is how he gained 30 seconds on Bobet." The day-long stage took them over the Galibier to the Col de la Croix de Fer but the final destination was far away. The Col de Porte and the Col du Granier in the Chartreuse Mountains were still waiting and Bartali cycled like a madman. With this effort he managed to win the yellow jersey and the overall Tour.

In 2006 the Croix-de-Fer was taken from Bourg d'Oisans via the Galibier. The elevation shows that this is a stage that shows no mercy.

At the Croix de Fer, Gino Bartali kept his competitors in check.

24 The notorious 21 bends
ALPE D'HUEZ

If you spot this sign, you are not far away from any cyclists' seventh heaven.

CLIMB TOP: 1850m

TOTAL ELEVATION: 1090m

DISTANCE: 14km

MAX GRADIENT: 13%

AVERAGE GRADIENT: 7.8%

STARTING POINT:
Bourg d'Oisans (3060 inhabitants), Département Isère (38)

APPROACH:
From Grenoble on the N91 to Bourg d'Oisans

PARKING:
At the supermarket just at the end of the town to the left

ROAD CONDITION: Perfect

SPECIAL FEATURES:
Velodateur at the campsite La Piscine, just before the ascent; on the mountain time trial

MOUNTAIN PASS OPENINGS:
All year

You are rarely alone at this ascent. Cycling fans around the world make a pilgrimage to the Alps to conquer the notorious 21 bends at least once. If you still have the TV images of the mountain time trials in your mind's eye, you will be doubly motivated. It is a special treat even for the professional cyclist. As Lance Armstrong said in an interview, "This is the most famous climb in the cycling sport, it is a mythical and historical place. Every racer wants to win once."

Along the legends

Alpe d'Huez has been part of the Tour 27 times now and you'll learn about the stage winners from the signs on the 21 bends. Meanwhile, there have been more winners than bends and often the signs bear two names. With your eye on the signs, the tough struggle also becomes a tour through the history of the Tour de France and reminds us of the greatest legends: all the important names from the cycling community are represented, from Fausto Coppi, Joop Zoetemelk to Marco Pantani and Lance Armstrong.

You will cycle from Bourg d'Oisans towards the left in the direction of Alpe d'Huez. You'll then pass the campsite La Piscine and after several metres you will ride up the perfect road. The bends are counted backwards and therefore the final metres are a countdown to the finishing line. After the first bend, the road goes straight uphill. You'll go directly along a crag but you won't be able to see the overall route yet. After three bends you will realise that this is not a Sunday outing. Given the gradient of 10 per cent, you will understand and literally feel the mythical reputation of this ascent. It is no coincidence that the French call this the '*muraille de l'Oisans*', the castle wall of Oisans.

Snow-capped giants in the background provide a spectacular backdrop for the most famous bends in the world.

Say 'cheese'

Cycling past a stone church, this section of the road is flatter and leads through La Garde en Oisans.

At the city limit, more beautiful hairpin

bends await you. One hairpin bend follows after another and with double-digit inclines,you'll have to pedal very hard. After bend 14, the road is a bit flatter so you'll be able to build up momentum before the next steep bends. At bend 8, the hotel bunkers of the alpine castle loom over you. You'll now no doubt be looking forward to the finishing line and will be surprised that the town is already in reach. It is only 4km to Alpe d'Huez but a bit longer to the finish. The route goes along gentle slopes and just before bend 4, take a deep breath and smile. In the summertime, a local photographer takes pictures of the amateur cyclists and hands out numbers. He then offers his photographs for sale on the Internet and the number indicates the right picture. However, these photos can be extremely expensive. It is worth taking your own photographs as you'll save somewhere between €12–79.

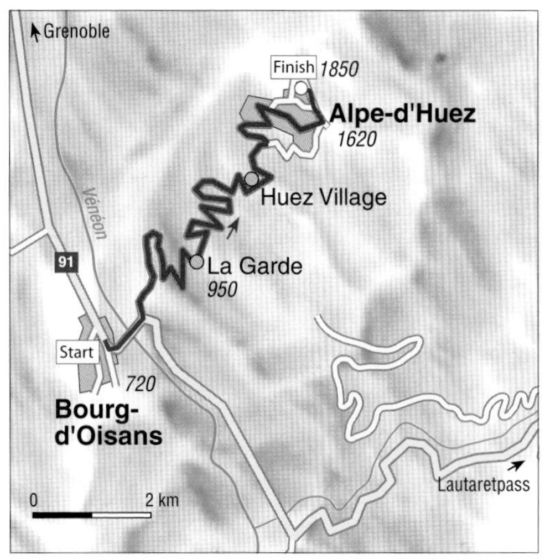

Not quite there yet

After the photoshoot, the place-name sign awaits you. One more bend and you'll see the entry to Alpe d'Huez. The finish is marked just before a small tunnel in front of the tourist information office and this is where most of the cyclists dismount. When comparing times, many amateur cyclists have only then noticed that they did not cycle to the actual finishing line. In order to reach it, you have to follow the road. Following the signs, you should turn right at the first roundabout and then uphill at the second roundabout around the Fausto Coppi monument. After 100m a lamppost indicates the finish. Opposite the Tour de France sign is a stamp site at the campsite. Many will take a deep breath and will be relieved that this struggle is finally over. Who is, indeed, able to stay calm on this mythical stage and resist rushing uphill?

Race against the clock in Alpe d'Huez

The tourist information office in Bourg d'Oisans offers a particular treat for all

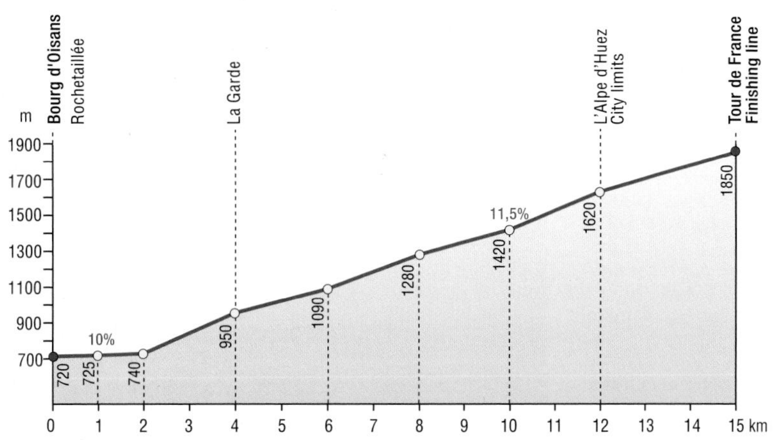

climbers: a mountain time trial is held every Tuesday at 10am during the main season for the general public. The start is from the office but you must register at least an hour earlier. There are two concession stands for beverages and one at the finishing line for food. The chosen route is 13.5km long and can be managed by foot. Naturally, these hairpin bends are also great for trained mountain joggers! If you do not want to participate in this race, but nevertheless want to have your achievement documented, you can buy a document at the tourist information office in Alpe d'Huez. You enter your own time. Cheating is obviously not allowed and will come back to bite you if your colleagues ask you to repeat your record time!

A fierce battle

Peter Winnen achieved his greatest success during his career in Alpe d'Huez. But all his stage victories were hard-earned. In his book *Post from Alpe d'Huez*, he vividly describes the last 2km on the way to his stage win in 1981: "One thing was clear: my liver was on the way out. With my stomach and other intestines it moved slowly up the oesophagus – not literally, obviously, but it felt like it. I already deeply regretted my breakaway attempt. [...]My muscles felt like snarled string. Inside me there was nothing else than an infinite void. All concrete thoughts had ended. Why someone struggles on in a moment like this remains a mystery to me." One should however not even attempt a comparison with the professionals: Marco Pantani darted up the ascent in 1995 and 1997 in approximately 37 minutes. Therefore, he averaged a speed of 22kph, even though he had already cycled 150 or 190km that day.

Opposite: Thomas Voeckler illustrates why the Tour is called the Tour of suffering (far right, top). Carlos Sastre is on his way to the stage win in Alpe d'Huez in 2008 (far right, bottom).

Right: The finishing line of the Tour de France in Alpe d'Huez.

VOECKLER
6552 WK 76
Rabobank
Rabobank

Formel 21 at the Dutch Mountain

Alpe d'Huez offers neither a significant part in the history of the Tour de France nor a spectacular landscape. Nevertheless, no other climb excites the cycling fans more. Up to a million spectators line the streets on the day of the Tour de France, leaving little space to pass through. Its popularity is due in no small part to television. It is the perfect medium to capture so dramatically the struggle up the mountain. It was a happy coincidence that in 1952 on its premiere at the Tour de France a cameraman was able to document the whole stage on film. Fausto Coppi won and thus inaugurated the mountain gracefully. The legendary 21 hairpin bends on the slope seem like a giant amphitheatre carved into a rock. In 1976, it became for the second time part of the 'Big Loop' and since then, the Alpe d'Huez has been a stage finish almost every year. The winner in 1976 was none other than than Joop Zoetemelk.

In the following years, it was the Dutch of all competitors who won the stage most often. This is why Alpe d'Huez is known as the 'Dutch Mountain'. Dutch fans made the pilgrimage to Alpe d'Huez and for a long time, the mountain was steeped in orange during the Tour de France.

Alpe d'Huez was also the stage for many thrilling duels. One of the highlights was the duel between Bernard Hinault and Laurent Fignon in 1984. Hinault, having not quite recovered from an operation and also recently joining a new team, sought his chance. During the stage between Grenoble and Alpe d'Huez, he attempted several times to break away. Even on the long straights on the way to Bourg d'Oisans, he cast himself to the wind. At the beginning of the ascent though, he was exhausted. On the 21 bends, Laurent Fignon took 4 minutes off him and secured the yellow jersey that he kept until Paris. However, not all was lost for Bernard Hinault. In 1985, he won the Tour thanks to the dedicated help of his comrade Greg LeMond. As a *quid pro quo*, he promised his full support in the next year. In 1986, he obviously had forgotten his promise as he launched attacks several times. Both cyclists crossed the finishing line in Alpe d'Huez simultaneously and the yellow jersey was therefore already awarded unofficially.

In the 1990s, the Italians took the reins. The mountain was ideal for climbers such as Marco Pantani; 'the pirate' holds the unofficial course record, which he achieved in 1997 at the end of the stage from Saint-Etienne to Alpe d'Huez. To all those watching on television, the Tour of 2001 remains unforgettable, when Armstrong bluffed his way through. During the stage, he repeatedly went to the back of the group, changed his face as if he was suffering and fiddled with his ear piece. The signs seemed obvious: Armstrong was having a bad day. The Telekom group did exactly what Armstrong wanted: the magenta-clad cyclists sped up and cycled forcefully against the wind. For 200km Armstrong hid in the group and only at the ascent did he drop the act and attack. He sped past the surprised Jan Ullrich who could not keep up with the speed. The Texan metronome was back and, at speed, he reached the stage win. At the end, he gained over 4 minutes and set his overall victory in motion. Armstrong admitted to his bluff openly in interviews: "I know I had to bluff so that the others cycle even faster. We made this decision on the road. Everyone watches the broadcast, tries to read the faces of the racers, including athletic managers of the teams in the

accompanying team cars. While I seemed to continue to suffer, team Telekom accelerated. I toyed with Telekom and I won."

In recent times, the highlight of the Tour was surely the mountain time trial of 2004. About a million television viewers watched the cyclists hounding each other up the mountain. Jan Ullrich even cycled with time-trial handlebars but stood no chance against the 'Tourminator' Lance Armstrong. As usual, he darted up the mountain with a high cadence. The Texan won with 1 minute over Ullrich and even overtook Ivan Basso who set off before him and had dreamed of a final victory. However, not even Armstrong could beat Pantani's best time.

Pantani's phenomenal best times and other records were achieved during a time when EPO was frequently used. However, it is doubtful that the competitors of the CERA (an EPO substitute) user Kohl were only on pure water.

There are 21 bends that await the cyclists on their way up Alpe d'Huez.

25 Fun from the first to the last minute
GALIBIER VIA THE COL

The peloton of the Tour de France on the climb up the Col du Galibier.

CLIMB TOP: 2645m

TOTAL ELEVATION: 1925m

DISTANCE: 50km

MAX GRADIENT: 12%

AVERAGE GRADIENT: 3.9%

STARTING POINT:
Bourg d'Oisans (3060 inhabitants), Département Isère (38)

APPROACH:
From Grenoble on the N91 to Bourg d'Oisans

PARKING:
At the supermarket just at the end of the town to the left; ideal parking facilities

ROAD CONDITION:
Generally good, but at the summit a bit bumpy

DANGERS:
Several tunnels, so possibly bring lights

MOUNTAIN PASS OPENINGS:
Middle of June to middle of October

Is there really a reason why you should not tackle the Galibier from the north via the Télégraphe? Both options are attractive but the southern route offers a more varied landscape. A beautiful reservoir and impressive roads offer distraction. Besides, it takes longer before it goes uphill; on the way to the Col du Lautaret, you have enough time to get into full swing. Even if it is not a classic climb, the Tour de France convoy has often used this approach to the summit. In 2006 the charge on the Galibier was sounded in Bourg d'Oisans.

A treat for the eye

On leaving Bourg d'Oisons you'll have to resist turning left to Alpe d'Huez as you should either savour this treat separately or add it to the end of a tour. The road remains flat and straight directly after the town. The traffic keeps within reasonable limits although the route is not free of cars.

You'll reach a crossing after 8km and remain on the main road which turns to the left. You'll then be noticeably cycling uphill and the landscape is a treat. In a narrow valley, you'll bike through rocks, to the right along a crag, and to the left you'll pass a mini-reservoir. After several hefty kilometres a brief restful section along small waterfalls follows. Shortly after that you'll reach the snug Le Freney-d'Oisans. If you are not sure if you can manage the whole route or have only limited time, you could start here and save on the 400m elevation gain and 14km. In the village to the left, near the tourist information, are parking facilities and a well to fill up your drinking bottles.

Focus on the tunnels

After Le Freney-d'Oisans you'll continue uphill in bends alongside a crag and through short tunnels. Near the Barrages de Chambon

The Galibier belongs to one of the most famous alpine roads of the Tour de France.

DU LAUTARET

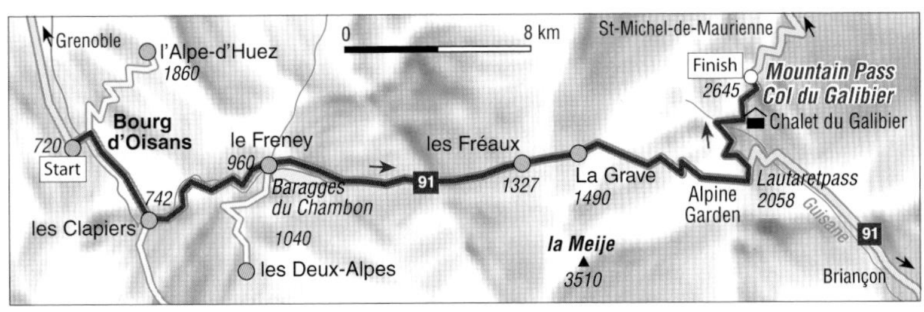

(1044m), a big reservoir, you'll continue to the left over the bridge.

The famous Galibier is not signposted yet, but it is nearer to Col du Lautaret. Incidentally, the road forks off to the right to Les Deux Alpes which has served as the mountain finishing line several times and is also the place where Jan Ullrich would be reminded of his bitter collapse in 1998.

The following kilometres are intoxicatingly beautiful, the hairpin route goes all along the turquoise Chambon Reservoir. You'll only really need to concentrate on the very slightly lit tunnels. Inevitably, with cars breathing down your neck, you'll cycle more nervously and yearn for the end of the tunnel.

Gaining in elevation

You'll then leave the Départment Isère and enter the Départment Rhône-Alpes. The road runs along the Romanche with leisurely incline. It is worth casting a glance up to the right where the massive rocky summit of Roche Mantel (3042m), Pic de la Grave (3669m) and the glacier Mont du Lans (3288m) will attract your eye. The incline only increases after 30km and you'll reach La Grave, with several restaurants and a supermarket. If you feel you need to stock up, now is the chance to buy food and/or drink. You'll have managed the first 1000m in elevation gain. A few kilometres after the village, the road leads through a 600m-long but faintly lit tunnel. The route then goes through an expansive valley towards the pass. It might seem odd to the cyclist that there are still no signs for Galibier. For the road traffic it is only the Col du Lautaret which is of importance and it lies directly on the way. Therefore, any fears you might have of getting lost are clearly unfounded. The route is set by the valley, and to the right and left of it you could only hike. You'll continue past several restaurants, always in the sunshine. After 42km you'll reach the summit of the Col du Lautaret (2057m). You do wonder where all these people suddenly come from who scatter among restaurants, hotels and giftshops. During fine weather, even

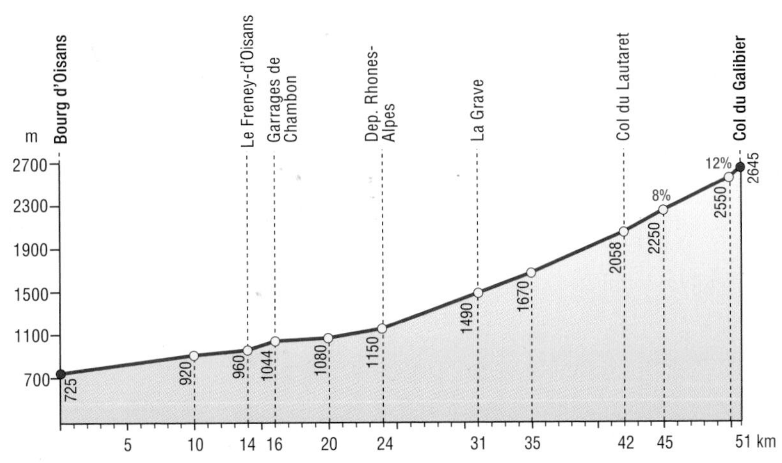

the motorcyclists will let the sun shine on their leather gear.

Ode to the Galibier

From now it is only 8km but 600m in altitude to the summit.

The traffic on the narrow road eases and the highlight of your climbing programme can really begin. The road immediately goes uphill and the first hairpin bend awaits you. The thrill of anticipation for the Galibier gains with every metre in altitude. While the road coils through lush meadowy slopes, you'll already have a fantastic view back to the summit of Lautaret and down into the valley.

A long-drawn stretch follows that meanders with constant incline uphill. Only after roughly half of the stretch will you finally be able to see the longed for, but still far away, summit. The road surface is good but a bit uneven which you'll notice on the descent. The last 5km again offer an athletic challenge. You'll pass the monument of Henri Desgrange, the first organiser of the Tour and remember his poetic celebration of the Galibier: "Oh Laffrey! Oh Bayard! Oh Tourmalet! I do not hesitate to proclaim to the Galibier you are but pale and vulgar babies. In front of this giant there is nothing more for you to do but take off your hats and bow from down below."

At the wrong spot

The restaurant Chalet du Galibier is placed only a few metres behind the monument and before the tunnel. (Be careful on the descent as there are treacherous traffic lights which are easily overlooked.)

You'll still continue on the final metres towards the summit. In the first years of the Tour, the route still went

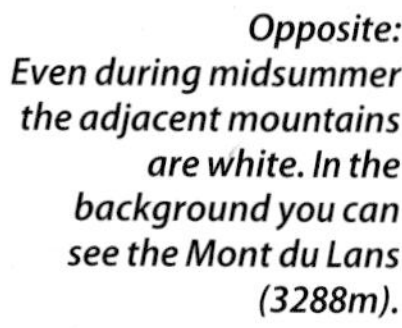

Opposite: Even during midsummer the adjacent mountains are white. In the background you can see the Mont du Lans (3288m).

Below: During the race, there is no time to take a breather at the Galibier. This stage is always accompanied by tough battles towards the summit.

Above: The last climb to the Galibier is challenging – you'll probably clench your teeth during the final metres.

Below: An expansive valley opens to the eastside of the Col du Lautarets.

through the tunnel. The champion of the first ascent, Émile Georget, commented with the ironic remark: "Instead of constructing the tunnel on the top, one could have built it at the foot of the mountain to spare us the climb in the snow. I would have loved to ride a cycle metro."

The final spurt

It is not far now but you really have to earn the final metres. The incline increases considerably. Even the bravest will need to ride out of the saddle to tackle the incline of more than 12 per cent. But you can nearly smell the summit and the sense of achievement is particularly gratifying when you reach the parking at the summit and are rewarded with a magnificent panorama. The view is indescribably beautiful: on both sides of the pass hairpin bends coil uphill and at least then you are inspired to tackle the Galibier from the other side. If you have planned a big circuit and cycle towards Saint-Jean-de-Maurienne, you need good breakpads. From here on the road goes downhill only, the small incline at the Télégraphe is negligible. On the way from the Col du Glandon or the Col de la Croix de Fer however you are quickly reminded what makes a real alpine pass. But it is worth the struggle as mountain air is the best after all!

Hard labour at the Galibier

When the Galibier was integrated into the Tour programme in 1911, many spectators showed great interest. They crowded alongside the road and waited eagerly to see whether this huge mountain could really be conquered by bicycle. Émile Georget, who was the first cyclist of the Tour to cross the Galibier, showed that it was in fact possible. Starting in Saint-Michel-de-Maurienne it took him 2 hours 38 minutes to get to the summit. Still, the person who went down in history was the second-placed Gustave Garrigou who scolded the officials after his exertions: "You are bandits!" His colleague Eugène Christophe was equally furious about the new highlight of the Tour. "This is not a sport anymore, nor a race, this is hard labour!" he protested. Nevertheless, despite all these protests, he did appreciate the exertions as the following year he came first crossing the pass, or we should say 'passing through' the pass as until 1979 the route led through a 365m-long tunnel just below today's summit.

In 1911 Tour organiser Henri Desgrange declared that the Tourmalet, Laffrey and Bayard were small hills in comparison to the Galibier. It is not surprising that the mountain became part of the regular Tour circuit in the following years. The races were filled with thrilling duels or momentous accidents that decided victory or defeat. Eugène Christophe, who went down in history because of his fork-break at the Tourmalet, was also unlucky in the Alps. In 1922, he changed his bike twice after a breakdown and arrived at the finishing line 3 hours late. Fortunately, time trials had not been introduced by then.

However, a few years later the Galibier made the headlines because of a tragic accident. On 11 July, 1935, the Spaniard Francesco Cepeda fell on the descent between the Galibier to the Lautaret and injured himself badly. He died a couple of days later in hospital and the Tour mourned its first fatality. This was a sad accident, but others followed.

In the following years, the Galibier remained a fixed component of the circuit, but there are few Tour winners who have not suffered at this mountain. Coppi, Bahamontes, Gaul, Merckx, Zoetemelk, Ocana, Van Impe, Indurain and Pantani all crossed the pass as winners with fantastic achievements and also won the Tour overall. This is a reward which sadly Alexander Vinokourov has not been granted yet despite the fact that in 2005 he darted up the Galibier at the front of the group. After his failure on the previous day, the Kazakhstani's victory of the 'royal stage' in 2005 proved his abilities.

Although the Galibier was supposed to be invincible, the vigour of the racers was infinite. In the early days, the escort vehicles had problems keeping up with the cyclists. The incline overwhelmed the vehicles and they often had to take compulsory breaks to let the motors cool down. On the route, which now resembles a ski-run and would be more appropriate for mountain biking, the cyclists speed past the cars on their descent. Maximum speeds similar to those reached by cars are possible if the roads are perfect.

Not everyone is comfortable with this high speed. In 1986, the radio reporter Jean-Paul Brouchon feared for his life when his motorbike accompanied Bernard Hinault and Greg LeMond on the descent. Undaunted by death, both cyclists raced towards Alpe d'Huez at a speed of 100kph. Meanwhile, Brouchon had lost all interest in the race. He only wanted one thing: to reach the finishing line in one piece.

26 The classic twin pack
GALIBIER VIA THE COL

To really worship the Tour de France at the Galibier you need to be up close and personal.

CLIMB TOP: 2645m
TOTAL ELEVATION: 2090m
DISTANCE: 34km
MAX GRADIENT: 10%
AVERAGE GRADIENT: 8%
STARTING POINT:
Saint-Michel-de-Maurienne (3000 inhab), Départment Savoie (73)
APPROACH:
On N90 and then N6 from Chambery to Saint-Michel-Maurienne
PARKING: There is parking at the station
ROAD CONDITION: Consistently good
MOUNTAIN PASS OPENINGS: Middle of June to middle of October

The Galibier is a mountain that excites cyclists for a reason. In most editions of the Tour de France, the Galibier features as the highest pass of the tour. This is why it is often called the 'Roof of the Tour' and indeed, the route via the Télégraphe is an ordeal. Who in fact knows the Col du Télégraphe? Although it is an inherent part of the tour, it has always been in the shadow of the great Galibier. But you'll soon find out that the 'green flag lap' for the Galibier is not for the faint-hearted. The double pack poses a real challenge and in the worst case scenario, a performance test under harsh weather conditions. For its altitude of over 2600m, it can be bitterly cold even during the summer months. It could even snow in July and cover the pass with a white blanket.

Towards the Col du Télégraphe

The point of departure is the uncomfortably loud town Saint-Michel-de-Maurienne. Wedged in between the motorway to Italy and the B-road, the town does not really invite you to linger. But its good transport connections is the town's advantage. Besides, you can find many shops in the vicinity of Saint-Michel-de-Maurienne and Saint-Jean-de-Maurienne where you can buy anything from batteries for your camera to sports equipment. But you'll actually be happy to leave the town behind. You'll need to follow the signposts from the station to the right, cycle across a bridge and then between the houses on the D902 to Saint-Martin-d'Arc.

From the first round of hairpin bends, you'll be expecting more will follow. You'll no doubt be happy to leave the noisy valley of the Arc behind you and you'll be motivated to pursue the road uphill. The view becomes more delightful as forested slopes

View back from the summit over the northern ascent of the Galibier.

DU TÉLÉGRAPHE

characterise the landscape, and they will accompany you for a while. Soon, the houses dissipate and are replaced by dense forests. You'll steadily push up the bends which are labelled by the first signposts of the Tour. In between the leaf trees, the road turns more bendy uphill. The surroundings becomes more beautiful and you'll see the summits slowly approaching. After around 12km, quite a lot of traffic and 800m elevation gain, you'll reach the Col du Télégraphe. The summit provides the opportunity to scan the valley but you'll have no use for the picnic tables. The fun has only begun, the majority of the struggle still awaits you.

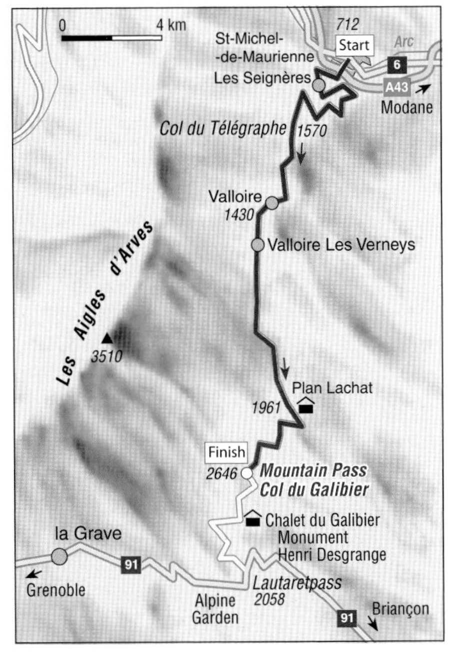

Interim downhill descent

The altitude will melt away under your wheels as the road plunges on the next 4km. You'll pass a line of hotels, trundle to Valloire, which you'll drive through on a one-way street, and leave at a roundabout to the right. If you do not want to miss out on the great Galibier but only have limited energy, you could of course mount your bike in Valloire. This is where the actual ascent to the Galibier begins and if you were to start here, you would only have to manage 1200m elevation gain. After the signposted turn-off in Valloire, you'll cycle uphill with an incline of about 8 per cent. The momentous Galibier will already be visible straight ahead of you. You'll then cycle through a wide valley with little traffic and relatively good road conditions. On the exit from the road, though, I made the acquaintance of some nasty loose chippings. You'll continue to pass restaurants and the first mountain huts. To the right, ragged rocks accompany you and in long straight stretches you'll steadily gain altitude with an incline of up to 8 per cent.

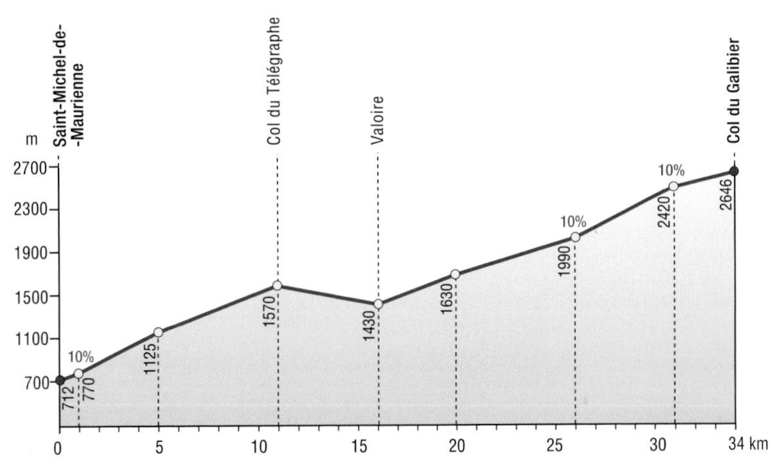

Vive le Tour

You'll now enjoy the wonderful scenery and the varied inscriptions on the roads. They bear witness not only to the current favourites of the cycling fans but are also quite funny. One fan took special trouble to indicate the exact distance to Paris. However, I doubt that the professional cyclists would be more motivated by being reminded of the 1600km-long agony to come! If you pay attention to the language of these graffiti artists, you notice how many faithful German fans have supported their team. The Galibier is of course one of the most popular destinations for cycling fans. The slope is populated with many tents and thousands of visitors create a buoyant atmosphere the evening prior to the race. The northern ascent in particular lends itself well to visitors and parking is relatively easy. Some grotesque scenes are created when the commercial displays crawl up the mountain just ahead of the cyclists. Mobile merchandise characters are in sharp contrast to the rocky landscape.

Mountain adventure

To the right, you'll be able to look down on to the narrow valley which has no roads but does have mountain bike trails. It is not the only worthwhile destination away from the road. Approximately 155km around the Valloire are at the disposal of mountainbikers. And you don't need your own bike to make the most of this offer – there are two shops in Valloire which rent out mountain bikes and the tourist information office sells a guide with routes and maps. As many other places in the Alps, Valloire has adjusted itself to a young and adventurous crowd. In addition to the mountain bike programme, a wide range of mountain adventures are offered. Several mountain schools offer mountaineering, alpine climbing or canyoning. During the winter the 150km-long ski slope occupies the centre stage. If you prefer the seclusion of the mountains, you can find suitable ski tour circuits.

Inhuman

Even if the landscape is a pleasure for the eye, the altitude has a powerful influence.

Opposite: The world divides underneath the summit – cyclists are on cloud nine, car drivers take the tunnel underneath the pass.

Right: The final kilometres towards the summit are covered with graffiti.

Human habitations stand no chance under these hard conditions, in fact the area above Valloire has never been inhabited. Spring arrives very late, the winter very early and even during the summer months long periods of bad weather turn the mountain into a cold and inhospitable area. There are even patches of snow left in the summer. It is similar on the other side of the Galibier. It is therefore even more surprising that a road was built in this hostile environment. As early as 1879 a wide lane was constructed and in 1891 a tunnel was added. Over the years, the tunnel had been closed but was reopened in 2002.

Hairpin bends and shoelaces

The road does not, as you would expect, lead up to the left to the col but turns suddenly to the right and climbs up a steep crag. You'll then get onto the most beautiful section of the route with tight bends along the crag and a gigantic view in all directions. After a few bends you'll already be able to see quite a bit of the summit. The road leads with a slight incline straight towards the pass. When you get within reach of the Col du Galibier, you'll get more wonderful and narrow hairpin bends. Motivated by the graffiti, you should be able to find the energy to climb the incline. While the tunnel branches off to the right, some more steep bends await you and then a straight but steep run takes you to the summit. The reward is a fantastic view over both slopes of the Galibier. The ample ascent to the Galibier seems wonderfully harmless from up here. The road winds down into the valley in small bends and you'll no doubt understand why the French language has just the one word for hairpin bends and shoelaces.

The proud summit around the Pic des Trois Echevés (3118m) – a wonderful panorama.

Jan Ullrich is hitting 'the wall'

Surely, the most famous collapse of the Tour de France is the one Jan Ullrich experienced in 1998. At the beginning of every Tour, Ullrich was under enormous pressure. Jan had no illusions and was sure that he could not match up to Lance Armstrong in the decisive minutes. If he regretted one thing, it was the victory of the Tour in 1998 which he gave away. He had been the champion and a silly mistake made him come second.

In 1998, during the 15th stage from Grenoble to Les Deux-Alpes, Jan Ullrich was wearing the yellow jersey. The Galibier was hidden behind constant rain and the temperature was a mere 5°C. On 27 July, 1998, the weather did not favour Ullrich. The peloton moved slowly towards the Galibier under the cloudy skies and only a sprint bonus livened things up a bit.

A small break away trio was leading the way up the Télégraphe in constant rain. The peloton sped up and thinned out even more but Ullrich was still in control. Even the television viewer shuddered with cold. The cameraman had to wipe the raindrops off the lens on a regular basis and image interferences indicated the tough weather conditions. Dense fog surrounded the mountain and 5km before the summit of the Galibier Marco Pantani sped up. In pattering rain, 'the Pirate' started a sprint towards the mountain with his hands as usual gripped around the lower handlebars. After 20 seconds he stopped pedalling and turned around: Ulle had not followed him and therefore it was worth fighting for the yellow jersey. Meanwhile, Ullrich sought help in his group but there was nobody able to come to his aid.

Others also had severe problems: the umbrella of one of the spectators ended up in Erik Zabel's spokes during a short sprint. He was not harmed but his bike was done for. There wasn't a team car with a spare bike to be seen. Of all people, it was the team of his competitor Mario Cipollini who assisted him: they gave Zabel one of their bikes. As the frame was too small, he had to cycle to the Galibier standing up.

In 2005, Alexander Vinokourov secured his stage victory with an impressive ride across the Galibier. In 2007, he was convicted of doping.

Naturally, the battle for victory was even more dramatic. Pantani had gained a considerable advantage on the top of the pass. What followed was a 35km-long descent. Ullrich had lost 3 minutes and launched himself into the downhill race. He was chilled to the bone and completely forgot to eat. To make matters worse, he had a puncture. Too weak on his own, he waited for Bjarne Riis and Udo Bölts who were way behind. Hitting 'the wall', completely exhausted, his ascent to Les Deux-Alpes became torture. Deep rings under his eyes marked his pained face: "My fingers were so clammy," he wrote in his biography, "that I could not steer anymore. I shivered with cold so much that I thought my frame was broken as it was wobbling. I felt dizzy and sick. I had no strength left to pedal. I don't remember how I got up that mountain but it must have looked as if in slow-motion."

Jan lost over 9 minutes and placed fourth in the mountain stage. Pantani could keep his yellow jersey until Paris and Ullrich was able to fight successfully for second place. But he was not able to forget this failure. In the end, 3 minutes were needed for his victory – the 9 minutes he lost at the Galibier were his undoing. If he had eaten two energy bars at the right moment, perhaps he would have won the Tour a second time around.

27 Sweaty climbing fun
COL DE LA MADELEINE

CLIMB TOP: 1993m
TOTAL ELEVATION: 1525m
DISTANCE: 19.5km
MAX GRADIENT: 10%
AVERAGE GRADIENT: 8%
STARTING POINT:
La Chambre (1100 inhab.), Départment Savoie (73)
APPROACH:
From Chambery towards Albertvillle, then turn right onto N6 towards La Chambre
PARKING:
At the church in the centre
ROAD CONDITION: Good
MOUNTAIN PASS OPENINGS:
All year

In order to keep up with the speed of the cyclists, even the directors of the Tour have to step on it.

The Col de la Madeleine is one of the most famous mountains on the Tour de France due to its favourable position. It connects the Arc Valley with the Val d'Isère and is therefore an ideal north/south transit route, although the more eastern situated Col de l'Iseran would be an alternative but is only navigable in stable weather conditions. Due to its lower altitude the Madeleine is less susceptible to summer snowfalls and therefore more predictable. A dozen or more steep bends lead from La Chambre to the Col de la Madeleine. You really have to work hard to earn the view from the summit and this is also why this ascent is ideal for the Tour de France. With maximum inclines of 10 per cent and at times a constant 8 per cent this mountain road sets a challenge.

To find the right rhythm

The route in La Chambre begins with a hardy incline that continues for a while. Your forward glance will always be an upward glance. You'll immediately have to negotiate several ramps as the road winds along rocks and lush meadows uphill.

Repeatedly, you will get a wonderful view across La Chambre and the valley. While you'll be bothered by a lot of traffic in La Chambre, it will cease suddenly after the first few metres out of town. You'll cross Saint-Martin-sur-la-Chambre and the incline of 10 per cent just before the turn to Montaimont demands great effort. At least you'll already have managed 300m in altitude and hopefully you will have found the right rhythm for this stretch of the circuit since it continues to go uphill steeply and continuously. Only after 9.5km will you get a bit of respite on a short, flat section. That is why you'll need to breathe in and out deeply as the incline increases quickly up to 10 per cent again.

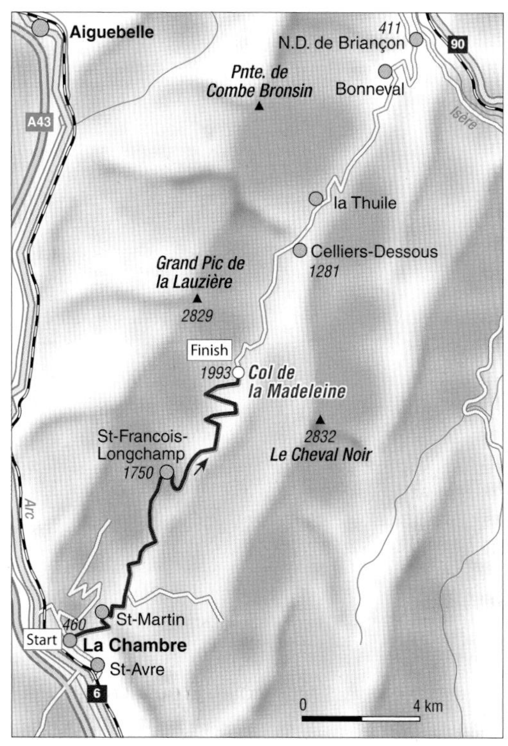

Restful interlude

The reward is a shady and woody section. Hairpin bends lead you towards Saint-Francois-Longchamp. Without waning incline, the route takes you through the small winter sport town. During the summer months the hotels of this ski resort seem eerily deserted. After the town, you'll already be able to spot the mountain pass. You'll meander along steep grassy slopes uphill. In the summer, this ascent is very challenging as you are exposed to the sun. It is worth getting up early on days like that to escape the midday heat. If you are lucky, you'll get some light wind, which offers refreshment. The remaining five ramps with 8 per cent incline offer the opportunity to show off your mountaineering skills and to exhaust yourself.

Ullrich in the climb

It is exactly here where Jan Ullrich launched his missile. After he had given away his victory on the previous day at the Galibier, the fighter in him awakened on the stage to Albertville. He lunged himself resolutely into the ascent to the Col de la Madeleine and proved why he is considered the greatest talent of German cycling sport.

He powerfully pedalled towards the summit in the highest gear; the incline seemed to have no effect on him. No

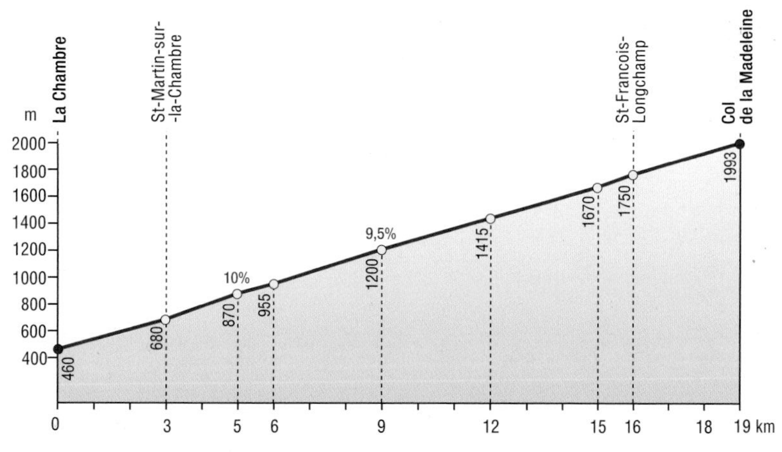

one could keep up with his devilish speed. Only Marco Pantani was able to follow him closely and he hovered over him until they reached the stage finishing line. Ullrich won the stage but lost the Tour overall.

View over Mont Blanc

The information about the exact altitude of the Col de Madeleine is contradictory. The traffic sign at the summit notes the convenient figure of 2000m. It seems that this figure is rounded to the nearest metre, though. Topographical maps note the pass' altitude to be 1993m and this is the officially confirmed altitude. If you have rocketed up the mountain too quickly and feel the first signs of exhaustion, you should feel comforted: even professionals have their weak moments on this mountain. Jan Ullrich described this graphically: "If you have exhausted yourself, if you are suddenly out of breath . . . You try to launch an attack, suddenly you hit the wall halfway through the race and you are at a dead end."

The reward for the exertions is a grand mountain view on the summit. In the distance Mont Blanc looms. Much nearer are the rocky Cheval Noir (2832m) and, opposite, the Pic de la Lauzière. So much beauty will take the last of your breath away. There is an inn on the summit that is particularly popular in bad weather. This is where the cyclists pause and hope that the rain clouds will move away. But their hopes are not always fulfilled and what remains is a wet and cold ride into the valley.

With an average incline of 8 per cent it is OK to be out of the saddle.

Jens Voigt in the yellow jersey

How can tragedy and triumph be so close to each other? The moment of glory of the 9th stage of the 2005 Tour de France belonged to the belligerent all-round cyclist Jens Voigt. With an excellent performance he was able to secure himself the yellow jersey and even made it to the front pages of the biggest German dailies. After Jan Ullrich had ruined all his chances for victory with his false start, Jens Voigt delivered an eagerly anticipated miracle. Even if it was not about the overall victory, it had to be a German again who would wear the yellow jersey for at least one day. The likeable Voigt ignited a true storm of enthusiasm, ending up on the front pages of newspapers and charming the fans. For years he had delivered impressive achievements and, in particular, had convinced everyone with his boldness. A reward therefore was long overdue.

During the 9th stage he had worn the yellow jersey, but two days later he was punished for his exertions. The success in the first stages had worn him out exceedingly. At the beginning of Stage 11, there were already warning signs. Voigt was ill and doctors recommended that he pull out of the Tour. But the man from Grevesmühlen was not prepared to surrender and mounted his bike. Although the stage from Courchevel to Briançon is only 173km long, it has three very difficult ascents. Voigt had already fallen behind at the Col de la Madeleine, the first mountain of the day. You could see the suffering in his face. But his lag kept within bounds and all was not lost at the Télégraphe. About 100 cyclists followed behind the group around Armstrong and Ullrich. Jens Voigt's battle at the Galibier was tragic but futile. With a lung inflammation and a temperature of 40°C, he battled up the Galibier and the 173km to the finishing line. It was a lonely battle against time; only the fans at the Galibier backed him up, the last cyclist at the mountain. With a time lag of 43 minutes, the completely exhausted Voigt reached the finishing line. Every metre was torture, the battle to the finish complete suffering. But even then Voigt was unlucky: he exceeded the time limit by 42 seconds and was therefore excluded from the Tour. "Damn," was his sad commentary on the following day. "I should be on the bike rather than drive the circuit by car." However, there should have been no cause for regret as he had a thousand reasons to be proud of his achievements. His fans agreed and the Mecklenburger was chosen as cyclist of the year 2005 by the journal *Radsport*.

Jens Voigt is a particularly faithful and dedicated cyclist in the peloton. The 'King of the Breakaways' radiates great enthusiasm for cycling.

The sign at the Col de la Madeleine offers a rounded up figure but 2000m seems to be a slight exaggeration.

28 Exhausting excursion into the high mountains
COL DE L'ISERAN

CLIMB TOP: 2770m
TOTAL ELEVATION: 2025m
DISTANCE: 50km
MAX GRADIENT: 9%
AVERAGE GRADIENT: 4%
STARTING POINT:
Bourg-Saint-Maurice (7600 inhab.), Départment Savoie (73)
APPROACH:
From Albertville on the N90 from Mountiers to Bourg-Saint-Maurice
PARKING:
In the city centre, next to the police station
ROAD CONDITION:
In the middle and upper sections, often very bad road conditions
DANGERS:
There are many unlit tunnels and covered galleries – it is crucial to bring lights
MOUNTAIN PASS OPENINGS:
July to the end of September

The Col de l'Iseran with its 2770m is considerably higher than the Galibier, and its northern position also makes it more challenging. Nevertheless, the Iseran does not play a great part in the history of the Tour. When you mount your bike in Bourg-Saint-Maurice, the high mountains seem far in the distance. But even if it is nicely mild in the valley, you should take warm clothes for the descent and listen to the weather forecast. On this tour you'll be climbing to about 3000m altitude and therefore, it can get uncomfortably cold and with a sudden fall of temperature, even dangerous. This is the main reason why the Iseran is so seldom part of the Tour.

Snowy chaos

The Tour of 1996 showed how changeable the weather at the Iseran and Galibier can be even during the summer months. The snow line dropped to 1800m and in the ski resorts, people joked that all they needed now was ski tourists. A stormy wind blew over the white mountain pass and alongside the roads were massive snow banks. Despite temperatures below zero and a wind velocity of 100kph, fans were lined up along the road and watched the caravan of cyclists. Even for the cars, members of the teams, journalists and organisers it was not an easy task. The stage was finally shortened by 140km and launched in the lower Le Monetier-les-Bains. It was a horrendous stage as its length of 46km made it shorter than some of the time trial stages.

The snow-covered summit of the Col de L'Iseran.

Finally uphill!

You'll depart from the police station to the right through the town and continue after the roundabout to the right and downhill. After you have passed the railway station, the Col de l'Iseran is already signposted. There is a lot of traffic on the first kilometres and it is even less enticing that the road is going steadily downhill. This explains the difference of altitude of 2000m. After 10km you'll be happy that it finally goes uphill. Your mood will improve with the gigantic mountains in the background and the first hairpin bends right in front of you. You'll arrive at Saint-Foy-Tarentaise with the first drops of sweat on your brows and you'll slowly climb up the hairpin bends to La Thuile. Expect a short section of restful cycling in the town before more hairpin bends take you uphill.

Through unlit tunnels

After a distinctly flatter section, you'll reach a wide valley. There is less traffic and the road conditions are good. The road winds up a steep hill and the rocky giants are slowly approaching. After approximately 20km you'll go through an unlit tunnel and several covered galleries. I highly recommend portable lighting, and at the very least you should take a tail light. As the road conditions in the tunnel are at times quite bad, I also recommend a front light. Short and flat sections take you nearer to a massive mountain (Dome, 3000m). Next, you'll go through a 200m-long and unlit tunnel with a bad road surface. After you have passed it, look immediately to the right where you should be able to catch a glimpse of the impressive Savine glacier. You'll then

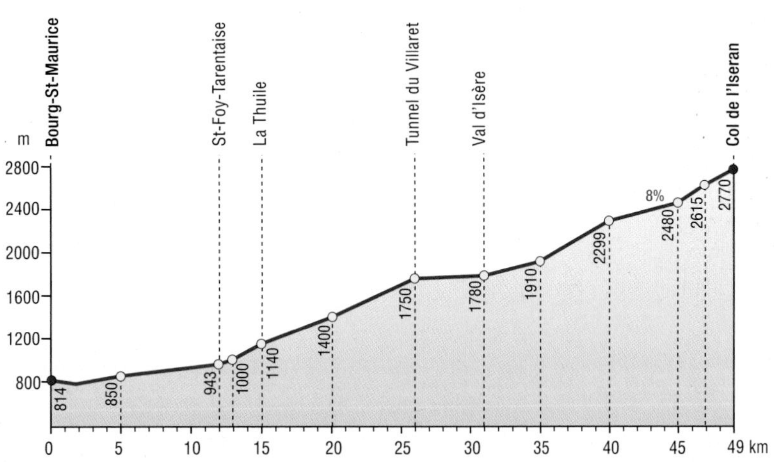

pass the Lac du Chevril Reservoir and will get a view of the ski resort Tignes across the valley.

Gigantic mountain world

You'll continue through many more tunnels and covered galleries and finally, just before Val d'Isère, through a very tight tunnel that has been carved into the rock. The town is spread out across different districts and once you have left it, you'll reach the next, slightly higher district. But none of them are too welcoming, as Val d'Isère is a typically French ski resort with big ugly hotel bunkers. If you want, you can briefly rest here as you still have 1000m in altitude to conquer.

After you have left the last ski resort behind you, you'll be cycling on a flat stretch along a creek. This is where the fun really begins because the most beautiful stretch of the day starts here. You'll find yourself in an isolated and tremendous mountain region. In front of you will be huge mountains around the Mont Iseran (3237m) and the Pers (3383m) which are covered in snow even during the summer. Steep sliprock extends down from the boulders and the temperature drops noticeably. The road winds up steep bends with a gradient between 7 and 8 per cent which will quicken the pulse.

No magic

From the sweeping bends you'll get a grandiose view down into the canyon – an ideal test to see if you have a head for heights. The vegetation above the tree line gets sparser and sparser, the finish gets nearer and nearer but suddenly the road turns to the left past the zenith. The prospect widens and reveals that you have to continue going uphill. The final metres, however, are an extraordinary experience. At the summit an icy mountain atmosphere prevails. There is a small restaurant with souvenirs and an invaluable alpine view. Even if the measurements sound fantastic, the Col de l'Iseran is not unconquerable. The route consists of only a few very steep sections and mostly of a constant incline. It is therefore easy to find a rhythm and slowly work yourself uphill. If you cross the pass and descend towards Lanslebourg, you'll need to have good break pads. The road is at times extremely narrow and the steep bends demand the greatest attention.

The road winds up the pass between bare slopes and sliprocks on the final kilometres.

Claudio Chiappucci – the devil at the Iseran

Full steam ahead: Chiappucci has moved onto the fast lane.

In 1992, Miguel Indurain had already captured the yellow jersey in the prologue of the Tour and had therefore declared his claim on an overall victory. But the tough Italian Claudio Chiappucci would continuously challenge him throughout the Tour. On 19 July 1992, Chiappucci entered the history books of the Tour with a spectacular breakout. A tough section with five high mountains was part of the daily programme. The 13th section from Saint-Gervais to Sestrières started after only 20km with an attack from the cyclist from Lombardy. He took the lead with an unbelievable speed, still accompanied by the breakout group. He traversed the Col des Saisies in first place, as well as the Cormet de Roselend and the Iseran. His head start on Indurain was so big that he was also leading overall. Alarm bells rang in the head of Indurain and he started a race to catch up Chiappucci. He collected all his strength to chase the Italian. But Chiappucci seemed to have supernatural powers: Even at Mont Cenis he maintained his speed and at the final ascent to Sestrières he did not lose it. After 254km he reached the finishing line, cheered by the Italian fans.

But Indurain had gained the advantage and had reduced his lag to 1 hour 54 minutes. With this result, he could keep his yellow jersey. Inevitably, newspapers started to compare him to Fausto Coppi. Chiappucci was a real fighter who signed his autographs with his nickname, 'El Diablo', the devil. His speciality was the alpine mountains, which he attacked, no matter what. His talents earned him the polka-dot jersey: in 1990 and 1992 he came second overall. But he never was able to win the Tour and in the subsequent Tours, he was not able to lead.

His solo escape was probably one of the most spectacular in the history of the Tour but not the longest. The record is still held by Albert Bourlon, who in 1947 attacked on the stage from Carcassonne to Luchon. At the Col de Port, he was in the lead and his excursion through the Pyrenees was an enormous effort.

His lonely position in the lead lasted for a legendary 253km. At the end he reached the finish with an average of 30kph and had crossed the Col de Port as well as the Portet d'Aspet as the winner. He gained an advantage of 16 minutes. But in the overall classification this was not enough to finish in the first three.

29 The stage with the time-recording system CORMET DE ROSELEND

CLIMB TOP: 1967m
TOTAL ELEVATION: 1240m
DISTANCE: 20.5km
MAX GRADIENT: 8.5%
AVERAGE GRADIENT: 6%
STARTING POINT:
Beaufort (2000 inhab.), Département Savoie (73)
APPROACH:
From Albertville on the D925 to Beaufort
PARKING:
At the entrance of the town, to the right of the petrol station. The tourist information office is 100m towards the centre of town
ROAD CONDITION:
With the exception of some short sections, very good
PARTICULARITIES:
Number to be collected at the tourist information office
MOUNTAIN PASS OPENINGS:
June to middle of October

Scenically this is the most diverse mountain pass of the Alps but you also get your money's worth from an athletic point of view. Beaufort offers everything that the racing cyclist desires: the tourist information office even hands out numbers to which 'signallers' are attached. When you leave the car park and go through the take-off ramp, a beep signals that your starting time has been recorded.

Acid test

Once you've left the take-off ramp, you'll cycle straight through Beaufort, along a small road with businesses and shops. Keep going. The route is signposted with C2 signs. In a narrow valley, edged in by crags, the road goes along a creek. After approximately 2km steep hairpin bends will take you uphill and along a woody slope. On the opposite slope lies a small village with traditional wooden houses. The valley narrows further and the road signs will remind you of the Tour de France.

The road continues uphill in bends and after a short and flat section you'll cross an idyllic wild river on a small bridge. After 5km you'll cycle alongside small creeks that meander down the slope. The route continues through forests that provide shade. You'll get a wonderful view across the surrounding mountain tops and long slopes. The landscape has a wonderful alpine ambience and tranquillity. The incline remains constant with protracted bends. If you notice the first signs of exhaustion, you can console yourself that even the stars have faltered at the Cormet de Roselend. In 1996 even the wearer of the yellow jersey, the Frenchman Stéphane Heulot, had to get off his bike. He abandoned in tears suffering from severe knee pain.

The peaceful Roselend Reservoir.

Breathtaking views

After 10km another view over the valley makes the 500m in altitude you've just mastered worthwhile. A few more hairpin bends follow from which the view changes from one mountainside to the other.

You'll enjoy the view into the valley as you approach the summit. But do not cheer too soon: you won't have reached the finishing line but the 1605m-high Col de Meraillet. The view after the bend is breathtaking: you'll see the turquoise Roselend Reservoir, surrounded by the grey summits of Aiguille du Grand Fond (2889m) and Mont Coin (2541m). It will no doubt suit you that you are able to trundle along the lake with a small downhill gradient. You'll then pass the aquatics club and a bar and will no doubt cherish the view to the right across the lake one more time.

Pleasure wins

The view ahead is intimidating because you'll be facing a rock face along which hairpin bends spiralling upwards. You'll ascend on the road passing graffiti and with a view onto the crag. The road is very narrow but in good condition. Arduous hairpin bends take you along a creek and a steep rock face, ahead of you rocky crags emerge. You'll then slip between the rocks through a narrow passage and you'll be pedalling along the crags, surrounded by momentous alpine scenery. Shortly afterwards, the view opens up to a huge high plateau, which is traversed by many hiking trails and characterised by barren vegetation. You'll pass a mountain hut and briefly go downhill. After a wild mountain river, the last meandering kilometre awaits you. A road blasted through the rock will take you uphill and the final metres are flat. Arriving at the Cormet de Roselend, an empty parking space will await you. Your eyes will no doubt run over the alpine landscape one more time and you may even forget the time-recording system. But to be honest: who can race through this imposing landscape without enjoying it?

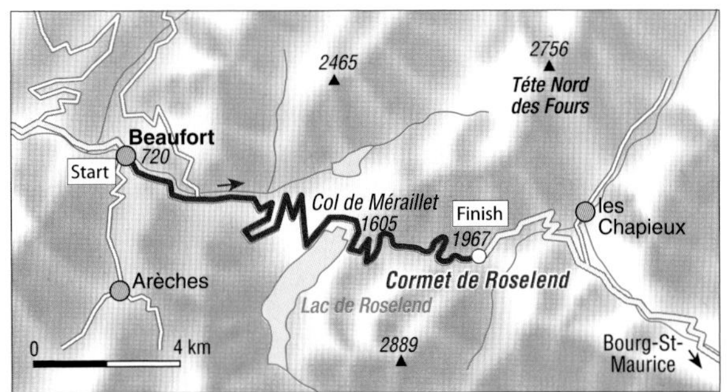

Away with the wolf

The Tour de France is the target of political activism on a regular basis. Racing fans have little sympathy for demonstrators abusing the race for political aims.

Protestors are repeatedly successful in interrupting the race or preventing the start. There are always reasons for protests. France has been in the headlines for years with violent campaigns by fishermen, farmers, truckers or youngsters from the suburbs. In 2005 protests by cattle breeders prevented the stage. Due to planned protests by local farmers against the wolf hunting prohibition, the starting point was moved quickly from Grenoble to Brignoud. The farmers

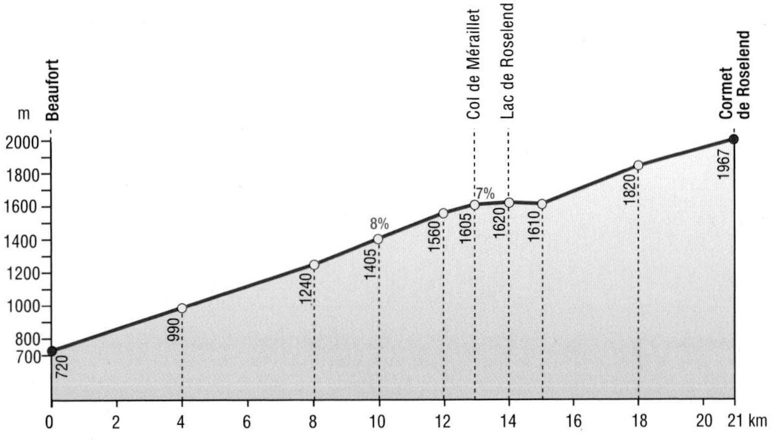

felt threatened by the wolves and campaigned against overzealous animal protection. This conflict was reminiscent of that of the Pyrenees where the battle against the bear is ubiquitous. The farmers promote a range of arguments for hunting the wolf. According to them, around 2600 animals are killed every year by wolves in the Alps. This includes many guard dogs, which are supposed to guard the herds. In 1992 the first two wolves were re-introduced to the Park national du Mercantour. Since then, the wolves have spread quickly. It is likely that several hundred wolves live in the area between the Southern Alps to the Jura.

Opposite: The Comet de Roselend is an ideal mountain pass to experience the Tour de France.

Below: The summit of Cormet de Roselend bestows a true mountain atmosphere.

Leader of the pack

Due to the protests, the Tour circuit was shortened by 12km to a still impressive 181km. The start of the stage had to be changed but the leader of the pack was not broken. As in previous years, Lance Armstrong proved that he would not tolerate any rivals on his territory. He was only briefly challenged when his helper Jaroslav Popovich crashed on the descent from Cormet de Roselend. The whole world followed what happened when Popovich clawed back his position. Instead of being thanked for his efforts, he was told off by Armstrong – the leader of the pack.

Phonak Cycling Team
6
262
BMC
BMC
ZH·703931
Škoda
www.phonak.com
Škoda
PHONAK
BMC
BMC
PHONAK
BMC

Racing tours around Beaufort

Steep mountains and little traffic around Beaufort delight the racer's heart. As the whole region focuses completely on winter sports, it is quiet in the summer. The organisers are therefore eager to fill the hotels with cyclists and hikers. In addition to the good idea of the number at the start, the tourist information office also offers a small guide with 13 cycling routes in the vicinity. The routes range from the Petit Boucle du Beaufortain (470m in altitude/31km) to the Grand Tour du Beaufortain (3850m in altitude/155km).

Your efforts can also be validated. If you show the stamps of the control points you will be given a gold, silver or bronze certificate. You certainly won't get bored!

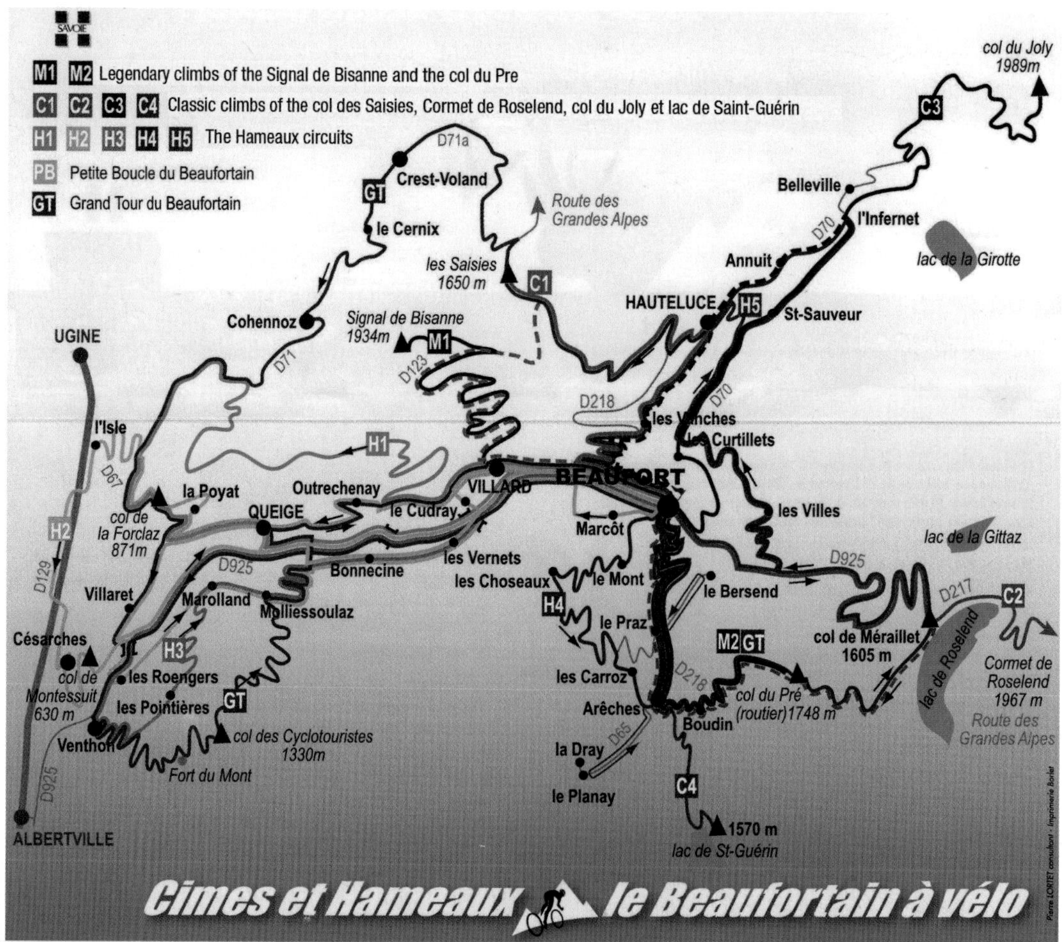

The Swiss at the Tour de France

In 1995, the Swiss professional Alex Zülle raced like a bat out of hell across the Cormet de Roselend as the winner. He pedalled particularly vigorously as at the beginning of this Tour, as the role of captain of the ONCE-team was still up for grabs – a difficult role to earn. Zülle fought and won. In addition to the stage win, he also won a place on the podium – overall success!

In 1998, Zülle was in the limelight. The Festina affair rolled over the team. Zülle also admitted to doping and was barred for half a year. The other teams feigned innocence.

It was only in 1999 when he gained success again in the overall race, finishing in second place. The Swissman probably could have achieved more but a mass crash at the Passage du Gois cost him 6 minutes. Nevertheless, the jubilation in his home country was great, as he had limited success in the preceding years.

The period of success of the Swiss cyclists dates back some years. Between 1947 and 1954, a proud number of 18 stage victories were achieved. During that time, the team had two extraordinary athletes in their midst: Ferdi Kübler and Hugo Koblet. At the start of the 1950 Tour, Kübler was still the outsider: "I have to admit," said Kübler to *Equipe*, "that at the beginning of the Tour, I was anxious. I have never had much success in bigger races. Incisive memories were invoked and I asked myself how I would survive 22 stages which were spiked with alarming difficulties." However, at the end of the scandal-ridden circuit, his worries were unfounded and he was the first Swiss cyclist to win the Tour.

His victory inspired his compatriot Hugo Koblet. His nickname was 'the handsome Hugo' as he had the habit of combing his hair immediately after arrival at the finishing line. In the 1951 Tour, he won with an advantage of 22 minutes. There was no shortage of prominent competitors, but Géminiani, Bartali, Bobet and Coppi stood no chance against the charming cyclist. The news of his Tour victory brought huge delight to all his supporters in Switzerland. On his return, Koblet drove in a convoy of cars through Geneva and Zürich. He had no doubt coiffured his hair with special care.

Alex Zülle in low-level flight across the Cormet de Roselend in 1995.

Since then, there has been no Tour victory for the Swiss. In 2010, Fabian Cancellara had the yellow jersey for five stages. He won the prologue, was in yellow in the second stage, lost it then got it back on the third through to sixth stage.

Tony Rominger is one of the most exceptional talents in the sport of cycling. He only discovered the bicycle when he was 20 years old, an age, when it is usually far too late to begin a high-performance sport. However, Rominger was determined to fight and trained in the Swiss Alps as if it were a matter of life and death. He won three stages at the Tour de France and in the race against the clock even defeated the time trial champion Miguel Indurain. Along with this, he managed to come overall second in 1993.

30 Beautiful summits beyond ragged crags
COL DE LA COLOMBIÈRE

Since its premiere in 1960, the Col de la Colombière has been on the Tour schedule twenty times.

1 ***

CLIMB TOP: 1618m
TOTAL ELEVATION: 1050m
DISTANCE: 17km
MAX GRADIENT: 10%
AVERAGE GRADIENT: 6.1%
STARTING POINT:
Marnaz (4500 inhab.),
Département Savoie (74)
APPROACH:
From Geneva on the N205 and just before Cluses, you turn to the right to Marnaz
PARKING: In the town centre
ROAD CONDITION: Good
MOUNTAIN PASS OPENINGS:
June to end of October

The motto for this tour is 'ingenious finale' as the steepest and most stunning section comes at the end of this stage. The contrast with the ugly and built-up Cluses could not be greater and you'll be happy to escape the Arve Valley.

Watch the signs

Leaving Marnaz you'll cycle uphill immediately between the houses, but the incline will even out quickly. At the beginning, the signposting is not clear; in the town centre, you'll need to cycle towards Mont Saxonnex until after 1.5km you'll see the sign to the Col de la Colombière. You'll leave Blanzy on an easy incline; the signs indicate that you'll be on the route of 'Grandes Alpes'. The road leads through leafy trees, which provide cool cover. You'll wind up the mountain in hairpin bends. To the left, a view towards ugly Cluses with its high-rise buildings is offered, but the prospect straight ahead of you will be much more inviting: a view across a valley enclosed by woody and rocky slopes.

Time for a panorama

After 6km, the road conditions decline again. To the left, you'll get a wonderful view across a slope covered with fir trees and rocks. The road levels out and with an incline of 2 to 3 per cent, which offers the opportunity for you to admire the slowly narrowing valley. You'll cycle past a wonderful old farmhouse, accompanied by a small and picturesque creek. Past the village with its beautiful stone church, you'll continue to the right following the signs.

In clear view, you'll spot the imposing crags of the Pointe Percée (2162m). The village offers a restaurant and a well next to the

On the final kilometres to the summit, the view opens up to imposing limestone.

church where you can refill your water bottles.

Mountain biker meets mountain hiker

You'll then leave the Le Reposoir on a very bendy line with an incline of up to 10 per cent. Although there is no longer any forest, you'll be compensated with a wonderful view across steep grassy slopes and an imposing mountain chain. On the last 6km, except for a short interlude, the road goes steeply uphill towards the summit. You'll get to enjoy the wonderful alpine landscape without much traffic. The straight road leads along a steep hill towards the summit. The rocks approach until the road literally nestles up to the crag. At the summit, you often meet the 'cycle-less climbing colleagues' as there are a lot of hiking trails around the Pointe Blanche. Only 25 minutes away from the summit, a calm and varied area offers trails with different degrees of difficulty. The limestone is covered in big holes, but the overhanging rock poses a great challenge to even experienced climbers. Between June and October, many regional climbers meet here and the metallic rattle of the quick-draws echo in the mountains. The summit does not offer much apart from a restaurant. If you plan to cross the path, you can look forward to a bendy descent (13.5km) towards Saint-Jean-de-Sixt. The hairpin bends in the first section in particular offer the greatest delight.

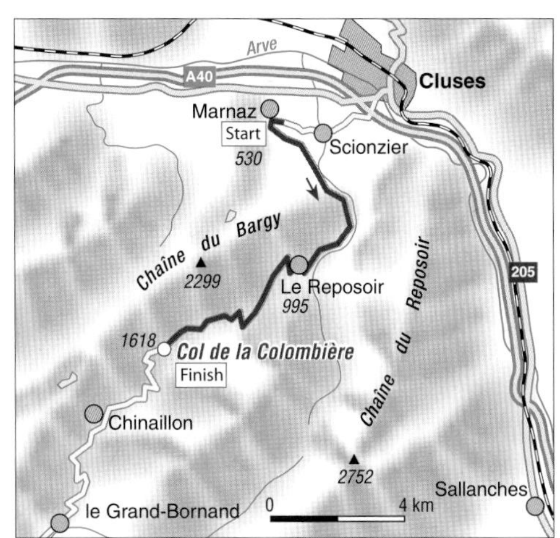

Voluntary extra task

If 1000m in altitude is not enough, you could also cycle across the Colombière towards Joux-Plane. However, for this route, you need to approach the pass from the other side. Many Tour stages took this route; the peloton of 2006 was the last one in addition to the 200km-long tour via the Col de Saisies and the Col des Aravis. This is an impressive programme that will allow you to forget your efforts on the 'short' ascent to the Colombière. If you want to tackle the Col de la Colombière from the south-west, you could start in Le

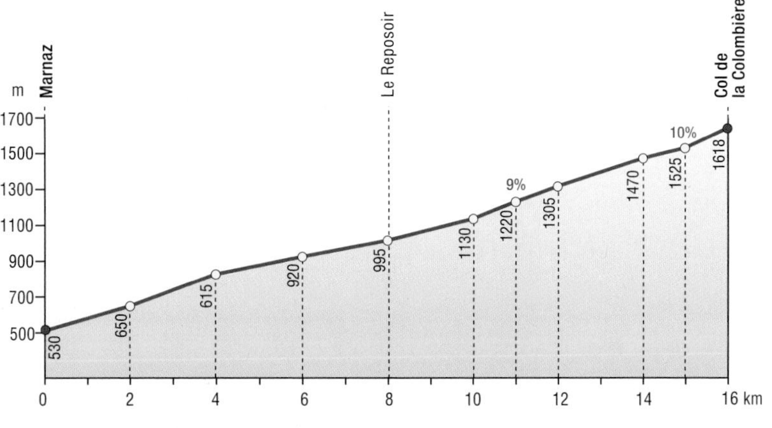

The tour for every man

Who does not dream of participating in a real stage of the Tour de France? But why merely dream if you can realise it? In 1992, the French magazine *Vélo Magazine* offered a stage for every man. Only a few days before the professionals started, amateurs could cycle the complete stage at the *Étape du Tour*. It goes without saying that the organisers favour alpine stretches. In 2002, the Col de la Colombière was part of the Tour. Although not very long with its 142km, the inclines were considerable. The Col de la Colombière was planned for the end of the route. The Col des Aravis, the Col des Saisies and the Cormet de Roselend had to be tackled first. In the region of 7500 competitors took part including cyclists from South Africa and the Arabic Emirates. The success of the cycling challenge was overwhelming. More and more starters from all over the world registered for the cycling challenge. In 2009 even 10,000 places weren't enough to satisfy the demand. Therefore in 2011 for the first time the ASO offered two *Étape du Tour* with 10,000 entries sold out at each.

Further information can be found at www.letapedutour.com.

The usual summit signpost stands on the Col de la Colombière.

Grand Bornand. The town is supposed to be particularly crazy about cycling and the inhabitants love the sport.

Le Grand Bornand is cosy in the summer but during the winter months, guests from all across Europe come to visit. Le Grand Bornand is at 920m altitude and to reach the summit you have to tackle 700m of altitude. Spread over 12km, this amounts to an incline of less than 6 per cent. While the first kilometres are easy, the last 3km get straight down to the nitty-gritty. The hairpin bends with an incline between 7 and 9 per cent offer wonderful climbing fun.

The landscape on the final kilometres of the pass is particularly impressive.

Farewell to 'the Pirate'

Marco Pantani had come first on a mountain summit or mountain section several times in his life. At the Tour de France, he had already won 16 times in the battle for the mountain. The three victories of Jan Ullrich look meagre in comparison. Climbing ran in the blood of the gladiatorial Italian. When he was young, he loved to overtake one competitor after another in the mountains. "In the mountains, I lift myself from the saddle to shorten the agony," he once explained in an interview.

No one therefore paid great attention when he came first crossing the Col de la Colombière on the 16th stage of the Tour de France 2000. The spectators saw the usual picture: Pantani's upper body was bent over, his hands clutched the lower handlebars and he pedalled regularly and gracefully. Only in hindsight did it become clear that this was the Italian's last performance. It was an invisible farewell to a hero which could not have ended more tragically. He hit 'the wall' that day and had to end the Tour. This was just the beginning of a downward spiral for him. On 14 February, 2004, he died of heart failure caused by brain and lung oedemas. An incurable mixture of cocaine and antidepressants caused his death. A sad coincidence: on his last stage victory, he arrived at the finishing line before the Spanish alpine specialist José-María Jiménez. In December 2003, only a few months before Pantani, Jiménez died in December 2003 in a psychiatric clinic in Madrid after years of drug abuse and depression. The decline of Pantani had started on 5 June, 1999 when he was excluded from the Giro d'Italia due to elevated haematocrit levels. It was a shock from which he never recovered, as 'the Pirate' had finished the race in the lead. He felt betrayed, even if the doping suspicion was not entirely unfounded. On the same day, he declared his resignation from the sport. For many years he was haunted by prosecutors and court summons. In 1995, the prosecutor came across a hospital file and discovered that Pantani's haematocrit levels had been between 59 and 61 per cent. The usual levels are around 40 per cent, therefore it was a clear indication for the misuse of EPO.

Even today, Marco Pantani has many fans. Every year, an 'Everyman' race is held in his honour.

On 13 May, 2000, he dared a comeback at the Giro d'Italia. He ended up well beaten in the general classification but his fans celebrated every appearance of the star. His whole focus was on the Tour de France. He managed two spectacular stage victories and after surrendering at the Col de Colombière, he was nevertheless confident. But hard times followed and he was broken by the accusations of doping, which meant he was unable to achieve his goal. He abused drugs again to deal with his frustrations. He didn't finish the Giro in 2001 and was suspended in 2002 under suspicion of the abuse of insulin. He tried one more time at the Giro in 2003 but finished in 14th place. When he was barred from the Tour in 2003, he fell into a deep depression and consumed a lot of cocaine. Several detox programmes failed and, after the tragic death of Fausto Coppi of Italy, cycling lost its second legend in a tragic manner.

31 An ideal training tour COL DES ARAVIS

The traffic on the main road between Thônes and Saint-Jean-de Sixt does not seem to bother these donkeys.

CLIMB TOP: 1486m
TOTAL ELEVATION: 860m
DISTANCE: 17km
MAX GRADIENT: 7%
AVERAGE GRADIENT: 5%
STARTING POINT:
Thônes (5500 inhab.), Départment Haute Savoie (74)
APPROACH:
From Annecy on the D909 towards La Clusaz to Thônes
PARKING:
Good parking opportunities near the Tourist Information
ROAD CONDITION:
Good, but partially dirty due to agricultural traffic
MOUNTAIN PASS OPENINGS:
May to end of October

The best scenic beauty usually awaits you at the end and it is no different on this circuit. Leaving the tourist information office in Thônes, you'll cycle along a very busy D909 to La Clusaz. The traffic is disappointing and will no doubt motivate you to speed up. It is sad, as the landscape is quite beautiful here. If you want, you can document your achievements by having the *vélodateur* (validator) stamp your times.

Creative restaurateur

The idea of a *vélodateur* came from a local restaurateur. Patrice Aupetit used to run an inn not far from Alpe d'Huez and was in constant contact with the cycling community. He too cycled a lot and loved to compare times with his colleagues. He thought that it must be easy to attach a mechanical device at the bottom and summit of a mountain pass that stamps your time card. When he proposed this to the Départment du Vaucluse at the Ventoux, his suggestion was met with great interest. The system also proved successful in the area of Thônes.

In the Pyrenees, Alpe d'Huez and several other unknown ascents the *vélodateur* has also been established. A robust, mechanical stamping device from the US was chosen. You buy a time card in the tourist office where you can register the beginning and end of your circuit. The second system that was established in the last few years at several famous climbs is the Timtoo Timing.

Among the shade

The incline increases after 3km on the wide road and soon you'll pass through Les Villards sur Thônes. To the right, you'll have a

The valley is surrounded by mountainscape on both sides.

view over an expansive valley and to the left, along the road, you'll see some very old farmhouses. You'll continue on ascending hills to Saint-Jean-de-Sixt, which you'll reach after 7km. You'll then continue straight on, passing a stone church and the tourist information office. You'll then enter a narrow valley in which the road gently winds uphill. In this section, you should enjoy the leafy trees that provide shade, as soon the road will be exposed again to the sun.

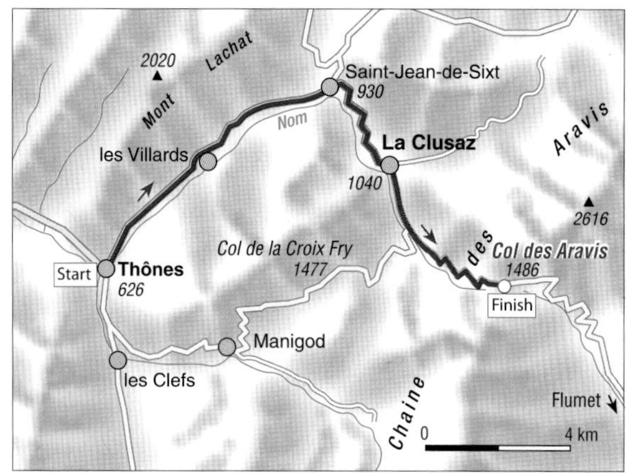

In La Clusaz

With 400m in altitude, you will have nearly achieved half the climb and you'll reach the ski resort La Clusaz. On entry to the resort, the 'Itinaire Cycliste Col des Aravis' branches off immediately. But do not worry – this is only the calmer route through the town. If you miss the turning, you can also go straight through the town. This will be your last opportunity to buy a *Carnet de Cols* to record your time. At the end of the town, the right exit at the roundabout will take you to the Col des Aravis. After 10m, you will see the stamping device attached to a lamppost. The road continues under two ski lifts with a gentle incline and distinctly less road traffic. You'll pass ski resort hotels and continue directly towards a massive mountain that is covered in ski lifts. But you won't conquer this summit, as the road passes it.

Don't forget to stamp!

About 4km after Clusaz, you'll reach the first steep bend. You'll have left the houses behind and you'll be able to enjoy the view over the green slopes along the road. The incline increases and you'll coil uphill in hairpin bends. The sounds of cow bells will accompany you while you gain altitude. Only 100m in altitude separates you from the summit and on the final metres, you'll even be spoilt with a flat section. Behind the grazing cows a wonderful rocky scenery emerges.

A small stone chapel sits on the summit and of course a restaurant. The *vélodateur* is directly next to the chapel, so be sure to get a stamp on your timecard. You should still have

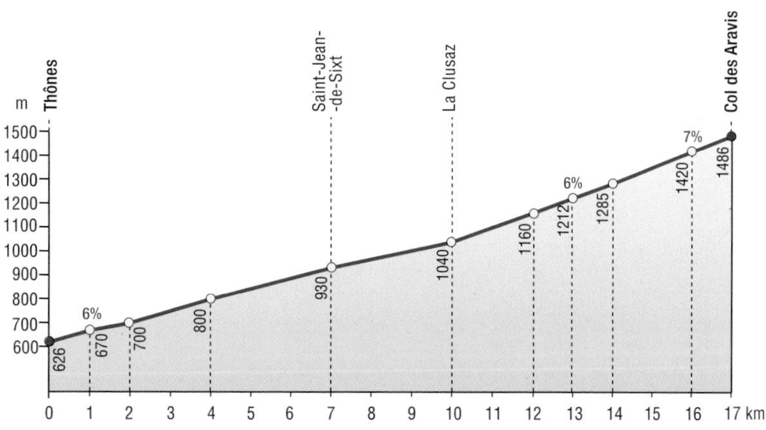

some energy left in your legs – there are so many mountains in this area that you are spoilt for choice.

Mini-circuit

It is rarely so easy to turn a mountain pass tour into a circuit. All you have to do is to turn around and roll back towards La Clusaz. After a few kilometres, a tiny road branches off to the left towards the Col de la Croix-Fry. With inclines up to 7 per cent, the D16 has very steep hills. But it is only 5km between the crossing and the summit so the exertions are limited. Downhill bends take you from the Col de la Croix-Fry to Manigod. It is however worthwhile to stop briefly and enjoy the view over the mountains Chaine des Aravis. In Manigod, only your speed will slow down but then again you continue speedily towards the valley of Chamfroid. You will lose considerable altitude and without much leg-work, you'll return to Thônes.

Always Aravis

The Tour de France has used the Col des Aravis 39 times now and the route always uses the south-western approach over the pass. The point of departure is often Bourg d'Oisans but sometimes it has been Aix-les-Bain or Valloire. The standard finishing line is Morzine. In 2006 the cyclists started in Saint-Jean-de-Maurienne and reached Morzine after 200km. This was a challenging stage, which led over the Col des Saisies (1650m), Col de la Colombières (1613m) and the Col de la Joux-Plane (1691m).

A small stone chapel stands at the mountain pass of the Col des Aravis.

Birth of the yellow jersey

In the year 1919 on the 11th stage of the Tour de France, the organisers launched their new distinctive jersey. It was 19 July and because it was a Saturday, the roads were lined with thousands of people. Eugène Christophe was the first cyclist to wear the yellow jersey. At the start in Grenoble, he had swapped his grey La Sportive jersey for a yellow one (perhaps it should really be called a long-sleeved yellow sweater). But when he crossed the Col des Aravis in his *maillot jaune*, only a few spectators recognised its symbolic value.

Even today, there are many legends surrounding the birth of the yellow jersey. One version is that the colour yellow was chosen because the magazine *L'Auto* was printed on yellow paper. Another simplistic but plausible explanation is that the tradesmen did not have any other colour in stock. What is clear is that it was intended to make things easier for the spectators. Often, they wouldn't have a clue who was in the lead.

The history of the second most important jersey is easier to trace. The polka-dot jersey was introduced in 1975 although the mountain prize had been awarded since 1933. The first champion of the polka-dot jersey was the Belgian Lucien van Impe, whose height of 167cm and weight of 57kg was ideal for a climber.

The winner of the Tour is, of course, established in a complicated points system. The points are calculated from the difficulty of a climb. The hardest grade is *hors catégorie* (literally outside or beyond classification) followed by *première catégorie* (first category). During the history of the Tour, different classifications were used for different climbs. The first 3 or sometimes 10 cyclists are awarded points according to their position. For the victory at the Ventoux, 40 points are awarded whereas a small mountain of the fourth category is only worth 3 points.

Until 2006, this was a famous image: Lance Armstrong in yellow.

Here comes the boss: The yellow jersey confers authority.

32 Small but mighty
CROIX-FRY

There is a vélodateur *at the Col de la Croix-Fry to measure your time.*

1 ***

CLIMB TOP: 1477m
TOTAL ELEVATION: 850m
DISTANCE: 13km
MAX GRADIENT: 10%
AVERAGE GRADIENT: 6.3%
STARTING POINT:
Thônes (5500 inhab.), Départment Haute Savoie (74)
APPROACH:
From Annecy on the D909 towards La Clusaz
PARKING:
Good parking opportunities near the tourist information office. Here you get the time card and the *vélodateur*
ROAD CONDITION:
Very mixed and at times, the road surface is very damaged
MOUNTAIN PASS OPENINGS:
All year

While the Col des Aravis is gently drawn out, this circuit gets down to business much more quickly. The same total altitude is spread over only 13.5km. However, this is isn't torturous but a slow-paced pleasure.

Country life

The parish of Thônes is only a few kilometres away from the Lac d'Annecy and the Aravis mountain range. This is why it is visited throughout the year by tourists and day trippers who venture to this idyllic area. The tourist industry has had a long tradition in Thônes and the Val Sulens. Recently, a centennial celebrated the opening of the area to tourism. Luckily, though, the valley has kept its originality, given that so many other areas in France are spoiled by bleak industrial sites and massive shopping centres. It is only the main road to La Clusaz which ruins the idyll. A highlight of the area is definitely the Saturday market, where regional specialities will provide you with great delight.

Cheesy business

A visit to Thônes isn't complete without tasting the local cuisine. The inhabitants are particularly proud of their cheese. The Reblochon and the Chevrotin have been served for more than three centuries.

During spring and summer, the cheese production is booming. Connoisseurs claim that the cheese is the best because of the blossoming herbs on the Alps. If you are interested in cheese making, you can visit the local cooperative dairies.

Less traffic, more of an incline

You'll start at the tourist information office and at the church, immediately turn to the right. This is your last opportunity to stock

Jalabert discovers his climbing talent.

up on food and drink. You'll leave Thônes through a small road lined with shops on the D12. One hundred metres later, the Col de la Croix-Fry is signposted to the left. The traffic suddenly stops and at the same time, the incline increases abruptly.

The road goes considerably uphill with only a few sections to rest. You'll cycle through the small and cosy villages La Combe and Villard Dessous. After having left the wooden houses behind us, a flatter road continues to Manigod. While you have to pedal hard in the village, the bike nearly rolls on its own once you leave it. On a bend after the village, you'll have a fantastic view over the mountain range on the other side of the valley. Just opposite looms the Tournette (2351m) which is flanked by impressive mountains. In the summer, you can spot paragliders sailing across the valley.

However, you won't have much opportunity to enjoy the view. The incline increases again and you'll need concentration for the road. The increase in incline is not surprising, as you'll need to conquer 500m in altitude before reaching the summit.

Landis at the Croix-Fry

In 2004, on the 17th stage of the Tour de France, the Col de la Croix-Fry became the stage for a demonstration of strength by Lance Armstrong. The pass is the closing climb of the 200km-long section where the T-Mobile and US Postal teams chase each other up the mountain.

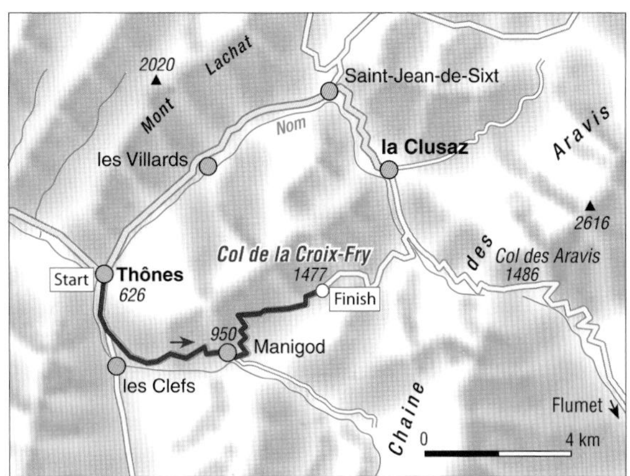

During the climb, Floyd Landis set the tempo for his team captain. On the descent, Andreas Klöden tried to leave in order to gain the stage victory. Nevertheless, Lance Armstrong proved himself again as a relentless competitor. He sprinted against Klöden for the stage victory and won by a few metres.

On the summit

The first hairpin bends will take you quickly up the mountain and you'll climb past small holiday homes towards the summit. On an exhausting incline, you'll pass Le Chenavay and Sous Le Rocher. You'll then coil up

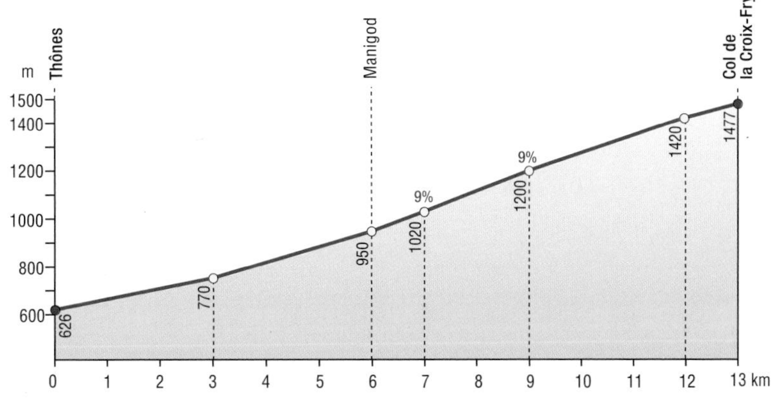

another hairpin bend and arrive shortly at the restaurant La Croix-Fry.

The signs are confusing, but do not worry – the climb is not over yet, as you will have to tackle another 150m in altitude. You'll continue to pass holiday homes.

In steeper hairpin bends, you'll climb further uphill and the view opens up to the first ski lifts. After a few final metres in altitude, you'll reach the summit and the small ski resort Croix-Fry. In addition to some ski lifts, the resort offers some hotels and restaurants. The onslaught of tourists however is limited and even during the winter Croix-Fry is quite cosy. The summit offers few attractions but the view across the Alps are wonderful.

If you want, you could cycle a circuit and go via Croix-Fry to the Col des Aravis (signposted). The eastern approach to the pass is distinctly easier and the 500m in altitude are quickly overcome. When you are back at the main road, you can either detour via the Col des Aravis or return to the point of departure via La Clusaz.

Small pleasures

If you want to stay in the region, you will find a selection of smaller climbs near by. The Tour 'Belvédère de La Forclaz' via the Col de La Forclaz (1150m) starts at the Lac d'Annecy. The 700m in altitude are impressive and maximum inclines of 13 per cent challenge even the professionals. It is therefore not surprising that the Forclaz has been part of the Tour de France. A good point of departure is Talloires, at the eastern bank of the lake. Via the D909 along the lake, you can easily return to Talloires.

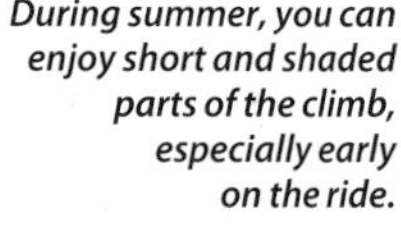

During summer, you can enjoy short and shaded parts of the climb, especially early on the ride.

France's late love for Laurent Jalabert

In 1997, Laurent Jalabert struggled up the Croix-Fry in first place. Nevertheless, he would not win the 15th stage from Courchevel to Morzine. It had not been a good year for him: he would be placed in 43rd position on entry to Paris. Two years earlier, everything looked much better for him; he even made it into 4th place. However, the pressure by the French public is enormous and the local press has not always treated him well. This is why he only gives interviews in Spanish.

'Jaja' has been through a lot during his career; the most momentous experience happened to him in the 1994 Tour. In the final sprint at Armentières he got caught up in a mass accident which a bystanding police officer had caused. He had to abort the Tour with serious facial injuries.

In hindsight, he conceded that this setback had actually worked to his advantage: "Every time that you have a tough time and survive it, you become stronger. Stronger than the person who is always successful."

Jaja is a very good all-round champion which is shown in his greatest achievements: in 1992 and 1995, he was given the green jersey, which is awarded for sprinting. In 1995, he won the Vuelta a España (Tour de Spain), in 1997, he won the individual time trial and in 2001 and 2002, he won the Tour polka-dot jersey. Only after he changed to the Danish CSC-team did he win the hearts of the French fans. His relationship with the media had improved and when he won a stage on their national holiday, he acknowledged his home country again.

In 2002, the son of a wine grower was at the peak of his career when he announced his resignation. He was very clear on the subject of doping. He saw the doping controls as mere harassment and had no sympathy for the anti-doping campaign.

Jalabert made some enemies with his stubbornness.

33 A wolf in sheep's clothing
JOUX-PLANE

On the summit, the ducks are enjoying the idyllic mountain lake.

CLIMB TOP: 1691m

TOTAL ELEVATION: 980m

DISTANCE: 12km

MAX GRADIENT: 13%

AVERAGE GRADIENT: 8.2%

STARTING POINT:
Samonfins (2300 inhab.), Départment Haute Savoie (74)

APPROACH:
On D907 from Geneva to Samofin

PARKING:
Parking in the city centre near the church and town hall

ROAD CONDITION: Dirty roads

MOUNTAIN PASS OPENINGS:
June to November

A thousand metres of climbing does not sound challenging but the excursion into the gentle foothills can still surprise you. The constant change in incline demands constant changes in speed and even the average gradient is not to be underestimated.

It is not surprising that on several stages of the Tour the climb has provided many surprises. The climb was last on the programme in 2006. In 1997, Marco Pantani had proved his top form with an average speed of 20kph and arrived at the summit after 33 minutes.

Bad road conditions

The pass is navigable on different routes and if you have time, you can try out the alternatives. This time you'll start at the car park (by the water fountain and toilets) and leave the town in the eastern direction. After a few metres, near the Hotel Edelweiß, the road takes a sharp left bend and the *été* (summer route) is signposted towards the Joux-Plane. A small road that takes you through the houses goes uphill immediately. Particularly in the first section, the road conditions are very bad with loose gravel. You'll continue past many houses, including a house painted with smurfs, on the small and very quiet D354.

The view stretches across the densely settled valley. You'll cycle between old wooden houses and will then turn to the right. The road goes uphill in stretched-out bends and through beautiful leafy forests.

There are few houses left and with a slightly decreasing climb, you'll reach La Combe aux Flés after 3km. The road in the town is very dirty and you need to be careful on the descent.

Many different roads go up the Col de la Joux-Plane. The main road is signposted and is easy to find.

A real treat

You'll then cycle along pastures accompanied by the calming ringing of cow bells. Next you'll wind up a hairpin bend through beautiful old wooden houses; goats, sheep and chicken contribute to the alpine idyll. The road continues in hairpin bends and takes you to the village Le Tour. After Le Tour, the road goes gently uphill in a long stretch. You'll get to enjoy a wonderful view over the Massif de Platé. Most cyclists on the Tour de France have by this point already lost interest in the beauty of this region.

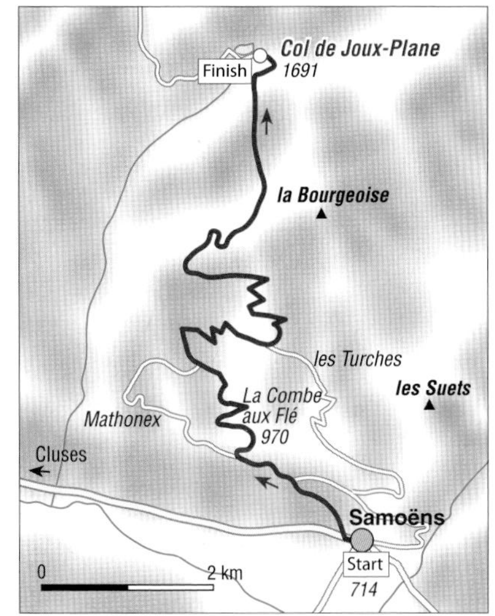

Now it is heating up

The road goes uphill in increasingly steep bends. The steepest section with a 13.5 per cent incline awaits you, stretching out over 200m. You shouldn't be in any doubt that the Col deserves an honoured place among the Tour de France mountain passes. In comparison, the 21 hair bends of Alpe d'Huez are a walk in the park!

The incline eases noticeably and you'll cycle through Combe Èmeru, a small hamlet with a few houses. The light leaf forest provides little shade and therefore on a hot summer day the climb is a sticky affair.

It was here when, in the year 2000, the iron Lance Armstrong suddenly had a collapse in strength and lost his position (see 'Tour History', page 166).

Two kinds of refreshments

From the hairpin bends, you'll have a wonderful view into the valley and the diverse and leafy slopes. You'll cycle past a small well and then a creek.

The road continues uphill with a constant but gentle incline and after all the chops and changes, this is very welcome. At a bend, the view opens up across the mountain pass and to the right, on to the beautiful Pointe d'Angolon.

Just behind the sign for the pass lies the small chalet – Chalet Joux-Plane.

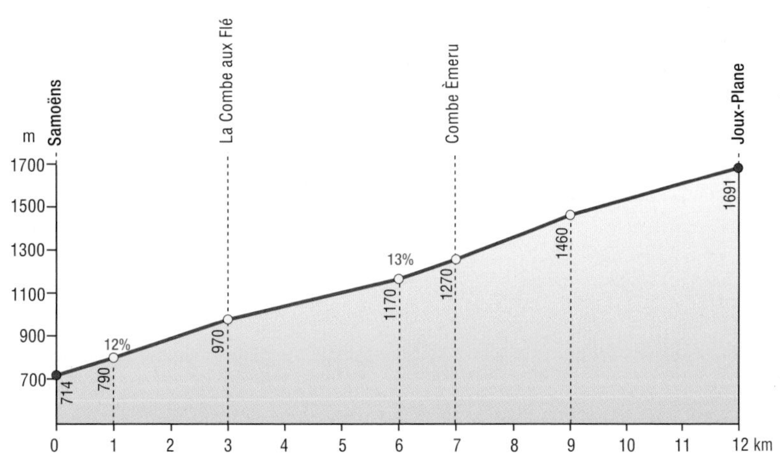

You should continue straight on as behind the summit you'll find a small and idyllic mountain lake where ducks splash about comfortably. A small break won't hurt. If you are hungry or thirsty, you have the restaurant Le Relais des Vallées to the left. On a hot summer's day, it is difficult to be restrained and not jump into the ice-cold lake. But you'll also be aware that a speedy descent provides refreshment too!

Opposite: The cool lake at the summit is a great temptation in the summer.

Below: From this view, you would not suspect that the Joux-Plane would be such an impressive incline.

Chaos of variants

The southern approach to the Col de Joux-Plane offers a confusing mix of varied routes. It is only on the last 6km where the routes unite again. Leaving Samofins there is an eastern and western variant. If you choose the western approach, you will have another opportunity to diversify if you cycle across the Mathonex. If you consider that, the average incline at the Alpe d'Huez is 9 per cent, and the one at des Joux-Plane is 8.4 per cent, then you'll realise how challenging this short climb is. It is worth returning for a second run, where you could take an alternative route – your training efforts will be rewarded.

The climb up the other approach seems relaxing in comparison. You are only met with 700m in altitude along the 11km between Morzine and the summit. This amounts to an average incline of 6.5 per cent, which is certainly more manageable than the above route from Samofin.

Lance Armstrong cracks

At every Tour from 1999 to 2005 he ran as reliably and as silently as a Swiss watch. For years, his competitors had to watch him speeding past; the spectators took his success for granted and watched his head bowed down in style, his neckchain dangling rhythmically from left to right and a murderous cadence of 115 revs per minute. While he was sweating profusely, the distance between him and his competitors was increasing. He was rewarded with a stage victory and the yellow jersey. Since his sensational recovery from cancer, he made few mistakes and he seemed invincible. Always? Nearly always! On the 2000 Tour, it was a small sensation when Armstrong cracked on the climb and was not able to stand the pace. However, it looked as if the stage would go according to the Texan's plans.

At the start, it was already clear that the day would be a tough struggle because anger was in the air. Marco Pantani and Lance Armstrong were at loggerheads and provoked each other via the press. The trigger was the stage at Ventoux where Armstrong 'bestowed' the Italian his victory.

But 'the Pirate' did not want the gift, seeing himself as the superior cyclist. Both pros tantalised spectators, who were expecting a thrilling duel. Needless to say that Armstrong was a different person when he had his second comeback in 2009 and 2010.

The toughest competitors for the Tour victory: Jan Ullrich and Lance Armstrong.

"If he believes that we are through with each other, he is mistaken," warned Pantani. Armstrong inflamed the situation by calling Pantani 'Elefantino', a nickname that made fun of Pantani's big ears.

Pantani let rip at the first climb. He set a murderous pace at the Col des Saisies. As usual, he placed his hands on the lower handlebars, sprinted forwards and left Armstrong behind. But underneath his cool demeanour, Armstrong was boiling. A lot was at stake for Jan Ullrich as he still came second in the overall classification. However, Pantani was only a couple of seconds behind. After 70km, it got worse: Pantani ousted Ullrich from his second-place spot and the alarm bells rang for the US Postal team. The pursuers put some oomph into their race and at the Col de Colombière, the distance to Pantani was melting away. In a breakneck speed, they raced downhill to the Côte des Châtillon-sur-Cluses, getting closer to Pantani.

The ascent of the Col de Joux-Plane was suddenly the most thrilling moment of the 2000 Tour: the group around Armstrong caught up with Pantani and finally passed him. The man in the pink jersey was beaten and fell behind. Now, it was Armstrong who determined the speed, and one cyclist after another fell behind. Finally, it was only Jan Ullrich, Richard Virenque and Roberto Heras who were game.

When Heras attacked, the sensation happened. Armstrong lost his rhythm and deep furrows appeared on his forehead. His legs were getting heavier and he dropped behind even further. Ullrich and Virenque followed the Spaniard closely and couldn't believe the spectacle. Was the American bluffing? But when they got closer and closer, it became clear that Armstrong was hitting 'the wall'. "First there was this peculiar tiredness in my legs, followed by a feeling of emptiness in my stomach. Virenque and Ullrich caught up and zoomed past me. First, I tried to catch up with them and force myself through the pain but inevitably, I slowed down. It did not take long and I felt that I was going backwards down the mountain. It was only 10km to the finish but it felt like 100km."

The Texan with jaundice: Armstrong dominated the race for years.

Jan Ullrich was close to a stage victory but on the ascent, he lost time changing his tyre. The break pads were too worn out. Heras was equally exhausted: he miscalculated and crashed into a gate just before the finishing line. Ullrich came second, 24 seconds behind Virenque.

However, the duel between Pantani and Armstong was much more exciting. Pantani lost over 13 minutes and was so tired that he had to quit the race. Armstrong was nearly delirious and his trainer was afraid that he had to quit the race too. But he scrambled for each metre and lost only 90 seconds in the end.

Though he again found himself on the podium, he had been very close to failure. "It was the worst day that I ever had on the bike. I nearly lost the Tour de France."

JURA AND VOSGES

34 An athletic collection of bends
COL DE LA FAUCILLE

The Col de la Faucille is also well known and popular amongst bikers.

CLIMB TOP: 1323m
TOTAL ELEVATION: 700m
DISTANCE: 12km
MAX GRADIENT: 8%
AVERAGE GRADIENT: 6%
STARTING POINT:
Gex (7800 inhab.),
Départment Ain (01)
APPROACH:
From Geneva on the N5 to Gex
PARKING:
Parking in the city centre of Gex in parking bays
ROAD CONDITION: Good
MOUNTAIN PASS OPENINGS:
All year

Previous double page: Racers on the way to the Grand Ballon.

The Col de la Faucille has been part of the Tour de France an impressive 40 times now. No other climb has been integrated so often into the programme since the creation of the Tour. However, even die-hard cycling fans could not place the mountain pass geographically . The Col de Faucille is a bit of a shrinking violet due to its relatively easy climbs. The pass only plays a negligible role in the Tour. Due to its low difficulty level and its peripheral position, few alterations in the overall ranking are made here.

Alternative routes

Generally the Col de la Faucille is approached from the west. For 8.5km, the road coils from the small town Mijoux to the summit. The drop on the western slope is only about 340m in altitude, while the drop on the eastern slope is 700m in altitude. However, I shouldn't keep a third variant a secret: if you approach the Col de Faucille from the northern Morez, you will accomplish 630m in altitude. The average incline is a cosy 2 per cent on 27km on the busy N5. There are many reasons why the route from Gex is favourable: it has athletic challenges and scenic delights, but it is also accessible.

Relaxing prelude

If you take faster routes to the Alps, you should not ignore this climb. It is a perfect route to train your legs after a long car journey. The Col de la Faucille is directly outside of the gates of Geneva and therefore for many on the way to the French Alps. It is only a stone's throw from the motorway to the point of departure.

Already a wide road leads from Gex uphill along several houses. After 2km, the traffic calms. It is now tourists who are on the move because they are hoping for a beautiful view along Lake Geneva. Despite the first bends, the incline is a pleasant 6 per cent. For the coming kilometres, the road goes steadily uphill and you'll be able to find your own rhythm. You'll now be in the nature reserve of Haut-Jura, which was founded in 1986 and offers a variety of flora and fauna. If you leave the road, you may see chamois, lynx and woodgrouse cocks. Above Lake Geneva, the mountains are crossed with a network of approximately 1000km of hiking paths. This is a true paradise for hikers and mountain bikers!

Opportunity for the final sprint

After approximately 6km, a bend offers a wonderful viewpoint. In good weather, you'll have an expansive view over Lake Geneva and, specifically, the white mountain giants near Mont Blanc. At around 1040m altitude, you'll pass Fontaine Napoléon. It's a reminder that that here has been a road here since 1805 – the year when Napoleon started his reign. The cool water is a welcome refreshment during the summer. After 8km, you'll start to sweat. With an incline of 8 per cent, you'll be expecting the hardest section of the route. But it is not far to the summit and the final kilometres have a little incline, which offers the opportunity for a final sprint.

Following in the footsteps of the Tour

In 2004, the 18th stage of the Tour led from Annemasse via the Côte des Collogner to the Col de la Faucille and further on to the finish in Lons-Le-Saunier. The peloton crossed the pass via the eastern ascent. If you want to follow in the footsteps of this stage, you have to cross the pass and cycle along the D436 towards Lajoux (1198m). You stay on the D436 and pass Saint-Claude until a turn to the right takes you on the D118 to Saint-Lupicien. Since Lajoux, you have lost about 600m in altitude. At the Côte des Crozet, after 30km, an incline with 200m in altitude awaits you but you'll find even this an easy task. Continue cycling until you turn left in Clairvaux onto the N78 towards the west. With a short interlude at the Côte de Nogna, you will continue downhill towards Lons-Le-Saunier (286m). The route is not easy to find as the organisers have chosen small roads. Therefore, you'll need to take a map.

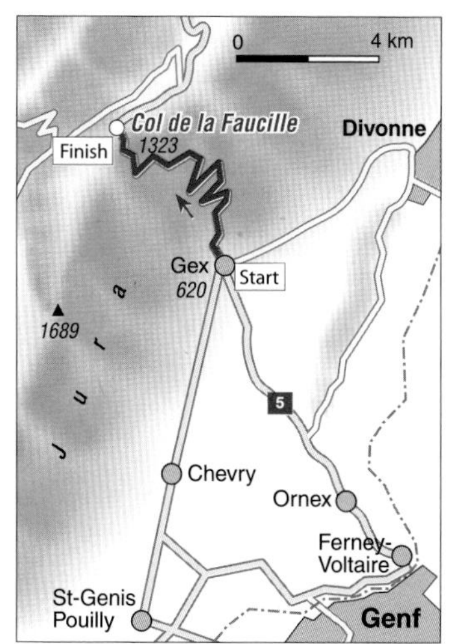

Unknown neighbours

If the Col de Faucille is already an insider's tip, then in comparison, the Côte des Rousses is entirely unknown. The mountain pass lies to the west of the Faucille. Since 1967, mountain points were given when the peloton crossed the Faucille from this side of the mountain. It is only 400m in altitude from Morez to the summit and the average incline is a limited 4.5 per cent.

Sightseeing by bicycle

If you feel at home near the lively city of Geneva, you could spend some days cycling around Gex. If you

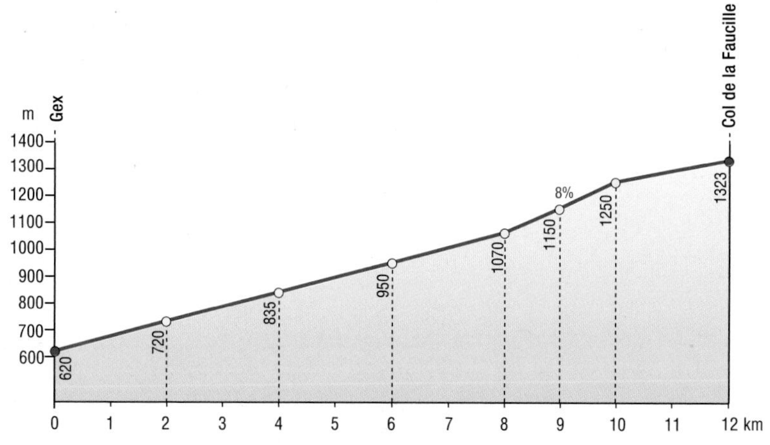

need ideas for the routes, it is best to go to the tourist information office and buy the booklet, *L'Ain à vélo*. It lists 34 cycling tours in Département Ain. Most of them vary between 50 and 70km, but there are a few with three-digit distances as well. The suggestions for sightseeing by bicycle are ideal. Every tour has a foldout that offers a map and information on sights. The only problem is the language – without French, you will not be able to use this wonderful information at all.

It seems that the climbs in the Jura are out of fashion. The touring of the small peaks is long past and many were only tested for the Tour. The Col du Berthiand (780m), Cerdon (595m), Croix de la Serra (1049m), Mollendruz (1185m) and Vue des Alpes (1283m) were mountain roads in the Jura that had only been used once or twice.

Local specialities

If, when back in Gex, you are tormented by hunger pangs, a hearty ploughman's lunch is recommended. In addition to the Comté cheese, the local speciality is the Bleu de Gex, a blue cheese with an aroma of hazelnuts and mushrooms. This does not only satisfy my hunger but leads me to imagine the alpine cheeses and alpine passes that are waiting to be discovered.

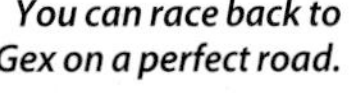

You can race back to Gex on a perfect road.

The 'Eagle of Toledo' learns how to fly

The big names in cycling history have left their trace at the Col de la Faucille. At the beginning of the last century, Eugène Christophe, Henri Pélissier and Ottavio Bottecchia crossed the pass first. Before the war in 1938 and after the war in 1951, Gino Bartali was in the lead. However, in 1958 the Col de la Faucille really made history. The Spaniard Federico Bahamontes crossed the Faucille in the lead and secured himself crucial points in the mountain trial. He ended the Tour as the winner of the mountain trial and no one knew that he would be included in the circle of famous climbers of the Tour.

His climbing talents were enormous. He raced up the mountains nimble-footed and put a great distance between himself and his opponents. But the 'Eagle of Toledo' had one decisive handicap: he was terribly afraid of descents. As a child, he had a severe bike accident and never got over his fear. His performance in 1954 remains unforgotten.

During the 18th stage from Grenoble to Briançon, he won a big advantage. But he did not dare to go downhill on his own. Therefore, he bought himself an ice cream at the Romeyère Pass and waited for his pursuers. "He is a great mountain cyclist but he is completely crazy," explained his fellow compatriot and colleague Jesus Lorono.

His hometown Toledo would stage a big fête every year on his return. After he had participated in the Tour de France several times, Bahamontes came under increasing pressure. His fans felt that he could achieve more than the mountain trials. If he were to fling himself downhill more bravely and not lose time in the flat stages, a Tour victory would be possible. In 1959, a highly motivated Bahamontes waited at the start. That year, the circuit was contested in national teams. The French team had the first-class cyclists Jacques Anquetil, Louison Bobet and Roger Rivière competing and that was the problem. All three wanted to win and saw their fellow compatriots as competitors. Bahamontes profited and won his first Tour.

His successes were not confined solely to the Tour de France. In 1956 he won the mountain trial at the Giro d'Italia, in 1957 he came second at the Vuelta a España and first in the Vuelta Ciclista a Asturias. His roots were down to earth. Coming from a farming family, he was accustomed to hard work and an austere life. In his youth, the harsh daily routine formed the basis for his climbing skills: When he was 15 he had to cycle through the mountains of Toledo to do the deliveries for his parents. Apparently, he carried sacks of potatoes weighing up to 25kg on his back. It is therefore not surprising that cycling light was so easy for him! He started his professional career at the age of 25 after he had not been very successful in the amateur races. The sensation at the Col de Faucille catapulted him to success. However, he remained a mountain specialist. He won the mountain trial six times and entered the history books as one of the best climbers.

The climbing 'King' Federico Bahamontes gains important points at the Col de la Faucille for his mountain stage victory.

35 The classic Vosges ascent
BALLON D'ALSACE

There are many different approaches to the Ballon d'Alsace.

1 ***

CLIMB TOP: 1178m
TOTAL ELEVATION: 720m
DISTANCE: 19km
MAX GRADIENT: 9%
AVERAGE GRADIENT: 4%
STARTING POINT:
Giromagny (3260 inhab.), Département du Territoire de Belfort (90)
APPROACH:
From Belfort on the D465 to Giromagny
PARKING:
In the city centre of Giromagny near the tourist information office
ROAD CONDITION:
Continuously good
MOUNTAIN PASS OPENINGS:
April to November

Ballon d'Alsace is known by every tourist. Even if the climb cannot boast impressive data, it is a substantial part of the Tour.

Slow start

You'll start the tour in Giromagny. You'll have hardly left the town and you'll arrive into the neighbouring Lepuix-Gy. The flat stretch takes you between industrial buildings but in front of you will be the first leafy slopes. After 3km the road goes uphill and you'll continue riding past houses. The imagination of the self-appointed garden designer has no limits: to the right a garden gnome villa shows a confident creative drive.

Cycling in circles?

You'll be very surprised to return to Lepuix-Gy after 4km. However, do not worry, you won't have cycled in a circle but will have reached another district (550m). After you have passed through this small village, the built-up area comes to an end and the more pleasing landscape starts. Right, have a good time!

If you want you could try out rope climbing on the way back, as there is a small climbing garden (Roche du Cerf) on the road. The road directly runs alongside a creek and big billboards entice you to the Grand Hotel at the Ballon d'Alsace. You won't be able to make it in the promised 15 (car) minutes – only Tour de France cyclists can nearly measure up.

At the summit

The road passes a restaurant and then goes in steep bends uphill through a forest. You will have reached just about 800m in altitude

Many parts of this section run through forests.

and you'll have to make another 8km to the summit. Beautifully wide bends lead uphill. The quiet road continues to go along rivers and creeks. After 10km lovely hairpin bends will delight you. The incline increases and you'll pass the Routes de Gouriettes (888m). You'll then continue through a dense forest. To the right, the road opens up onto the section below and after another hairpin bend, you'll reach a crossing. For the Ballon d'Alsace you have to take the left turning.

After 15km the road passes a lodging house and crosses over a peak. Here there are many more lodgings that advertise specifically for cyclists. During the summer months this is a meeting place for hang gliding tourists. The flat road continues towards the pass and after 17km you'll reach the Auberge du Ballon d'Alsace. Souvenir shops and in the winter, a ski hire, are located at the summit.

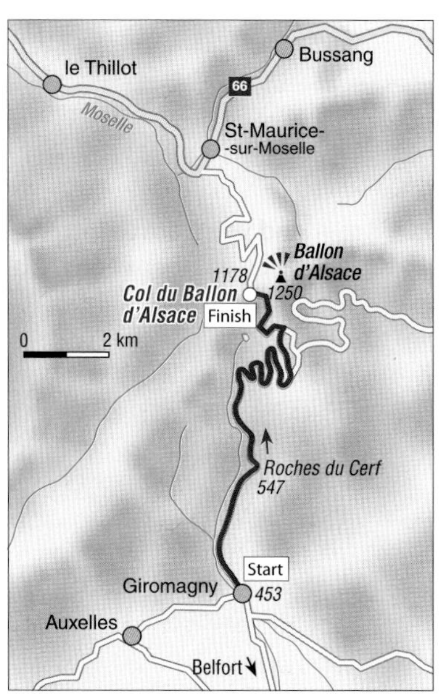

Voluntary extra task

It is hard to imagine that between 1871 and 1919, the German border ran along here. Historical postcards, which are sold here, still show the old border station. The atmosphere at the border to the 'arch enemies' was rarely relaxed. If you have come to like the Ballon d'Alsace, you could consider a second visit. An alternative to the southern approach is the climb via Saint-Maurice-sur-Moselle. This northern approach offers an average incline of 6.5 per cent and 630m in altitude over the 10km. If you are looking for a day-long excursion, you should integrate the Ballon d'Alsace into a round-trip tour.

Panorama

If you are spending several days in the Vosges, you won't necessarily get a very varied landscape, but you'll get many different climbing possibilities.

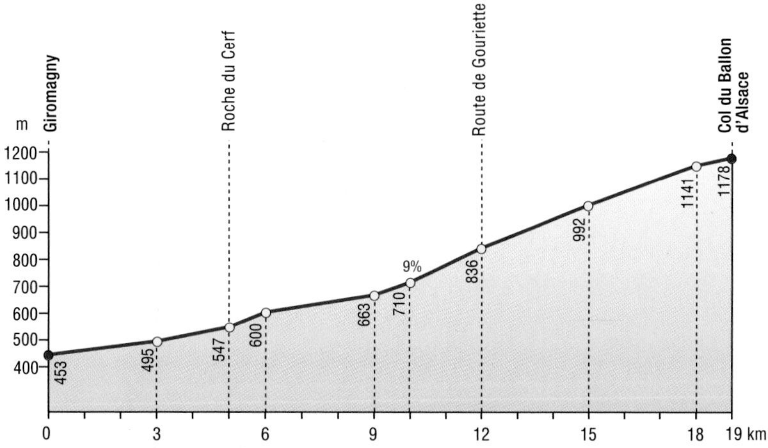

Amateur race 'Les 3 Ballons'

The race 'Les 3 Ballons' which takes place every June proves that you can collect your mountain points in the Vosges until you drop. Amateur cyclists can struggle across the Grand Ballon, the Ballon d'Alsace and the Ballon de Servance. However, the organisers have integrated some additional highlights of the region. The result is an impressive package of 4300m in altitude over 200km. Considering these impressive figures, some tours in the Alps seem like a mere walk in the park. Depending on your time, you will be given a golden or silver certificate. If you want to eat humble pie, you could also cycle the 100km circuit.

Further information is available at: www.sportcommunication.com.

The Route des Crêtes is ideal to really enjoy the ups and downs of the Vosges. The mountain panorama road runs in a north-south direction near the ridgeline of the Vosges and offers fantastic panoramas. After World War I, the road was built as a military access and mountain defence against the Germans. The road is particularly popular among cyclists but has one disadvantage: it is very busy during the summer months. Many day trippers use the road to enjoy the view without breaking into perspiration. The Southern Vosges are particularly busy during July and August. In the wintertime, the road cuts right through a ski area, therefore it is closed until May. Only snowshoe hikers, ski tourers and cross-country skiers are able to enjoy the fantastic panorama. The beginning of the scenic route is in Sainte-Marie-Aux-Minnes, which takes you immediately across the Col de Bagnelles (911m). The official finish is Cernay. The high points in both senses are the Col de la Schlucht (1131m) and the Grand Ballon (1324m).

Cycling at Easter time can be a cold amusement. Even if the road is clear of traffic and people, the snow is still there.

The first mountain of the Tour

It is hard to believe that at the beginning of the last century the Ballon d'Alsace was seen as an extreme challenge. But when the newly founded Tour de France travelled via the Ballon d'Alsace in its third year, many watched the race eagerly. In 1905, the first official mountain climb was a challenge with unusual road conditions and a big gear ratio. René Pottier managed the 12km-long ascent in about half an hour and took the lead. But two days later, he had to quit the Tour due to injuries.

Nevertheless, it did not prevent him the following year attacking at the Ballon d'Alsace and racing across the summit into the lead. That time, he had prepared directly for the mountain. Pottier attacked at the foot of the mountain, took the lead and after 416km and a 250km solo run, he finished in Dijon with an advantage of 48 minutes. He won the Tour in 1906 and was considered the finest climber in the field. But only 6 months later, his life ended tragically: due to a broken heart, he took his own life.

The Ballon d'Alsace has always had an important political meaning. After France lost the war of 1871, Alsace and Lorraine were annexed and the mountain became part of the border to Germany. The French cyclists were therefore particularly patriotic about the mountain. It represented not only an athletic challenge, but also the vicinity of the German nation meant every Tour victory was an heroic act. This is why in 1905 and 1906 Pottier was celebrated as a national hero. A memorial stone was erected in his memory at the top of Ballon d'Alsace. The German occupiers provoked the Tour organisers with morning blasts of trumpets. The cyclists waiting at the start responded with the French national anthem. This provocation had consequences. The next excursion of the Tour de France to Metz was outlawed by the German occupiers.

In 1933, the mountain trials were introduced and as the Ballon was the first steep obstacle of the Tour, the Spaniard Vicente Trueba won the polka-dot jersey. Only four years later, a German cyclist secured his yellow jersey here. Erich Bautz from Dortmund realised on the stage between Metz to Belfort that he was in good form. When he started to pedal hard, no one could keep up. At the Ballon d'Alsace, the German road master left all favourites behind and crossed the summit first. He increased his advantage under cheers of encouragement from the French. Surprising everyone, he reached the finish line with a great advantage and after Kurt Stöpel in 1932, became the second German to win the yellow jersey. He wore it for several days but then had to hand it over due to technical glitches: three punctures at the Galibier ruined all his chances of victory.

After World War II, the mountain marked either the beginning or end of the mountain trial. In both cases, the stage was particularly important. The Ballon d'Alsace had its heyday during the first years of the Tour. Fortunately, the political dimension of the Ballon has become irrelevant in united Europe. Thus, the big party at the mountain in 1997 had near-mythical meaning. Hundreds of thousands of German and French fans lined the road and celebrated Jan Ullrich's victory. The young man from Rostock won the hearts of both nations with his fearless style.

36 The easiest tour of this guide
COL DU HUNDSRUCK

Following in the footsteps of Armstrong and Ullrich, this U-13 cyclist mastered the climb to the Hundsruck.

2 ***

CLIMB TOP: 748m
TOTAL ELEVATION: 390m
DISTANCE: 7km
MAX GRADIENT: 7.5%
AVERAGE GRADIENT: 3.1%
STARTING POINT:
Bitschwiller (2160 inhab.), Département Haut-Rhin (68)
APPROACH:
From Thann to Bitschwiller
PARKING:
In the city centre in front of the church
ROAD CONDITION: Perfect
MOUNTAIN PASS OPENINGS:
All year

This mountain is made for the first practical experiments with altitude. The climb is not long and sporty teenagers can get their first climbing experiences here. Even if they do not have to manage an impressive altitude, the incline will give beginners a taste of what is to come on the other routes in this guide.

Pure pleasure

The Hundsruck is, of course, only a brief pleasure for persistent climbing experts. Therefore, it is advisable to combine it on a round trip with the Ballon d'Alsace. The climb up the Hundsruck will not take longer than a morning. However, its classification is valid, as the point of departure is at the southern end of the Alsace wine route. The pronunciation of the name varies from 'u' to 'ü' and the pass therefore is signposted as Col de Hundsrück or Hundsrueck. Generally, it is tackled from Thann. The following route avoids the main road of Thann. Although it is only short, it is very busy with traffic.

Keep it simple

This is the motto of the climb. From the church in Bitschwiller, you'll cycle towards Thann and turn to the right after 100m. The pass is already signposted, which should not be taken for granted. Not many visitors will look for this by-road. After a few metres, the road narrows considerably and leads along a meadow-ridden slope. After a farm, a wonderful bend awaits you and is a delight for all newcomers to climbing. You'll then vanish into a forest and continue uphill.

The cool air is a blessing, as the incline of over 7 per cent will make newcomers break out into a sweat.

Only hikers climb the Hundsruck; this is why the roads are quiet.

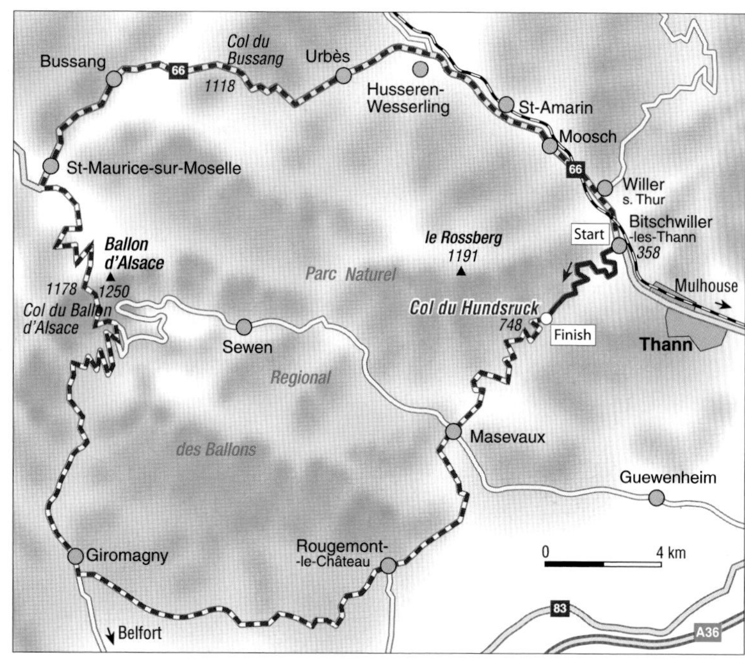

It's a wrap

After 4km, very narrow bends will take you up to 600m in altitude. You will have managed the majority of the challenge already. With the higher altitude, you will have gained a sublime panorama. The silhouette of wooded slopes on the other side of the valley appears between the trees. You'll pass mossy rocks on the final metres up the hill and – you may not believe it – but you will have reached the summit. There is an Auberge and a war memorial for the *Troupes de Choc* (the French troops). Two different hiking routes branch off from the summit. They also offer something to athletes that is a little more ambitious. The Marathon du Ballon d'Alsace starts right at the summit and continues to the west to Col de Perches. The route continues on the GR5 to the Ballon d'Alsace and then in a big sweep to the finish in Masevaux. This is an unusual route, which bears little resemblance to the usual road marathon through a city. While the marathon distance is of course a challenge, this route has another hidden advantage. As you start at the summit, you enter the race on high altitude. While the route goes uphill several times, the finish is situated at a lower altitude.

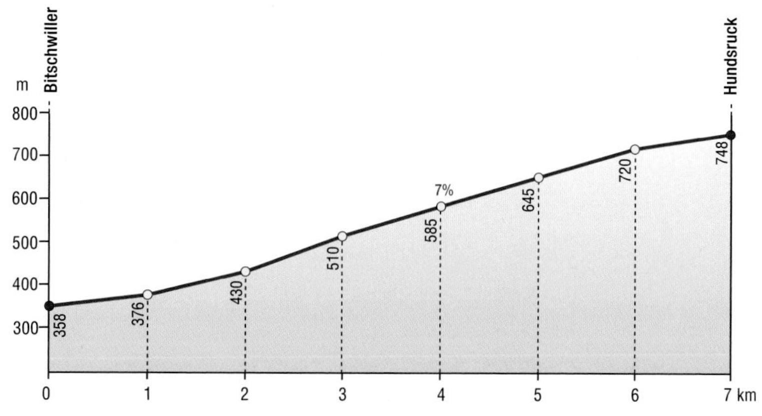

Hiking paradise

The Vosges provide more than only small day excursions. The GR5 is a good example: if you want, you can combine this long-distance hiking trail with the GR531 and spend days in the mountains without having to descend into the valley. In the high Vosges, you often hike across stretched-out mountain meadows. The absence of forests is not down to the altitude but to centuries of alpine farming.

Since 1872, about 16,000km of hiking trails have been maintained by the Club Vosges Club in this region. They lead from the peaks around the Alsatian wine villages high up to the regional national parks of the Vosges-Belchen and the Northern Vosges. The Parc Naturel Régional des Vosges was designated as a biosphere reserve by UNESCO.

Forwards and onwards to the Ballon d'Alsace

Barely 6km and 400m in altitude is a mere warm-up programme for experienced racers. But, luckily, you can combine the pass with the Ballon d'Alsace. It takes barely 26km to the start of the ascent, Giromagny. On this variant, you cross the pass and continue to Bourbach-Le-Haut. The road meanders through a forlorn landscape and through a small farming village. It is only the cobblestones that will tarnish your enjoyment of the descent. You'll go straight on to Rougemont, continue on the D2, then on the D12 to Giromagny. The Ballon d' Alsace is signposted from there.

Wine trail

If you don't feel like exercising, perhaps because the weather does not play along or because you need to give your body a rest, you can devote yourself to pleasure. Thann is located at the southern end of the Alsatian wine trail. On the stretch of 170km, you'll find many wine bars and wine tasting cellars. If you follow the route of Marlenheim, you will have the opportunity to hike through the signposted vineyards. The reception at Thann will give those of you who like to learn about wines information about the wine trial, the different grapes and the work of the viniculturists. The House of Alsatian wine, located north of Colmar, offers the opportunity to get to know the Alsatian vineyards and wines. Between April and September over 50 wine festivals along the Alsatian wine trail provide cheerfulness and many opportunities to enjoy the juice of the grape with the authentic Alsatian *tarte flambée*.

The view from the edge of the road reveals this route is not as flat as you might think.

The amateur Tour de France

Cycling along the routes of the Tour de France is great fun. It is even more fun, though, for some amateur cyclists to conquer the whole route. Over recent years, the route has been cycled repeatedly by non-professionals. The ability spectrum ranged from well-organised group tours to the solo efforts of extreme cyclists. More often, the subject of doping will be addressed. The motto of many of these tours is: "See, you can also manage it clean." The most popular tourers in recent years were:

Guillaume Prébois

You can only cycle the Tour 'on water', was the proposition by Guillaume Prébois. In order to back this up, the French sports journalist together with Fabio Biasiolo cycled the route of the Tour de France 2007. In the following year, he cycled all three of the Tours before the professionals. In 2008, he cycled the Giro, the Tour and the Vuelta in one year and wrote a book about it.

Info: www.guillaumeprebois.com.

Guido Kunze

The German extreme sportsman did not want to just trace the Tour de France 2008. On his 'Tour non-stop' he cycled 3500km and 50,000m in altitude in 10 days instead of the 22 days professionals take. He clocked up 160 hours' cycle time on his speedo. He cycled between two and three original stages before he allowed himself to sleep. "To arrive in Paris is the reward for all the strains."

Info: www.guido-kunze.de

Pre-Tour

In 2007, a group from Dortmund, Germany, had the goal to cycle along the complete Tour. Fourteen men and one woman wanted to cycle in front of the professionals from London to Paris. It did not quite work out like this as they skipped some kilometres of the original route. During their tour, the cyclists made it clear that this project meant a lot of suffering. Gabi Möller reported honestly in her online diary on her difficulties on the tour:"Cycling-wise this Tour is incredible. No one can doubt that! How can you tackle the Col de Columbière and not be overwhelmed by a feeling of happiness?" she raved after having arrived at the finish.

Info: www.pulsschlag-dortmund.de.

In 2007, the cyclists of the Pre-Tour cycled from London to Paris.

37 To the highest summit of the Vosges
GRAND BALLON

2 ✱✱✱✱

CLIMB TOP: 1343m
TOTAL ELEVATION: 860m
DISTANCE: 25km
MAX GRADIENT: 8%
AVERAGE GRADIENT: 3.5%
STARTING POINT:
Kruth at the Lac Wildenstein (1000 inhab.), Département Haut-Rhin (68)
APPROACH:
From Thann on the N66, then turn off in the direction of Fellering/Le Markstein
PARKING:
In the city centre in front of the church
ROAD CONDITION: Good
MOUNTAIN PASS OPENINGS:
May to October

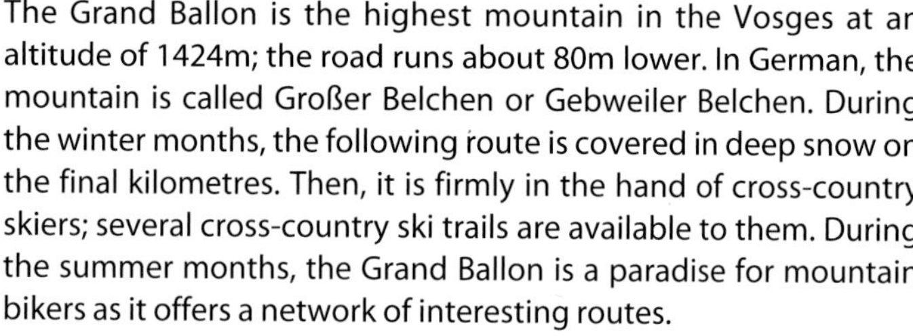

The Grand Ballon is the highest mountain in the Vosges at an altitude of 1424m; the road runs about 80m lower. In German, the mountain is called Großer Belchen or Gebweiler Belchen. During the winter months, the following route is covered in deep snow on the final kilometres. Then, it is firmly in the hand of cross-country skiers; several cross-country ski trails are available to them. During the summer months, the Grand Ballon is a paradise for mountain bikers as it offers a network of interesting routes.

Cold shock

If you cycle in springtime on the Grand Ballon, you get a frozen shock. If the figures don't impress you, the geography will convince you otherwise: the Grand Ballon is very high! In April, the road is still covered by snow and impassable. The last cross-country skiers are still trekking along where just several weeks later bicycles will be buzzing by. Even in May and June, an ice-cold wind blows at the summit that will cool you down quickly. You are accustomed to this in the Alps but you do not expect such low temperatures in the Vosges. However, the neighbouring passes of Col de la Schlucht or Ballon d'Alsace are after all 300m lower in altitude.

Pedalo or racer?

Apart from the church, the little village Kruth does not offer any sights. It is still very cosy there. Stress is a foreign word in Kruth. If you want, you can refill your water bottles at the well as if you had all the time in the world. The D13 leaves the village towards the left in the direction of Wildenstein. After 3km, you'll reach Lake Wildenstein where in the summer you can rent pedalos. You'll want to stick to a cheaper alternative by turning right towards Markstein. At the first ascent, your legs will be adequately occupied.

The ascent to the Grand Ballon via Kruth is a secret tip; this is why the traffic is limited.

Small excursion

Now the traffic should have calmed. In the beech forest, the road goes steeply uphill and after 5km, the field of vision opens up again. You'll be high above the valley and looking down onto Kruth and a ruin on the slope opposite. The road winds uphill past the birch trees and you'll reach the first flat section of the route. The road continues in long hairpin bends along the slope. After approximately 10km a sign indicates the distance to Markstein.

The leaf forest thins out gradually and the warming sun will accompany you on the coming kilometres. You'll pass a small hamlet called Le Treh that does not offer much apart from a chalet. You'll then trundle along meadowy slopes and reach the crossroads of Le Markstein after approximately 17km. You'll then turn right and the Grand Ballon will be signposted from then on. Strictly speaking, you will now be following in the footsteps of the Tour de France but the peloton of course has no time for the idyllic ascent from Lac Wildenstein. Mostly, the Tour cyclists come from Géradmer on the Route des Crétes and only join your route in Markstein.

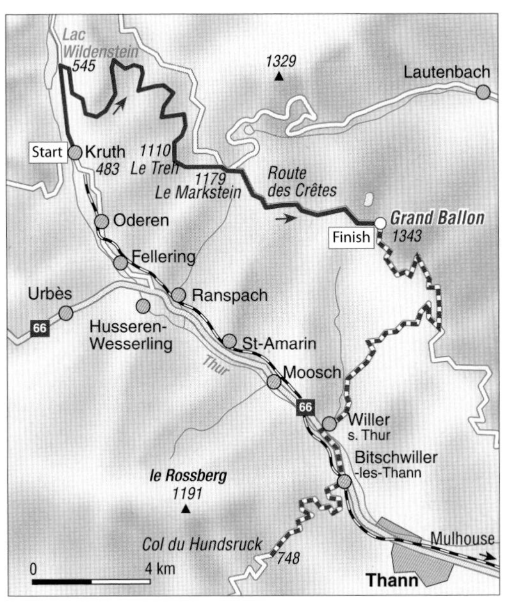

A slight mountain detour on foot

You'll pass the restaurant Ferme de Markstein towards the summit. You'll be exposed to sun on the final kilometres but you'll rarely get too hot. It is very windy on the Grand Ballon and you'll find yourself at the coldest spot in the Alsace. On 10 February, 1956, an all-time low was recorded at -30°C and the climatic map shows that in the summer it is several degrees cooler than in the valley.

On a beautiful day, you'll have a view across gentle slopes. Once you've arrived at the summit of the Grand Ballon, you won't be so grateful of the cooling wind. You won't have quite reached the summit, as it is only navigable on foot. If you can leave your precious means of transport for a brief time and have taken your mountain-bike shoes, you have a great advantage. The walk from the parking area to the summit plateau takes only 10 minutes. You will get a wonderful view that stretches from the summits of the Vosges across the Black Forest to the chain of the Jura.

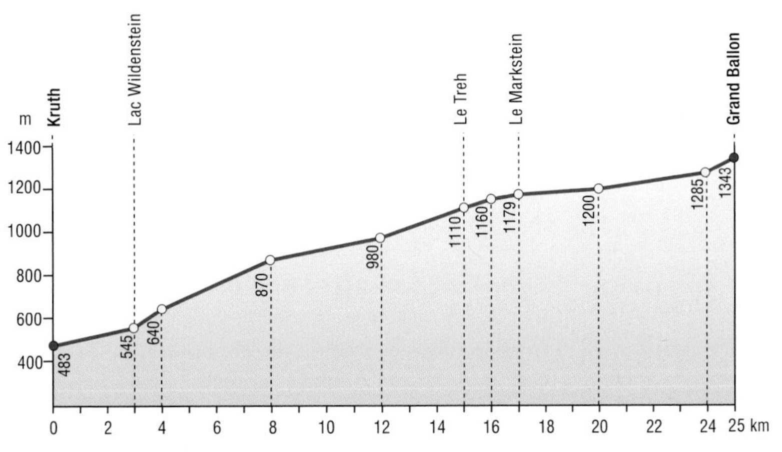

Military past

From photographs, we are familiar with the monument for the Diables Bleus, the French mountain troopers who fought during World War I. Under dramatic conditions, they defended the summit of the Vosges. The monument, erected in 1927, consists of a stone pyramid and a bronze mountain trooper.

During World War I, the Grand Ballon was fiercely fought over and a French trooper remembers how he hid in an earth hole at the summit, shell splinters buzzing around his ears. Nevertheless, he did not feel animosity when he met a German prisoner of war: "The Germans were like us, poor devils who had to sacrifice themselves for nothing."

Excursion number one

Only during bad weather will you find quietness and calm at the weekend. The Grand Ballon is one of the most popular tourist attractions and is therefore always busy. You'll now be grateful that you cycled via Kruth. The secret of this particular ascent has not got out to the motorised weekenders. The beautiful restaurant and the Hotel Du Grand Ballon invite you to stay but we cyclists are drawn again into the valley.

Some other alternatives

If you are planning a longer day trip, you could combine the Grand Ballon with the Col de la Schlucht, which is only 29km away. A shorter alternative is the descent towards Willer-sur-Thann. You simply cross the pass. Unfortunately, the road downhill is a bit bumpy and has two bends with cobblestones. However, the beautiful and narrow descending hairpin bends are a pleasure and the round tour is a worthwhile experience. A glance at the map reveals that there are a series of different ascents to the Grand Ballon. If you leave Cernay, the official finish of the Route des Crêtes, you have to manage 1000m in altitude with only a 4 or 5 per cent incline. In comparison, the second, alternative approach from the south is a bit more demanding. The average incline on the route from Willier-sur-Thur is 6.1 per cent. However, these are not all of the possibilities, as there are more on small by-roads. If you leave from Saint-Amarin and Moosch, the average incline is over 7 per cent. The Tour de France has not tested all of these approaches, but most of them and Mulhouse was often chosen as point of departure or as a stage finish.

Above: A cyclist signpost at the Grand Ballon.

Right: Only at the beginning of the tour, the road is flat – later the ascent will live up to its name.

The Grand Ballon – late addition to the Tour

The Grand Ballon was only integrated into the Tour rather late in its history. The summit, often also called Ballon de Guebwiller, became part of the Tour only in 1969. On 15 July, 1992 the Grand Ballon witnessed one of its moments of glory when the brave solo run of Laurent Fignon delighted the whole of France. Fignon is a distinctive character in the annals of the Tour de France. His glasses made him look like an intellectual and he ended up with the nickname 'Professor'; his ponytail underscored his striking appearance.

When in 1992 Fignon raced up the Grand Ballon, he remembered bygone days. The winners of the Tours in 1983 and 1984 were not the same cyclists in the lead in 1992. The country was even more enthusiastic when he pursued the stage victory on the 11th stage from Strasbourg to Mulhouse. His getaway lasted over 55km and at the end, he managed in a thrilling finale, to finish with an advantage of 12 seconds. For 3 years, he had been unsuccessful, so his joy on that day was particularly great.

In 2005 Michael Rasmussen was equally chuffed. The Dane cycled nearly the complete 9th stage from Gérardmer to Mulhouse solo. Rasmussen would not be deprived of his polka-dot jersey until the end of the Tour. At the start of 2007 the Dane was seen as the favourite. Missed doping tests and lies however sent him home and plummeted the Tour into another crisis. It was apparent later that on the 2007 Tour he had tested positively for Dynepo.

Rasmussen didn't get to enjoy the yellow jersey for long.

38 Constant climbing in dense woodland
COL DE LA SCHLUCHT

The centre of Munster offers wonderful house fronts. A stroll through town is a definite must.

2 **

CLIMB TOP: 1139m
TOTAL ELEVATION: 760m
DISTANCE: 19km
MAX GRADIENT: 5%
AVERAGE GRADIENT: 4%
STARTING POINT:
Munster (5000 inhab.), Département Haut-Rhin (68)
APPROACH:
From Colmar on the D417 to Munster
PARKING:
In Munster in front of the tourist information office
ROAD CONDITION: Good
MOUNTAIN PASS OPENINGS:
All year

The Col de la Schlucht is already signposted and this reflects one of the problems with this mountain road: the road is busy and depending on the time of the day, in addition to trucks and motor bikers, many cars are on the road. The mountain pass offers a constant incline and therefore relaxed cycling, mostly through dense forest.

The Col de la Schlucht is the most important mountain pass road of the High Vosges. It was constructed under Napoleon III in around 1860 and was seen as a miracle of technology. In contrast, to the then-common road-building techniques, it was not adapted ruthlessly to the cross-country tread but was blasted into the rock.

Unmissable town

Munster has a long history as it grew out of a Benedictine monastery founded in AD 630. Due to its position so near the frontline, it was destroyed heavily during World War I. Nevertheless, the Place du Marché and the ruins of the Benedictine monastery Saint-Grégorie are worth a visit.

Highlights of the town are the white storks that build their nests on the stork tower in the centre of town. Unbothered by gawping tourists, they sit on the roof and guard the town. You'll meet these birds with their long beaks all across Alsace. The birds are virtually a landmark of the region. Also inextricably linked with the town is the distinct and tangy Munster cheese. You should definitely combine your city tour with a purchase of this speciality.

Before you stroll through Munster, you should ride the Col de la Schlucht. Munster is stretched out long; it takes 2km to get to the place-name sign and then you'll plunge into the next village. The Vallée de Munster pushes its way between the peaks. On the D417 the route is easygoing; only in Stosswihr will you have to pedal

Pieter Weening at the Col de la Schlucht.

harder. To the right, a beautiful creek winds into the valley and straight on, you'll have a view on to Soultzeren.

Theatre of war

After 7km, the road turns to the right to the Col du Wettstein; you, however, will turn to the left into a big hairpin bend towards the Col de la Schlucht. Between 1914 and 1918, Wettstein was the site for many bloody Vosges battles during World War I. On both slopes of Le Linge (Lingenkopf in German), war cemeteries document the human loss: 3535 soldiers who died for France rest in the Cimetière des Chasseurs, the hunter's cemetery. The graves are marked by stone crosses. Name, rank, unit and day of death are noted on small signs. The cemetery was set up in 1919 in the former combat area.

Varied pleasure

On the road you'll see the faded lettering of the Tour de France. To the left, deep below you, you may recognise the pointed church towers of Munster and Stosswihr. The meadowy slopes are covered in holiday chalets, which are particularly popular during the winter. You'll cycle uphill in long bends and with gentle incline. After 11km, you'll pass the station Tanier du Lac Vert on the right. The road leads through shady spruce and silver fir.

After about 16km, the incline increases a bit and you'll wind up beautiful hairpin bends. On a flat bend, there is an impressive

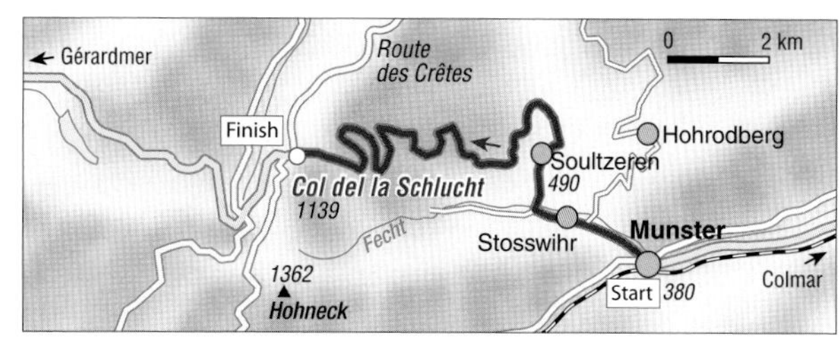

view onto 100m of rocky landscape. You could climb it but it is easier to take the road.

The last 2km are a varied pleasure but with the decreasing treeline the view changes. To the left, you'll have a wide prospect into the valley and across the opposite slopes. The road will take you along a low crag towards the top of the pass. You'll then slip through a small tunnel hewn into stone and steer towards the Col de la Schlucht.

The Alsace

For German cyclists, when the tour visits the Alsace it becomes like a home game to them.

Throughout the whole year, German tourists visit Alsace and when the Tour de France takes place there, they visit in droves. The whole of the

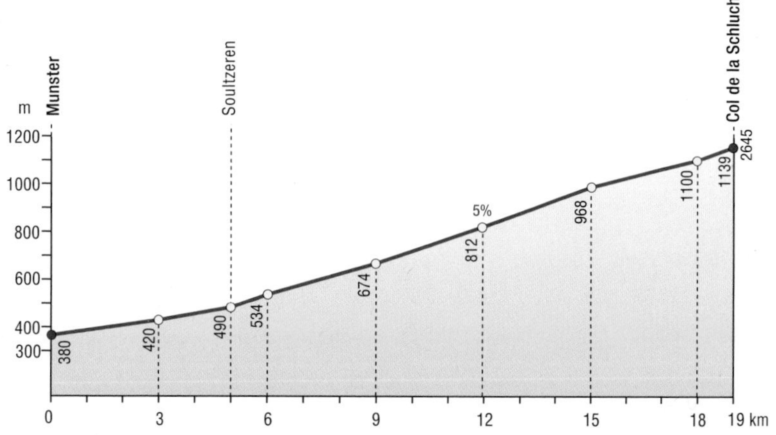

region turns into a cycling arena and the enthusiasm of the fans inspires many a cyclist. Andreas Klöden crossed the Col de la Schlucht first in 2005 after he arranged an attack. He nearly won the whole stage (see 'Tour History', page 189). In addition to its historical importance, the exalted atmosphere is one of the outstanding features of Alsace. This is why during the 2006 Tour, the first three days' races remained in the region. Tradition has made Strasbourg a key fixture in the race. The Tour has been a guest here 24 times, the first time in 1919. Other stage places were also Mulhouse (15 times) and Colmar (7 times).

What the pass has to offer

The Col de la Schlucht has always been an important mountain pass, as until 1919, it marked the border between Germany and France. Meanwhile the summit is covered with restaurants but it depends on the season as to whether they are busy or not. During the winter months, the pass is firmly in the clutches of skiers, snow boarders, snowshoers and long-distance skiers. In the summer, hikers who are drawn to the Martinswand (1258m) or the Botanic Garden, meet up here. The Botanic Garden was created by the University of Nancy and assembles 3500 alpine species over 10 hectares. It is open between June and September.

Another attraction is the summer sledging. However, there is no competition between this short, not very athletic ride on fixed chutes to the ride on your hot bike into the valley!

Fallen heroes: Klöden and Ulle.

The tragedy of Klöden

Generally, during the Tour de France hundreds of kilometres decide victory or defeat. But sometimes very small distances are decisive in the Big Loop. On the 8th stage of the Tour de France in 2005 not even a centimetre decided between glorious victory and tragic defeat. At the Col de la Schlucht, Andreas Klöden started an attack, as planned. The T-mobile team member was able to suddenly break out from the leading group. At the descent, he managed to increase his advantage and only Pieter Weening was able to get to his tail. The clever Dutchman let Klöden cycle against the wind and saved his own energy for the final sprint. At the final manoeuvre, Weening was the lucky strategist. With a flimsy advantage of 9mm, he won the stage. It was impossible to pick a clear winner on the television footage and even the moderators were clueless. Only the finishing photo could reveal the winner.

No one could have predicted how quickly Klöden's popularity would decline in Germany. His second place at the Tour de France in 2004 could have been the beginning of a great career. In 2005, he had to quit the Tour due to a scaphoid fracture in his wrist. In 2006, the revelations around Fuentes distracted from the 2006 Tour. Without his captain Jan Ullrich, Klöden came third. The winner was Floyd Landis who was later convicted of doping. Surprisingly, Klöden changed to Team Astana in 2006. He vehemently defended the dubious reputation of the team. But events started unravelling very fast: fellow team member Eddy Mazzoleni was confronted with suspicions of doping at the 2004 Tour, Matthias Kessler tested positive for testosterone, and it all came crashing down in 2007. Astana captain Alexander Vinokourov, one of the favourites for the overall classification, tested positive for doping by blood transfusion. The team returned home. Andrey Kashechkin was tested positive, but was let off. Andreas Klöden continued to protest his innocence and felt the public treated him unfairly. In 2008, he declared that he would never ride for Germany again. He never understood the 'sudden' efforts to make cycling dope-free. After revelations from the University of Freiburg, the doping doctor Eufemiano Fuentes and other related doping cases, the suspicions around Klöden's involvement are still debated.

Klöden has achieved a lot during the Tour.

39 Summer fun on the ski slopes
CHAMP DU FEU

Decorative half-timbered houses adorn the old town of Villé.

CLIMB TOP: 1100m
TOTAL ELEVATION: 840m
DISTANCE: 14km
MAX GRADIENT: 9%
AVERAGE GRADIENT: 6%
STARTING POINT:
Villé (1700 inhab.),
Départment Bas-Rhin (67)
APPROACH:
From Sélestat on the N59 towards Saint-Dié and after a few kilometres continue on the D424 towards Villé
PARKING: In the centre of town
ROAD CONDITION:
No significant road damages
MOUNTAIN PASS OPENINGS:
All year

The Champ de Feu also has a German name, Hochfeld: in fact, most towns, rivers and mountains of the region have bilingual names. The Champ is the highest point in the middle Vosges and is in the Départment Bas-Rhin. The French name means 'fire field', a relic from the Celtic period. At that time, fires for solstice and sacrifices were burned at the summit, whereas today the lights of the ski-lift stations glow. During the winter months, the Champ du Feu is very busy. With 13 ski lifts, the mountain belongs to one of the most popular ski areas in the region.

A view onto the weather

Many mountains in the Vosges are winter ski resorts. This is beneficial for cyclists and hikers as all ski areas are equipped with a webcam, which facilitates the planning of the trip. With one mouse click, you can see what the weather is like. This is particularly useful in spring because the white colour in the image indicates that either it has snowed recently or there is still snow remaining from winter. This is not rare: in the higher altitudes of the Vosges it can snow at the beginning of June.

In addition to the Champ de Feu, the Ballon d'Alsace, the Col de la Schlucht, the Grand Ballon, Le Markstein and the Col de la Faucille in Jura are equipped with webcams. The Internet addresses are easily found if you type the name into a search engine.

All directions

You'll need to begin on the D424 towards Villé. You'll quickly reach Saint-Martin with its outstanding church.

In Saint-Martin, you'll turn to the right in the direction of Champ du Feu/Breitenbach. On the D425, you'll be aiming directly towards

The second part of the Champ du Feu takes you through forest greens.

the small Breitenbach, which is surrounded by a hilly landscape. After 3km, you'll reach the village and you'll need to turn left just before the church (*'toutes directions'*, all directions). A long left bend will take you along the slope and offers you a view onto Breitenbach, which is situated directly below you. On the following stretch, the road leads through a thick forest and next to the road, small creeks burble along. After 9km the forest opens up and to the left, you'll get a view across the rolling hills in the surrounding area. Hiking trails are continuously branching off the street but today you'll no doubt prefer the gentle cycling pleasure. Meanwhile on the D57, you'll cycle uphill.

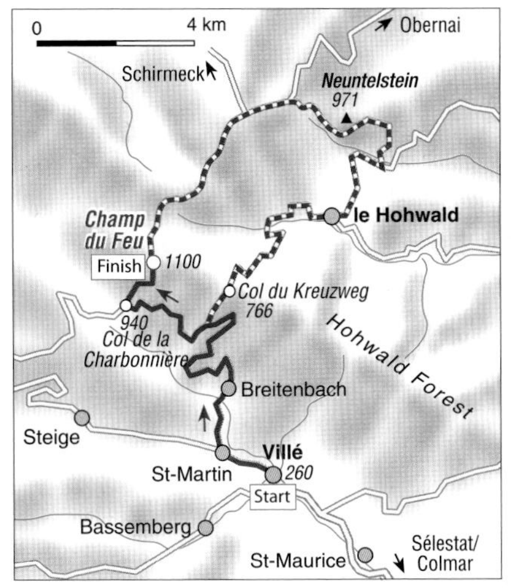

The final metres to the finish

After approximately 11km, the fir forest changes into a leaf forest. In one bend, you'll reach the Col de la Charbonnière, and a signpost stating a 960m total elevation indicates that the end is in sight. The road signs change again and you'll follow them on to the D214 to the Col du Champ du Feu. After a restaurant, a pleasant incline awaits you before you'll have to manage the final rather steep metres. After just about 14km, you will have reached the summit. If you want, you can cycle to the right over the pass and return via Le Hohwald to Villé. The special feature of the Champ du Feu is that it consists of granite whereas the mountains of the Northern Vosges are of full-colour sandstone. It is the highest elevation in the Middle Vosges with an altitude of 1100m.

The history of the chapel at the mountain is very unusual. In 1952 the Chapelle du Champ du Feu was erected from donations to enable skiers to attend local mass. Every Sunday the mass took place even in snow so the skiers could plunge back onto the ski slopes. However, this mass is not held anymore and the chapel is rarely used now.

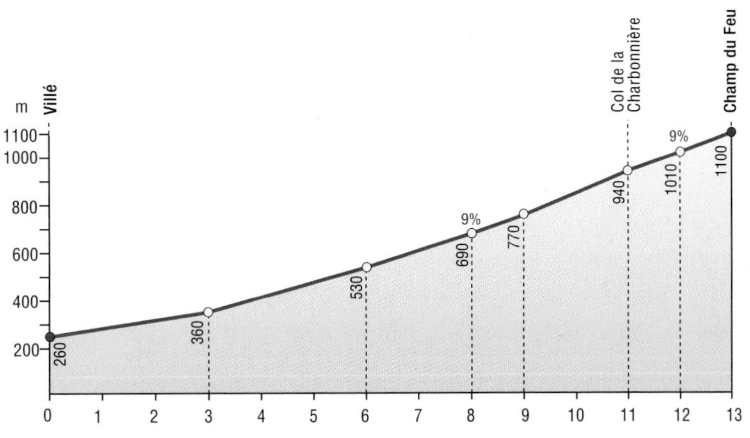

The old stone cross at the roadside is a reminder of a local family.

To take part is the most important thing

If you want to see the Tour on site, you should find standing room at the Champ du Feu. The proximity to Germany guarantees that every stage in the Alsace is accompanied with a festive atmosphere.

If the organisation of this event is too complicated and you find the long struggle for a good view too tiring, there is an alternative. Since 2006, fans have had the opportunity to experience the Tour more directly. Six travel agencies across the whole world were given permission by Tour organisers to sell special cycling package tours. The participants are able to experience the Tour close to the action and are able to visit sites, which are not accessible to other spectators. However, perhaps best of all is the fact that participants are able to cycle the stage hours before the professionals. After the stage finish, the photo shoot for the winners is done on the official podium. However, as so many things in life, these tours come at a price. The three-day tour, for example the alpine stages at the Alpe d'Huez, costs over €3000 when booked through one of the licensed travel agencies. For a mere €1000, you can extend the journey to an eight-day trip and participate until Paris.

As expected, the interest in the stages with challenging climbs is huge. In the first year, the tour packages to the Alpe d'Huez quickly sold out. The participants could really cycle the complete stage between Gap to Alpe d'Huez. If you have survived these 187km over the Izoard and Lautaret, you will enjoy the luxury menu for dinner. Participants agreed that the finale in Paris was worth the effort and money and they were offered helicopter transfers.

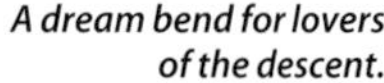

A dream bend for lovers of the descent.

It's free

The self-organised tour however is completely free. Mostly, you can pitch up your tent next to the road and, if you leave early enough you can use your own bike. While the road is blocked to traffic, as a cyclist you can move around freely. If the peloton is nearing and the spectators are bored, you can expect cheers of encouragement. Naturally, given the limited window of opportunity, you are not able to pedal the whole stage and you have to waive the luxury of an escort vehicle. However, in some cyclists the desire to participate in the real thing is too great. Therefore, amateur cyclists have actually mingled with the professionals several times. One story that has become legendary is that of a cyclist who hid in a tunnel and joined the professional cyclists that passed him by. The same sometimes happens in mountain stages when suddenly the solo frontrunner is joined by a companion. Given the high speed, it only takes some seconds until the impostor's cover is blown lagging behind, gasping for air.

Light and dark

Many cyclists lost their lives in the two World Wars. Octave Lapize, the winner of the 1910 Tour, died as a fighter pilot in Verdun, and both François Faber, who won in 1909, and Lucien Petit-Breton, who won in 1908, died on the frontline in World War I.

In 1932, only national teams were allowed at the Tour. In the previous year, Kurt Stöpel had proved he had strong legs. Nevertheless, in 1932, the cool outsider created a sensation: on 7 July, 1932, he wore the yellow jersey as the first-placed German. The Berliner earned his stamina in special training units. As he worked during the day, he set his alarm clock for 3am and always trained before work.

The second stage of the 1932 Tour led from Caens in Normandy to Nantes with over 296km covered. After 170km, a group of racing cyclists were in the lead including Stöpel. He even managed to break into a finishing sprint. Due to a time advantage, he was in the lead at that stage. However, the German team didn't have much money and had pretty shoddy equipment. Several breakdowns prevented Stöpel riding to victory. However, his second place in the overall classification remained the highest ranked position of any German for many years after.

At the finish line in Paris, the French winner André Leducq and Kurt Stöpel hugged affectionately. The gesture came from the heart and the French spectators welcomed the German outsider with great sympathy. At the Champ du Feu the memories of past Tour highlights are overshadowed by a cruel past. In 1941, a concentration camp for men was erected at the 800m altitude level. Hard labour in the quarry and medical experiments by Professor Hirt became notorious. Thousands of people lost their lives in an unbelievably brutal way, including many members of the French Résistance. The concentration camp Natzweiler-Struthof existed until September 1944 and cost thousands of people their lives.

At the summit: In front of the tower which was erected in 1889, there is a wonderful panoramic view across the Vosges and the Black Forest.

40 The only German mountain in the Tour NOTSCHREI

On the small Notschrei the incline is quite significant.

2 ***

CLIMB TOP: 1121m
TOTAL ELEVATION: 741m
DISTANCE: 15km
MAX GRADIENT: 7%
AVERAGE GRADIENT: 5%
STARTING POINT:
Kirchzarten (9700 inhab.)
APPROACH:
From Freiburg on the B31 towards Titisee and then you turn off to Kirchzarten
PARKING:
There is parking at the railway station in Kirchzarten
ROAD CONDITION:
The descent is at times quite uneven
MOUNTAIN PASS OPENINGS:
All year round

At the edge of the Vosges, right in the Black Forest, a rarity is hidden: the only German mountain of the Tour de France. After all, it was only used once, so it did not leave too much of a stamp in the history books. By contrast, the Notschrei and Feldberg have been crucial parts of the German Tour and have been decisive. This is why the Notschrei is a popular training resort for many professional cyclists. Naturally, Jan Ullrich trained for years at the Notschrei. So, if you are being passed on this tour by a cyclist at breakneck speed, you should perhaps glimpse into his face.

Past the Steinwasen-Park

From the railway station, you'll cycle through the town towards Oberried. After 1.5km you'll need to turn onto a rather busy road towards Schauinsland/Oberried. In front of you you'll see gentle slopes. The road goes slowly uphill through Oberried. You'll quickly reach a construction that looks like an aqueduct on the right side. Built in 1938, it is still used to generate electricity from water.

You'll then cycle through dense spruce forests. The incline increases only after 9km and you'll reach the steepest section of the route. The slopes are intermingled with big rocks and next to the road a ski lift appears. You won't have time for the Steinwasen Park but you could make a stop on the return trip if you are addicted to constant action. The Steinwasen Park boasts the longest 'adventure rope bridge' in Europe. You can swing across on the 218m-long rope bridge at a height of 30m above the valley. In addition, the summer bobsled run and over 20 kinds of games attract visitors to the region.

High-percentage incline

You'll leave the Park behind you and you'll be delighted by a simple traffic sign: for the first time, the Notschrei is signposted. The sign is impressive as it promises an incline of 14 per cent for the next 7km.

The initial kilometres in Kirchzarten are flat.

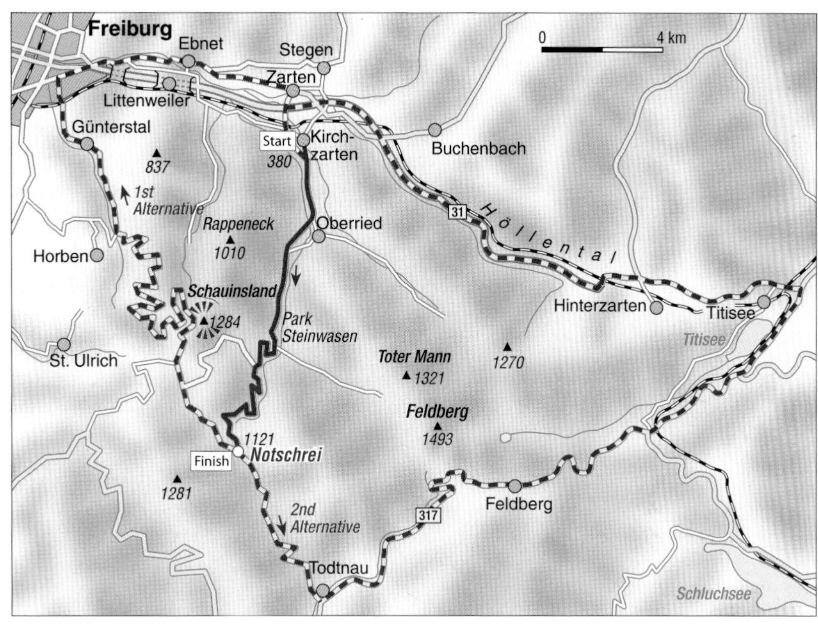

One bend to the left will take you uphill; the right leads to the mining museum. The incline decreases a bit but you'll only reach a longer and flatter section after 12km. The hairpin bends will take you through mixed woodland towards the summit. The four-star hotel Waldhotel is situated here but there is no significant view. Once you have reached the Notschrei, a detour to Schauinsland is recommended. Even more fun is the round trip to the Feldberg: if you choose this route, you will kill two birds with one stone. This variant takes you directly back to Kirchzarten and at the same time you cross the Feldberg, a mountain of the German Tour. In 2005, in cold drizzling rain, the decision over the total victory was made here. The former Telekom professional, Cadel Evans from Australia, won this cold climb by a few seconds ahead of Jörg Jaksche and Levi Leipheimer. Just 4km before the summit of the Feldberg, Jan Ullrich had to break off and lost his last chance for the overall victory.

Black Forest Marathon

In the middle of June, thousands of mountain bikers come to Kirchzarten to the annual Black Forest Ultra Bike Marathon. Behind this bold and simple name lies a race with four different categories that attracts 4000 competitors. In the category 'Ultra Marathon', competitors in 2006 had to manage 116km of forest and meadow paths. In total, this variant offered a total elevation of 3150m. If you did not trust your fitness, you could cycle the 'Short Track'. On 43km, you would

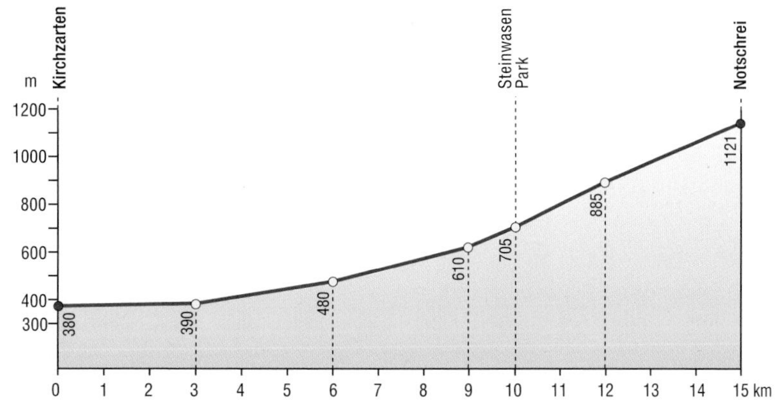

have to conquer only 1040m in altitude. In between these two extremes is the 'Marathon' and the 'Power Track'. According to organisers, the biggest mountain bike race in Europe has been attracting thousands of spectators.

Training area in the Black Forest

The Black Forest is an ideal training resort for newcomers to the alpine cycling community. In a beautiful landscape you can collect many kilometres and practise on gentle inclines. Traversing the Black Forest lengthwise, you have to cycle over 600km. A constant change between picturesque valleys and clear heights provide great fun for the cyclist. The routes are not difficult and run mainly across quiet by-roads and cycling tracks. The climbs are generally gentle; only three or four climbs are a bit more challenging; ideal conditions, therefore, to train for the Galibier and co. A glimpse at the map shows that the Black Forest has no shortage of mountain passes: Feldberg (1493m), Belchen (1360m), Kandel (1241m), Schauinsland (1200m), Hochblauen (1165m), Hornisgrinde (1150m) and Wiener Eck (1035m) are all worthy goals. Between 500 and 1000m total elevation have to be overcome and, given their variety, you will not get bored even after a few days. While the Feldberg is the most famous pass, it is not the most challenging. It is possible to compile a route that collects challenging metres in altitude. The Internet presents you with an idea for a challenge such as this. An ambitious amateur designed a tour that manages 6200m total elevation over 250km. This route would challenge most amateur cyclists and is adequately described as: 'A dream for every trained cyclist – a nightmare for untrained ones'. Info: www.blackforest-tourism.com.

The finish line of the only German Tour mountain is located here.

The Tour is a guest in Germany

The Notschrei (1121m) is unusual in the history of the Tour. It is the only German mountain that has ever been used in the Tour de France. The visit to the Black Forest was also a rarity in another way. On 27 June, 1971 the stage was divided into three sections. First, it lead from Mulhouse to Basel with a detour via the Black Forest.

In a mass sprint in Basel, Zoetemelk lost his advantage. Only a short while later, the cyclists had to continue. The second section took them from Basel to Freiburg, again with a final mass sprint. Shortly after the third section started, and also ended in a mass sprint in Mulhouse. As a mountain of the third category the Notschrei did not play a significant part in the race. However, it was an honour that it was integrated into the Tour. In the German Tour, the Notschrei, together with the Feldberg, are a part of the circuit. Nevertheless, the Black Forest cannot measure itself against the giants of the Pyrenees and the Alps.

The Tour had been a guest in Germany many times, but it is the flat stages that make for an adequate schedule. In 1907, the Tour ventured to Germany. The destination was Metz, which was occupied by Germans. This was a political hot potato and the Tour was banned from crossing the border through Germany in 1910 by the governor of Alsace-Lorraine.

It was only in 1964 when the peloton rolled again to Germany. The whole country was champing at the bit as Rudi Altig took the yellow jersey for a while in Freiburg. The following year, the Tour even started in Germany. The cyclists started in Cologne and went to Liège. Freiburg seems a good choice: in 1977 Didi Thurau rolled through the Black Forest in a yellow jersey.

In 1987, the longest visit of the Tour de France to Germany took place. The prologue was staged on 1 July in Berlin. The first stage went across Berlin, the team trials around Berlin and three stages went across West Germany. It wasn't until 5 July that the cyclists reached French soil in Strasbourg.

The enthusiasm for cycling in Germany is huge at every visit. Millions of active and passive fans follow the annual Tour of the Giants. Twenty-four stages have touched German soil and visited six different districts. When, as in 2005, millions of spectators were lined up along the route, even the director of the Tour was impressed. His verdict was: "The German fans and their enthusiasm are unique."

The Black Forest is an ideal training area. The diversity of circuits allows you to accumulate kilometres by way of variety.

THE MOST IMPORTANT

Pyrenees

Argelès-Gazost 1,2,3,4

This small town (3500 inhabitants) is not far from Lourdes in the Hautes-Pyrénées . It is ideal as a starting point for many classic tours. The Col d'Aubisque, Luz-Ardiden, Hautacam and the Tourmalet are only a stone's throw away. In Argelès-Gazost you have all opportunities to shop, several restaurants, hotels in all categories and along the road a selection of campsites. The area is focused on tourism and cyclists, hikers and canoeists get their money's worth.

Tourist information office:
BP 35
65400 Argelès-Gazost
Tel: (+33) 05 62 97 00 25
Email: infos@argeles-gazost.com
Website: www.argeles-gazost.com

Camping:
Camping Les Trois Valées
Avenue des Pyrénées
65400 Argelès-Gazost
Tel: (+33) 05 62 90 35 48
Website: www.l3v.fr

If you come from the direction of Lourdes, there are many other campsites along the RN21, which are signposted with large signs.

Saint-Lary-Soulan 5, 6, 7

Saint-Lary-Soulan has become in recent years one of the most important winter sport resorts in the region. This is why the infrastructure is very good. There are many gift shops, shopping opportunities, and the many hotels in different categories don't usually book out in the summer. Excursions to the Col d'Aspin, Col de Peyresourde and of course to Pla d'Adet are possible. If you want you can enrich your stay with hikes in the picturesque Réserve Naturelle Néouvielle:

Tourist information office:
37, rue Vincent Mir
65170 Saint-Lary-Soulan
Tel: (+33) 05 62 39 50 81
Email: info@saintlary.com
Website: www.saintlary.com

Camping:
Camping Lalanne
65170 Saint-Lary-Soulan
Tel: (+33) 05 62 39 41 58
Website: www.saintlary-vacances.com/camping/

There are eight campsites in total in and around the town. Even during the busy season, you will not have any problems finding a place.

Bagnères-de-Luchon 7, 8, 9

Luchon only has 4000 inhabitants but is one of the most popular thermal springs in the Pyrenees. It is busy with visitors throughout the year. The Col de Peyresourde and Superbagnères (see pages 34 and 38) are at every cyclist's disposal. You can also conquer the Col du Portillon and the Col de Menté from here.

Tourist information office:
18, Allée d'Etigny BP 29
31110 Bagnères-de-Luchon
Tel: (+33) 05 61 79 21 21
Email: luchon@luchon.com
Website: www.luchon.com

Camping:
There are two campsites in Luchon, four more in the region.

STARTING POINTS

Camping Beauregard
Avenue du Vénasque
31110 Luchon
Tel: (+33) 05 61 79 30 74
Website: www.camping-beauregard.eu

Ax-les-Thermes 11, 12, 13, 14

The thermal baths bring a constant stream of visitors throughout the year. The combination of thermal regiments, hiking trails and winter sports has given the town some wealth. In search of a restaurant or hotel you are spoiled for choice and naturally, you have great shopping opportunities.

Cyclists can tackle the climbs at the Ax 3 Domaines/Plateau de Bonascre, Plateau de Beille, Col du Chioula and Port de Pailhères. There are also several additional touring possibilities: for instance, you could attempt to climb the Port d'Envalira (unfortunately very heavy traffic) or tour in the quiet hinterland of the Col du Chioula.

Tourist information office:
La résidence
6 Avenue Delcassé
09110 Ax les Thermes
Tel: (+33) 05 61 64 60 60
Email: vallees.ax@wanadoo.fr
Website: www.vallees-ax.com

Camping:
RN 20
09110 Ax les Thermes
Tel: (+33) 05 61 64 69 14
Email: camping.malazeou@wanadoo.fr
Website: www.campingmalazeou.com

The campsite in Ax is not inexpensive. There are cheaper alternatives in Savignac-les-Ormeaux, Les Cabannes, Verdun and Ascou.

Southern Alps

Malaucène 15, 16

This is how you imagine a beautiful town in the South of France: a cosy city centre with a small market place and a wide range of little cafés and restaurants. In Malaucène everything focuses on the famous Mont Ventoux and therefore racing cyclists are often visitors here. But there are other excursions into the region as even without the mountains there is a lot to experience.

Tourist information office:
Place de la Mairie
84340 Malaucène
Tel: (+33) 04 90 65 22 59
Email: ot-malaucene@wanadoo.fr
Website: www.lemontventoux.net

Camping:
Camping Le Bosquet
Route de Suzette
84340 Malaucène
Tel: (+33) 04 90 65 24 89
Website: www.guideweb.com/provence/camping/bosquet

Barcelonnette 17, 18, 19

Barcelonnette is relatively manageable with its 3000 inhabitants, despite the fact that it gets a lot of through-traffic. The infrastructure leaves no stone unturned and the town is an ideal starting point for the Col d'Allos and to Pra-Loup. Also near by is the Col de la Cayolle, a bit further away are the Cime de la Bonnette, Col de Vars and the Col de Larche.

Tourist information office:
Place Fréderic Mistral
BP 4, 04400 Barcelonnette
Tel: (+33) 04 92 81 04 71
Email: info@barcelonnette.com
Website: www.barcelonnette.com

Camping:
Camping du Plan
52 avenue Emile Aubert
04400 Barcelonnette
Tel: (+33) 04 92 81 08 11
Website: www.campingduplan.fr

Northern Alps

Bourg d'Oisans 23, 24, 25

The most popular pilgrimage destination is of course Bourg d'Oisans. At the feet of the mythical 21 bends of the Alpe d'Huez, cyclists and fans from all across the world meet. The town is therefore adapted to the two-wheeler: even in the window displays you cannot escape the Tour de France. Of course you will not lack anything here, there is even a very good racing cycle shop. It is an ideal base camp for the climb up the Galibier, Télégraphe, Lautaret and Crox-de-Fer as well as a sprint up Alpe d'Huez.

Tourist information office:
Quai Girard
38520 Bourg d'Oisans
Tel: (+33) 04 76 80 03 25
Email: infos@bourgdoisans.com
Website: www.bourgdoisans.com

Camping:
Camping La Piscine
Route de l'Alpe d'Huez
Tel: (+33) 04 76 80 02 41
Fax: (+33) 04 76 11 01 26
Email: infos@camping-piscine.com
Website: www.camping-piscine.com

There are a number of campsites in and around Bourg d'Oisans which are also open outside of the season.

Saint-Jean-de-Maurienne 23, 26, 27

Admittedly, Saint-Jean-de-Maurienne is not one of the most homely towns listed here. Massive shopping malls in the vicinity and the main road to Italy cause heavy traffic, particularly during rush hour and school holidays. It is nevertheless a good starting point for tours to Galibier, Télégraphe, Croix de Fer and Col de la Madeleine.

Tourist information office:
Place de la cathédrale
73300 Saint-Jean-de-Maurienne
Tel: (+33) 04 79 83 51 51
Email: info@saintjeandemaurienne.com
Website: www.saintjeandemaurienne.com

Camping:
Camping Municipal des grands cols
422, Avenue du Mont Cenis
73300 Saint-Jean-de-Maurienne
Tel: (+33) 04 79 64 28 02
Email: info@campingdesgrandscols.com
Website: www.campingdesgrandscols.com

La Clusaz 30, 31,32

In this holiday town, you can anticipate the hustle and bustle of the winter season. The whole of Clusaz is dominated by winter sports with its ski shops, ski hire stations and ski schools. This is why in the summer, it is quiet, with enough possibilities for experiences. Hiking tours, riding, gliding and golf are on offer to fill the hotel beds during the summer months as well. Cyclists can go directly from the town to the Col de la Colombière, Col de la Croix-Fry and the Col des Aravis.

Tourist information office:
161, place de l'église
BP 7, 74220 La Clusaz
Tel: (+33) 04 50 32 65 00
Email: info@laclusaz.com
Website: www.laclusaz.com

Camping:
Camping Le Plan du Fernuy
1800 route des Confins
74220 La Clusaz
Tel: (+33) 04 50 02 44 75
Fax: (+33) 04 50 32 67 02
Email: info@plandufernuy.com
Website: www.plandufernuy.com

Vosges

Munster 38

Munster is a small and cosy town in the Vosges. It offers a historic town centre where the storks also feel comfortable. The ascent to the Col de la Schlucht starts in Munster. In the vicinity you also have the Col du Bonhomme and the Route des Crêtes.

Tourist information office:
1, rue de couvent
68140 Munster
Tel: (+33) 03 89 77 31 80
Email: tourisme.munster@wanadoo.fr
Website: www.la-vallee-de-munster.com

Camping:
Camping municipal du Parc de la Fecht
Parc de la fecht
68140 Munster
Tel: 09 89 77 31 08
Email: info@campingterreoceane.com
Website: www.campingterreoceane.com

Thann 35, 36, 37

Thann is a very busy town, which is why it is worth a miss. The campsite in

Ransbach is directly on the way to Kruth where the tour to the Grand Ballon starts. For a longer day excursion a round tour over the Col du Hundsruck and the Ballon d'Alsace is available.

Tourist information office:
7, rue de la 1ère Armée
68800 Thann
Tel: (+33) 03 89 37 96 20
Email: contact@ot-thann.fr
Website: www.ot-thann.fr

Camping:
Camping Les Bouleaux
8, Rue des Bouleaux
68470 Ranspach
Tel: (+33) 03 89 82 64 70
Email: contact@alsace-camping.com
Website: www.alsace-camping.com

INDEXES

Place index

General index

K

L

M

N

P

R

S

T

U

V

W

Y

Z